Gratitude in Education: A Radical View

Gratitude in Education

A Radical View

Kerry Howells
University of Tasmania, Australia

SENSE PUBLISHERS
ROTTERDAM/BOSTON/TAIPEI

A C.I.P. record for this book is available from the Library of Congress.

ISBN: 978-94-6091-812-4 (paperback)
ISBN: 978-94-6091-813-1 (hardback)
ISBN: 978-94-6091-814-8 (e-book)

Published by: Sense Publishers,
P.O. Box 21858,
3001 AW Rotterdam,
The Netherlands
https://www.sensepublishers.com/

Printed on acid-free paper

For my students

TABLE OF CONTENTS

ACKNOWLEDGEMENTS

"I can no other answer make, but, thanks, and thanks." – William Shakespeare

I am forever indebted and deeply grateful to all those students, teachers, pre-service teachers, academics and parents who participated in tutorials, workshops and research projects on the role of gratitude in education over the past 15 years, and who provided the inspiration for this work; to Christine Thambipillai for your unconditional support, friendship and powerful vision of the potential of this work in education; to Jan MacLean for believing in the worthiness of my pedagogy and for creating opportunities for me to present it in the world of academia; to Professor Jane Watson for patiently mentoring me to have the courage and determination to keep my focus on this project and for believing in its importance; to Roya Pugh for our philosophical discussions, for helping me to free up my writing, and giving invaluable early editing suggestions; to Therese Smith for your commitment to the topic of gratitude, your insights, and for giving me strength while tirelessly working beside me for hours into the night as we did the final edits; to Perri Wain for your loyal and encouraging friendship and the photo on the front cover; to Judith Deans for your diligence in assisting with the final layout of this book; to Hisashi Doi for being an inspiring leader and opening my eyes to hidden dimensions of gratitude; to Atsuko Ono for your significant insights and invaluable support; to Maki Umeyama for your wise counsel and skilled assistance; to Lyn Russell (recently deceased) for instilling a sense of playfulness and possibility; to Jessie Cumming for your joy and enthusiasm for this work; to Laraine Donnelly for your great wisdom and guidance; to Erica Nathan for being an insightful critic and friend; to Catherine Morse for your perceptions and encouragement; to Judy Nicholas for supporting me in my early days of writing; to my daughter Amrita for your unique way of being in the world, and for taking me into areas of gratitude where only a daughter like you can; and finally to my loving and wonderfully supportive husband, Lynden, for your proofreading assistance, for being my rock and staying by my side every step of the way.

INTRODUCTION

Where there is no gratitude, there is no meaningful movement; human affairs become rocky, painful, coldly indifferent, unpleasant, and finally break off altogether. The social 'machinery' grinds along and soon seizes up.[1]
– Margaret Visser

Why gratitude in education?

Many frown upon the use of the words gratitude and education together. It seems like a strange combination. We might perhaps be able to contemplate the place of gratitude in aspirations for wisdom or transformation, but to picture how it relates to learning for information or understanding content may require a greater leap than many are willing to make. Gratitude could be seen to be more relevant to lists of values or mission statements rather than as a thread that can run through our curricula. Schools such as those based on the Montessori and Steiner traditions or those of a religious denomination often proudly advocate gratitude as one of their core values. Initiatives such as service learning[2] and 'Tribes'[3] capture the spirit of giving that is also embraced by gratitude. Recent studies in the field of positive psychology herald the potential of gratitude for enhancing the wellbeing of students.[4] However, it is still difficult and extremely rare for much of mainstream education to make links between gratitude and teaching and learning pedagogy.

I first stumbled upon gratitude as a powerful learning strategy for students nearly two decades ago. I was teaching a philosophy unit called 'Cultural and Ethical Values' at a university which had the reputation of being the domain of the 'privileged' few. Students from all faculties were obliged to take the unit, alongside three other core units. I was filled with appreciation that so early in their university studies they had the opportunity to gain a foundation in ethics and be in touch with the greats of ethical philosophy – Plato, Augustine, Kant, Mill, Nietzsche, Sartre, Confucius, and Buddha. A large number of students, however, wandered into my tutorials full of complaint about being required to study something they did not choose, and which they believed had no links to their other studies or vocation. Other tutors in the same course were reporting similar resistance and low levels of student engagement. After the first two semesters of teaching the course and unsuccessfully trying to whip up enthusiasm, exuding my passion for the subject, using all the best teaching techniques I knew, but receiving the same negative and unmotivated reaction from a large number of my students week after week, I decided that something had to shift. We were at a stalemate.

I took a different approach in the following semester. I facetiously informed my students, to their surprise, that I refused to teach them unless they chose to be 'present' enough to learn. I spent the first half of the tutorial in the first three weeks trying to understand what it was that was underneath the students' refusal to learn and be engaged in the unit. I asked them to write non-stop for twenty minutes on topics such as their obstacles to learning and their perceptions of why they found it difficult to engage; and followed this with group discussion. I came to discover a number of incongruences that I believe are as prevalent in today's university and school students as they were then. Although we may think that our students might be making conscious choices not to pay attention, to drift off, to be disengaged, in actual fact they want to be present, but do not know how to be. Most seem thirsty for answers about how to be more engaged, and look to us as educators to provide these for them.

I also discovered that the majority of students, no matter how privileged, were full of complaint about what they did not have, or about how their expectations were not being met, or that they wanted things to be different and were resentful that someone else was not initiating that change. They wanted to be engaged, and yet did not feel they were actively choosing not to be engaged. They were firmly entrenched as receivers, complaining about not receiving enough and feeling they deserved more. They were not seeing that their complaint and resentment could be undermining their ability to be engaged.

Without much preconceived intention at the time, I suggested that perhaps gratitude could be a valuable alternative paradigm to the one of resentment that predominated. Interestingly, many students started to approach their studies with more gratitude. They reported that as they practised more gratitude when they studied, they experienced increased engagement, greater connection to the subject and teacher, a deeper understanding of content, and increased motivation.

From that point onwards, the *educational* value of practising gratitude became my imperative. I started to embed gratitude as a learning strategy in each of my units, no matter what the subject. I have since taught the relationship between gratitude and student engagement in a number of different contexts and institutions – first-year orientation and transition programs, pre-service teacher education, Years 10, 11 and 12 high school studies, and other learning strategy courses at undergraduate and postgraduate levels. Many of these students went on to apply an increased consciousness of gratitude to their learning of subjects traditionally immersed in the objectivist framework. They reported the benefits of applying gratitude even when they were studying information-dense subjects such as tax law, economics, psychology, and business administration. The contexts and age groups may be different but the outcomes were consistent: attention to gratitude serves a very important need for students to attend to their being at the same time as their thinking. If they think about what they have been given rather than looking only for what they can receive, their learning transforms and they are able to be more present in their learning.

While teaching these students, I came to see that the number one condition or teaching strategy for discussing gratitude as a learning strategy is my own practice of gratitude. As I reflected why some groups of students were able to embrace the place of gratitude more than others, or even why some seemed to express more gratitude than others, I discovered that there was an uncanny relationship between my own level of gratitude and that of my students. Before we can expect students to practise gratitude, teachers need to be practising. This is the rationale for my approach to this book, and why I have written it about teachers' gratitude before addressing students' gratitude.

From this realisation I developed a pedagogy for teaching gratitude to teachers and school leaders, and started to offer this in the form of professional development and action research projects at several schools and universities. Most seemed to embrace gratitude as a powerful way of combating the resentment they themselves were carrying into their classrooms and staffrooms. Instead of blaming the system, they felt empowered to investigate the part they could play and respond proactively. Most were motivated by the inherent wisdom that their students' sense of entitlement and ensuing complaint affected their learning, and that gratitude presented a positive way forward.

Yet for some the concept of gratitude, especially the radical one I was proposing, was difficult. They were uncomfortable with connotations of indebtedness, reciprocity and obligation. I learned that unless this proposal is explored within a critical framework and in a way that empowers teachers, it could be seen to be adding to the heavy load of civic debt teachers already feel they carry. Indeed, they might ask, at a time when we have codes of ethics in education telling us that we are to act with 'dignity', 'integrity', 'respect', 'empathy', and 'justice', was I adding yet another weighty word, another loaded concept, to this ever-growing list? Am I also suggesting "another new technique" to teachers who complain already of an overcrowded and demanding curriculum and the most difficult generation of students they have ever had to teach? Some warned of the inherent dangers of suppressing negative emotions; of the possibilities of abuse of power where teachers expect their students to express gratitude to them; of the irrelevance of gratitude to the main game of teaching content; and of accepting the status quo in situations of inequity where much change is needed.

These teachers' responses helped me realise that I needed to listen more closely to the underlying difficulties that students may have with the notion that they should be more grateful. If we agree that gratitude has a place in our students' learning, and if gratitude is something that needs to be directly and consciously nurtured, where and when in the education system does this occur? Is it the place of education to nurture gratitude, or is this stepping over the traditional divide between the objective and subjective domain of the student? Can gratitude be 'taught' to another, in the traditional sense of imparting content, or is it so complex, so subjective, and so far away from 'the main game of teaching and learning' that all we can hope for is to pass it on through our own example?

Over time, I came to discover it was the dual challenge of the mismatch of the concept of gratitude, and how it plays out when teachers consciously practised it in the classroom or staffroom, which they struggled with. Yet it is this complexity that gives real meaning to the term, and where its potential for enriching our lives is found. When educators practise gratitude in the midst of time-poor and stressful conditions – where their self-efficacy, collegiality and resilience are most under threat – gratitude takes on dimensions that are far deeper than those that come out of most other academic discussions and clinical research.

When I first started to discuss the role of gratitude in education, I received all manner of looks and recriminations – especially in the world of mainstream academia. Now I am invited into faculties such as accounting, optometry, and law – faculties that in the past were dominated by the positivist framework, considering the subjective domain of the student to be irrelevant to higher order thinking. Their interest in the role of gratitude is indicative of a wider phenomenon, a change in consciousness that reflects what thinkers such as Charles Taylor[5], Anthony Giddens[6], and Richard Tarnas[7] discuss as a "radical reflexivity", or Ronald Barnett[8] calls an "ontological turn", where we not only reflect on our thinking, but on the interrelationship between our thinking and our being.

My aim is to make the principles underlying this book appealing and accessible to those teachers who may see gratitude as part of their professional identity, but whose feelings of disempowerment and disillusionment often work against this. *Gratitude in Education: A Radical View* thus directly addresses factors that, I argue, strongly impact on student engagement and teacher presence, efficacy and resilience.

Why gratitude?

We live in a time when we are constantly exposed to the suffering of those less fortunate than ourselves, or those who have had the world at their feet snapped away by an earthquake, a wave, a bomb, a fire, or a rampant storm. As they plummet into chaos or flee for refuge, we are summoned to answer just how to respond to the millions reaching out for our regard. If we have our own fortunes intact (for the moment) just one glimpse of others' suffering, can, if we allow it, generate a deep moral questioning of how we should react. A common refrain is that we should be grateful for what we have. But for gratitude to be an effective and moral response, we would need to embrace it as more than something that makes us feel good or reminds us of how good we have it. For if we were to meet gratitude face to face she would say 'take action that serves others', 'give back', 'give up', 'say sorry', 'let go', 'clear the air', and 'connect'. We are in danger of staying with an impoverished sense of gratitude if we only entertain it at the level of our intellect, or indeed if we consider it in isolation from its meaning in our interactions with others. To reach into the true nature of gratitude, we need to engage with it through action, and discover an embodied understanding through our lived experience, our connectedness to the other.

There is much in today's world that can numb our gratitude. Our excuses lead us to indifference when wholly reasonable indebtedness to each other and the environment knocks at our door. We have found numerous places to hide from gratitude. Some hide behind their concern about simplistic Victorian notions of gratitude where they may have felt they were required, ordered in fact, to put themselves in the shoes of others and never complain about their own pain. Some believe gratitude should remain in its cathedrals and religious inscriptions, neither to come out into contemporary discourse nor guide our secular life. Others are encased by a resentment that they have made their mission in life to protect. They take umbrage at any whiff of the word 'gratitude' as they think it suggests we ignore their pain.

In many circles, the greatest hiding place is in watered down versions of the word gratitude itself, so its role is as something that can make us feel good. It seems that the more we reach into the power of gratitude to answer some of our current psychological and social ills, the more the word is used to serve the very self-interests it wishes to destroy.

To hear the power of gratitude we need to listen with our heart. If we listen to one beat of nature, we would hear her crying out for us to give back for what we have received. Governments around the world are hearing that cry, but most do not hear it in their hearts. To take the kind of brave and urgent action our earth and humanity require, we need to be deeply moved by a force that connects us with each other, our environment, and perhaps to something greater than ourselves. If we allow gratitude to come out of hiding, and live in our hearts in an authentic and contemporary way, it can offer that bridge to community connection and action.

Many great thinkers of the past[9] including Seneca, Aquinas, Hobbes, Einstein, Chesterton, Shakespeare and Kant have spoken about the place of gratitude in enriching our lives. For hundreds of years, gratitude has been discussed in many diverse fields. When we read or hear the word 'gratitude' it can often be enough to remind us of a missing piece, an incomplete part played in our giving back, a strength we gained from expressing gratitude in times past. For some it can be a source of pain. The word gratitude reminds them of how deep is the wound when they give and give to others and nothing is returned, or where all they seem to receive is ingratitude.

In the past decade we have witnessed an exponential growth in explorations of gratitude in both academic journals and general texts. Perhaps this signals a rising interest in sources from where we can enhance our wellbeing or reach a higher consciousness? Yet if our discourse wholeheartedly embraces gratitude without an awareness and respect for those who do not warm to its powers or value its intent, we can alienate them unintentionally.

We do not need another book that simply adores and adorns gratitude. Nor do we need one that prescribes how to be or how to feel good, or which assumes a neutral starting point that discounts the culturally rich and deep understanding of gratitude that many readers already bring to the text. We need a book that can explore the dilemmas raised when we place this giant of a term amidst a complex, pluralistic, secular context, so that we can better understand its contemporary meaning and potential. We do not need a book that patronises or offers a panacea for all of the world's problems, but we do need one that mirrors the kind of dialogue we need if we are to bring gratitude to the table as we consider it as a meaningful way to respond and to be.

Why gratitude in education now?

Students orientate themselves to where they can feel valued and where there is trust. It is not until they find this safe haven that they can settle and be present enough to learn. Many of our educational environments – be they schools or universities or colleges of advanced education – are breeding grounds for conditions which make it difficult for gratitude and trust to take hold. Conditions that are the antithesis to gratitude – resentment, victim mentality, envy, or a sense of entitlement[10] – are toxins that kill off goodwill. A toxic environment of ensuing complaint culminates in good teachers and leaders walking out wounded by ingratitude, extremely unlikely to return. It is our lack of consciousness of the impact of this malaise that keeps us in the dark, and stops many wonderful education initiatives from taking hold. At a time where measurement and economy are our guiding lights, we are neglecting to attend to our ontological domain, our way of being in the world, and the impact this has in our education communities.

We often condemn students for their disengagement and for their blatant displays of negative complaint and blame. Some say these are characteristics of a typical generation Y student, who is totally absorbed in his or her own needs and interests. Yet it is also the environment we provide that allows such attitudes to prevail. Although Charles Dickens' satire of where gratitude has no place in Gradgrind school (described in his book *Hard Times)*, was published as long ago as 1854, it bears a scary resemblance to the ethos that predominates today.

> It was a fundamental principle of the Gradgrind philosophy that everything was to be paid for. Nobody was ever on any account to give anybody anything, or render anybody help without purchase. Gratitude was to be abolished, and virtues springing from it were not to be. Every inch of the existence of mankind, from birth to death, was to be a bargain across the counter. And if we didn't get to heaven that way, it was not a politico-economical place, and we had no business there.[11]

As the philosopher Michael Dale[12] notes in his exposition of how the characteristics of Gradgrind philosophy play themselves out in our times, much of our current educational discourse is dominated by language that reflects a bargain across the counter, or by what some call an 'exchange paradigm'. Genevieve Vaughan and Eila Estola describe the underlying logic and values of this paradigm as being ego-oriented, and something that "requires equal payment for each need-satisfying good".[13] In education this paradigm is characterised by individualism, instrumentalism and consumerism. For the philosopher Charles Taylor[14], the result is fragmentation and disenchantment, which has dissolved community and "split reason from self."[15]

As Dale notes, our present educational discourse is dominated by words that reflect this 'bargain across the counter' mentality – words like 'client', 'service', 'stakeholders', 'consumers', and hyphenated words such as 'performance-referenced', 'outcome-oriented', 'competency-centred', as well as unhyphenated ones like 'cohort groups', 'market demand' and 'standard variations'. He then goes on to ask what is it that we teachers do at university? "We 'deliver instruction'. Teaching in a classroom is an 'instructional delivery system', and the latest technology simply an 'alternative delivery system'."[16] Instead of reflecting on the Socratic question of "How should one live?" Dale says, we are instead focused on "How to make a living?"

In his address to the House of Lords in August 2011, the Archbishop of Canterbury, Rowan Williams, spoke of his views on the riots of the youth – as young as seven years old – across Britain. In his impassioned plea, he said:

> ...I believe one of the most significant questions that we ought to be addressing in the wake of these deplorable events, is what kind of education we are interested in, for what kind of a society? Are we prepared to think not only about discipline in classrooms, but also about the content and ethos of our educational institutions – asking can we once again build a society which takes seriously the task of educating citizens, not consumers, not cogs in an economic system, but citizens...[17]

The archbishop issues a challenge for Britain to reconstruct its education not by using an instrumentalist model but one that builds "virtue, character and citizenship". This echoes a cry from many quarters around the globe, for some time now, for character education to be at the heart of our curricula. Indeed through the ages, it has been at the forefront of debates about the purpose of education.

I propose a way forward is to embrace a paradigm that stands at the opposite end of the exchange paradigm alluded to in this speech. If the exchange paradigm is self-orientated, then a radical counterpoint would be a 'gift paradigm', which is other-oriented. Vaughan and Estola describe the gift paradigm[18] as one where "a giver unilaterally satisfies the need of a receiver and thereby establishes bonds of mutuality and trust."[19] Gratitude embodies a dynamic interrelation between giver, receiver and gift, and as such can provide a powerful dimension to the gift paradigm. Philosopher Robert Roberts describes gratitude as comprising of

> ...givers, gifts, recipients, and the attitudes of giver and recipient toward one another. It is a deeply social emotion, relating persons to persons in quite particular ways...[20]

By encapsulating the relationship between giver, receiver and gift, gratitude is highly relevant to the educational context. The receiver of education recognises that what they receive is a gift, and this prompts them to give back. When the giver of the gift of education sees that what they give is perceived as a gift, they are motivated to give and give, without necessarily wanting anything in return. A true dynamic is restored where education encompasses a healthy flow of giving and receiving amongst all parties. In most contexts, education is currently constructed as the teacher who is giving the gift of education to the recipients, the students, and there is an absence of students being educated to give back for the gifts of education. Too often education is not seen by its receivers as a gift or privilege, but only as a right or expectation.

This book neither presents gratitude as *the* answer to how we might educate better citizens, nor as a panacea to cure all of the ills of society. However, it does present a strong case for why we may consider gratitude as an important missing piece of current educational practices and why it may play a part in being a powerful antidote to the exchange paradigm.

Archbishop Williams goes on in his speech to draw our attention to a need for greater awareness of a deepened sense of "empathy with others", and "our involvement together in a social project in which we all have to participate". Yet to rally us *all* to participate in a social project – particularly one that aims to consider the kinds of virtues, character and citizenship we wish to promote in education – we need to consider, intelligently and wisely, the global, pluralistic and post-structuralist society we cohabit.

Just around the corner, or at least somewhere in the vicinity of the parliament where the archbishop was speaking, there are a growing number of philosophers and educators who take issue with educational policy that advocates what they call the "happiness agenda". In their recent work, educational philosophers Kathryn Eccleston and Dennis Hayes[21] present an important and convincing warning against the rise of "therapeutic education", which they define as "...any activity that focuses on perceived emotional problems and which aims to make educational content and learning processes more 'emotionally engaging'..."[22] They object to the large amount of funding being poured into education programs that focus on emotional wellbeing, and the picture of the "diminished self" as being vulnerable and fragile, that lies behind these initiatives. They regard such therapeutic education as "profoundly anti-educational", as it attempts to "coach appropriate emotions as part of developing emotional wellbeing and happiness."[23] Moreover, they cite many poignant examples where education in these emotions is common across all levels of education, and is socially engineered by the state.

When Adam Smith, in his 1759 work *The theory of moral sentiments*, recommended gratitude as a crucial antidote to self-interest if we were to have a healthy political economy, and when G.K. Chesterton wrote of gratitude as the source of human happiness in the early 1900s, they were doing so at a time when society was much more malleable to embracing a common identity that was prescribed by the church or the state. The most we should aim for today is an invitation to engage in healthy and open dialogue. If a commitment to a particular aspect of character education should arise from this dialogue, it needs to be chosen consciously and critically, and be informed by a plurality of views and concerns.

This book is not aimed at prescribing a certain way of being, nor is it offered as something that can be considered in isolation from other dimensions that contribute to effective education. Rather, I am inviting my readers to engage with the hypothesis that gratitude may be one important aspect that, for reasons I explore in the following chapters, has been overlooked.

Lived experience as my field of inquiry

As a custodian of gratitude I would not consider letting it loose in education without a critical framework that honours its strong historical and cultural roots. If we introduce gratitude poorly, it could be swept up as part of the 'happiness agenda' (which is currently its place) and miss its educational purpose and potential. In order to examine the role of gratitude critically, we need to listen to the difficulties the term raises; we need to awaken to what these difficulties can teach us about ourselves and about the term gratitude; and we need to make time for our understanding of gratitude to evolve. To this end, this book engages with hermeneutic inquiry to invite the reader to explore both dilemmas and possibilities. By taking this approach, I consciously rebel against the simplistic ways in which the concept of gratitude is used in some of the contemporary discourse that dominates the so-called 'positivity industry'.

Gratitude in Education: A Radical View uses impressionist ethnography[24] to explore the potential of gratitude, and to bring to life the complexities which educators grapple with when practising gratitude. My approach is narrative and interpretive as I recount stories of academics, school leaders, teachers, students, pre-service teachers, and parents, and interweave them into an account of my own discovery of the significance and challenge of practising gratitude in my life as an academic, teacher educator and parent, and about gratitude as a radical act of agency in education. It is impressionistic because, using strategies of remembering, recalling, and imagining, I deliberately attribute certain characters, parts of conversations, circumstances and events to players in my narratives in order to bring to life the dilemmas and give fullness to each story. In doing so I am able to bring the lived experience of gratitude to life in all its complexities and subtleties.

My ethnographic impressions draw together interpreted threads of teachers' and students' reflections, personal interactions, transcripts from interviews and focus groups, class discussions, and extracts from emails and student journals.[25] The characters portrayed are real people, though some are composites. Sometimes I have embellished responses and dilemmas by incorporating those experienced by others in different contexts. The institutions where they are positioned are real places. All identities are masked. I do not wish any character or place to be associated with a particular portrait. My purpose is not to tell the story of a particular character or a particular institution, but to draw out general points that may be relevant to many.

I have extended some questions and answers or reinterpreted them to tease out the dilemmas more fully for the reader. Large bodies of text such as excerpts from transcripts remain true to their original form.

Through my years of study as a practising educator, many thinkers in the fields of philosophy, education, sociology, positive psychology, spirituality and anthropology have caused me to reflect deeply about the place of gratitude. Rather than looking to these texts to provide a unifying theory underlying my approach to gratitude, I propose that they each offer lenses of wisdom through which those who work in the field of education may view their experiences of gratitude. To this end, I interweave theoretical insights with the exploration of the complexities and potential of gratitude.

Each chapter starts with a scenario in a school or university setting and uses dialogue to tease out the possibilities and dilemmas regarding the chapter's topic. After introducing the reader to various dimensions of gratitude practice for teachers, the book turns its focus on teaching gratitude to students, and invites the reader to further consider its pedagogical significance.

Although the effects of gratitude have been explored in other fields, this is the first full text to explore gratitude in the context of education, and the first to present gratitude as a pedagogy that underlies effective teaching. It acknowledges that gratitude is only one aspect of a teacher's pedagogy, but argues that it is so important that it is worthy of this work in its own right.

I invite you to join me in an exploration of the worthiness of a greater consciousness of gratitude in your vocation and life.

A LANDSCAPE OF GRATITUDE

The voyage of discovery is not in seeking new landscapes, but in having new eyes.
– Marcel Proust

In this chapter I use a school workshop on gratitude as a backdrop that sets the scene for the various dilemmas and complexities that will be investigated in the book. As the responses from these primary school teachers show, for many people their notion of gratitude is inseparable from other notions, or can even be comfortably replaced by them. Through the enthusiasm of some and the reservations of others, I hope to pave the way to a deeper appreciation of the depths of gratitude that reflect its cultural and historical richness, and also its ambiguity.

Leaders first?

For many weeks I had been anticipating the prospect of introducing a gratitude workshop to twenty-five teaching staff at Eastgates Primary School[26]. The nearer the time for the workshop, the more excited I became. Eastgates is situated within a large Australian metropolis, in a district where there is a distinct socio-economic advantage and wide multicultural representation amongst the people who live and work there. Eastgates' students represent many different ethnic backgrounds. Some of their teachers come from South-East Asian, Indian and Maori cultures. As in many other schools, a few teachers are nearing retirement, some have been teaching at the school for over a decade, and others are at the very beginning of their careers. Two or three have just started teaching there.

Claire, the school principal, came to Eastgates less than a year ago from a school she described as amongst the most disadvantaged of the schools in the city. She was already growing tired of the complaints of some Eastgates' staff and what she perceived as their petty behaviour, and so she was excited about the prospect of teachers practising gratitude and hopefully "waking them up to how lucky they are to teach in *this* school!" I was optimistic and pleasantly nervous because this was the first primary school where I had had a chance to introduce my workshop, called *Gratitude in Education: Worthy pedagogy or prosaic hopefulness?*

Over more than a decade of introducing a pedagogy of gratitude in high schools and universities, I had learned to modify the ways I was leading educators in workshops. When teachers see leaders practise gratitude, and see others benefit from their practice, it is likely that they would follow those leaders. Similarly, when a teacher practises gratitude, students are more likely to follow their teacher's example. I will rarely accept invitations to introduce gratitude as a learning strategy for students, without first offering it to school leaders and then after that, to teachers and parents.

With this idea in mind, I had visited Eastgates Primary a few months before to introduce my gratitude research to a group of six school leaders, including Claire. My inquiry into the effects of other school leaders practising gratitude had revealed some positive effects.[27] They reported enhanced wellbeing, better relationships with colleagues and students, increased self-awareness, and improved student learning outcomes. As one of these leaders wrote:

> *I made the effort to think about the students (and) be grateful for this environment with so many delightful cooperative intelligent students and even those who may not have met my expectations – and thought about how good it was to be here working and interacting with students.*

After discussing the potential of gratitude to be an antidote to a culture of complaint, and to enhance student learning, all the leaders enthusiastically resolved to include the rest of the Eastgates' staff in a forthcoming gratitude workshop. They could also see that first the leaders must practise gratitude. They knew this, although they wanted to jump right in and find a place for gratitude in the curricula for all students. All six leaders were keen to join what I called a 'gratitude project', which invited them to consciously focus on a gratitude practice and deliberately note the effects and challenges of their individual efforts. However, within the first week of practice, two members emailed me to apologise that they had too much on their plate and that they felt that it was too hard to be conscious of gratitude all the time. Two months later, only one of the school leaders had stayed on board with me. This was Julie, the assistant principal.

Claire agreed wholeheartedly with the idea of promoting more gratitude, but she said she would like to sit the year out and watch how the project progressed with the rest of the school, and let her staff get to know her first. As I had already sensed that all eyes were on Claire's performance as a newcomer to the school, I could understand her dilemma. However, as an outsider and relative stranger, I did not feel that I was in a position to advise Claire that it was likely that the other staff would not benefit from the project as much as they would if she were involved.

Voluntary participation is an important ingredient for any gratitude initiative in a school. Unfortunately the principal was so eager to make an impact on what she perceived as a culture of negativity amongst some of the staff, that she insisted that it would be essential for all the teaching staff to hear about the benefits of gratitude. Claire was so confident that this initiative was going to make a positive impact that she was proud to announce this in her targets for accountability in the following year. Dysfunctional and disharmonious relationships amongst colleagues in schools appeared to be of sufficient concern to school principals, to the extent that Claire could feel confident about announcing her goals so publicly.

I wanted to proceed with caution, to firstly see if this context was welcoming the gratitude initiative, and indeed if teachers also gave priority to Claire's message of "turning the culture of negativity around this year". I thought that because I was offering the workshop for free, coming in as a university researcher, I could somehow take a neutral position, be a free agent, and separate myself from Claire's larger agenda. The politics of the situation spoke otherwise. My workshop was to be presented to all staff whether they liked it or not. To make matters worse, Claire's express wish was that each one of the teachers would continue with the project for the remainder of the year. I needed to respect Claire's desire to create a more harmonious school and that her heart was yearning for the atmosphere of respect and value that permeated her previous school. The most I could do was to share with Claire my view that the gratitude work was not a quick fix for the problems she perceived amongst her staff.

Leading with grace

On the day of the workshop, I flew into the city on a very early flight, accompanied by an array of mixed emotions. I was excited and wanted to put my best foot forward, but I was also apprehensive, disoriented and tired. I was struggling with my confidence to run a workshop on the topic of gratitude in my present state. I was exhausted from being immersed in marking hundreds of students' essays for many weekends and late nights. The question of where I stood in relationship to Claire's larger agenda and how this would affect my relationships with her staff weighed heavily on my mind.

Most of the time I espouse and do my best to follow Parker J. Palmer's[28] philosophy of teaching: "we teach who we are: good teaching comes from the identity and integrity of the teacher"[29]. On my way to the workshop I questioned the worthiness of anything much from inside myself. I felt divorced from integrity as I reflected on the amount of complaint I had been recently engaged in. I had had to do double the amount of teaching and marking of students' work compared with many of my colleagues. Although I had tried to reach into gratitude and whip myself up into a more positive state, I could only stay there for short bursts before negativity took hold. Gratitude could not live up to its derivative, grace, in me at this point of the workshop. I feared the ungraciousness I saw concealed inside me might reveal itself to the participants.

My state of apprehension and exhaustion lessened quite dramatically on my arrival at the primary school, when I was greeted very warmly by Julie, who Claire had appointed to be in charge of the gratitude project.

"I've had all these amazing experiences," she said. "I can't believe how different I feel and even my husband and friends are noticing a positive difference. I feel calmer, more at peace, happier, and closer to my colleagues than I ever thought possible. I also feel more deeply connected to many of my students – even the difficult ones. "

In Julie's office, posters on the wall seemed to envelop me from many sources of wisdom about gratitude. One by Balduin Schwarz caught my eye:

> Gratitude is vital for each of us
> if we are to understand ourselves and others;
> for gratitude sees, and fully affirms,
> our dependency, our lack,
> our need to receive all that
> which we cannot provide ourselves. [30]

At the moment of writing this down, I recognised my dependence on Julie's enthusiasm. The grace her increased gratitude had brought wrapped itself around me, and my own sense of gratitude was renewed. Julie said that before the project she had not thought much at all about consciously practising gratitude, but by valuing people more, thanking students and staff with real heart, and finding little ways of telling people that she noticed their contribution, "there was an unbelievable shift." Julie's newfound joy infected me, filled me with energy and confidence. I was deeply relieved when she agreed to share her experiences of her gratitude practices at the opening of the workshop. It was the power of gratitude, not me, that was to do all the transformative work. I needed to let my fragile ego, my self-assuming importance, off the hook.

Are teachers hot or cold on gratitude?

The workshop started on Wednesday at 3.15pm. Most of the twenty-five teachers walked in exhausted, more ready to go home than to sit through a workshop. Soon many sat up straighter in their chairs as Julie inspired them with her experiences and enthusiasm. She talked glowingly about gratitude as the answer to many problems in the school. However, I noticed that some of the teachers were cringing. Might they have been thinking that her uncritical embrace of the concept was naïve, that we have at least one 'Pollyanna' in the room? I decided to come clean as I introduced myself. My instinctive response was to reveal some of my tussle in getting there and to be honest in saying that I felt the least suitable person to conduct a workshop on gratitude. Many in the audience smiled as I told my story. I sensed the possibility of connecting with them.

I asked the teachers what gratitude meant for them. Their responses were many and varied. Gratitude was something they did not contemplate. Gratitude was something that they thought about deeply and practised. Heartfelt definitions of gratitude rolled off some tongues – giving thanks for the people and resources in our community and acknowledging their importance in our daily lives was one of them. The word 'gratitude' was uncomfortable for some, and one teacher pleadingly asked, "can't we call it something else?" Many wondered if it would be better to use words like optimism, positive attitude, appreciation, thankfulness, praise, recognition or thanks?

When I moved on to discuss the question of the challenges raised by the notion that 'gratitude' should have a more prominent place in our education system, I immediately sensed that there is nothing like involuntary participation – and the absence of the principal – for strong opinions to be aired. Many teachers gave impassioned replies. Some felt that the idea of gratitude in schools was absurd. Even if there were some possible relevance for gratitude in other aspects of their lives, its place *in education* would be under scrutiny. Gratitude would be deemed the least appropriate response to all the perceived inequities and injustices teachers were suffering in a system that they believed was in rapid decay.

What was the big deal was a question asked by others. Gratitude was something they actively embraced to be a good teacher. They could not imagine a classroom or school without lots of praise and many utterances of thank you.

"But is that just a blind, ritual thankyou?" Bill's question challenged them. "I'm tired of the empty words that lack the authenticity to inspire real gratitude!"

Hyun Ji was a teacher from South Korea. She agreed with Bill wholeheartedly. Her culture had instilled in her from a very young age many rituals and customs of gratitude. Yet she felt that these rituals and customs were rarely performed with much sincerity or real feeling behind them.

Bill's doubting question and Hyun Ji's disappointment charged the discussion with energy. Kathryn sat forward in her seat. She said how much she valued the gratitude of her own child's teacher who would write notes of thanks in the school diary. She appreciated the teacher sharing these things with her. It had boosted her confidence as a parent and made her feel closer to the teacher.

"Funnily enough," Kathryn said, "it would be so easy to do this for the children and parents in my own class." Her eyes lit up as if she had not made the connection until that moment of speaking.

Some noted that were other teachers within this school community who radiated gratitude. It was uplifting to be in their presence. Nothing ruffled them. The atmosphere in their classes was "heavenly". But it was difficult to be like those practitioners all the time. These observations turned our talk to the difficulties of maintaining our gratitude when we face long hours, difficult students and their parents, sickness, tiredness, systems not working, not being listened to, stress, our problems with our own children or ageing parents.

Robert rose to emphasise these issues. I was to find out later that he was the union representative for the school's teachers. He said that promoting gratitude was like sitting back and accepting the *status quo* and this would place one in a passive position. Heads nodded as he explained.

"Current disputes between the Education Department and the Teachers' Federation highlight how little the teaching profession is understood or valued by our employer and society. If we have to be grateful, surely that is just going to give the message that all is okay when clearly it's not!"

Then a woman of great presence and serenity called us to consider another aspect of gratitude. As a Maori woman, Tipene said that she was very protective of what gratitude meant to her and told us that her culture had other names and meanings that went beyond the normal everyday notions of gratitude. One cannot be a teacher in her culture without a profound sense of the importance of gift-giving as part of the act of teaching and learning.

I invited the teachers to work in small groups to further pursue their responses to points already raised. While everyone else jumped eagerly into deliberation and debate, Marie who was sitting close to me, asked quietly, "Are you promoting a particular religious viewpoint?" Perhaps her question was one of acknowledgment that gratitude is at the heart of many religions and spiritual paths, but Marie, who told me she was a Christian, seemed to need my answer. Possibly it was so essential for her to connect her notion of gratitude with her own faith that she needed to know about mine.

With Marie's permission, I asked the whole group if they thought that the word gratitude had any religious overtones. My question revealed that there was disquiet similar to Marie's amongst some participants. Others were critical of what they believed smacked of New Age, or another slogan, another ideal, another quick fix, or someone telling them how to be.

From another perspective, Ashok quietly shared threads of Hindu teachings about gratitude that ran from the Upanishads right through to his dinner table where he and his children offered thanks for their day and then sat in silence as they tasted and ate their food with 'thanks'. As he spoke in a kind and unassuming manner, it seemed that Ashok's whole being exuded relief at the thought of being able to bring his sacred world into what he considered to be an overly-secularised education system.

Meanwhile, two older male teachers slumped back in their seats, chins dropped to chest, legs stretched out, as if mimicking and in compliance with one another. Perhaps it was just sour grapes on my part because they were not engaging in the workshop, but I allowed myself to judgementally wonder whether they were complacently nesting and hatching their superannuation eggs. They were easily distracted and made underhand comments throughout the discussion. Their negative attitude was difficult for me, and others, to accept, and stood in stark contrast with a group of young teachers on the opposite side of the room, who were openly enthusiastic about the potential of gratitude. Where was the place for their own gratitude when they could see that some people at the end of their professional lives were cynical and disenchanted with the vocation of teaching?

These young teachers reminded me of many of my student teachers, who seem to be more highly evolved in their consciousness than many who are twice their age. They might want everyone around them to embrace the wisdom of gratitude that they can so easily accept. Until it is pointed out to them, they might neglect to empathise with the conditions that have led to the resignation and cynicism they see in some older teachers. These two older Eastgates' teachers may well have embraced gratitude as part of their natural response. They may have given a lot by devoting long hours and much of their energy to their teaching. Over the years, they may have felt undervalued or under appreciated by the parents and students, and in some cases their principal, receiving nothing but complaints or disrespect. They could be too tired and in too much pain to reach into the wisdom that was so accessible to the younger teachers, and thus unable to move past their resentment. They could have put up walls, withdrawn and found refuge in each other, in order to be able to protect themselves from being asked to give when they had nothing left inside.

The young teachers were cautious about the principal's role. "Is Claire joining this project?" Katie asked me softly. She believed the project would only work if Claire came to the party and changed her habit of valuing some staff members and not others. Again, I wondered if this young teacher was expecting too much of her principal and was not able to put herself in Claire's shoes. Katie also asked me if I was going to do something about paper wastage and lights being left on unnecessarily. "Surely gratitude for materials comes into the picture somewhere?" she asked.

Dianne tapped my elbow as I walked from the room for a coffee break. She said she did not want to be overheard and asked to speak to me privately. Almost whispering, she told me about the woman in her discussion group who recently came back to work after the death of her son who was killed in a car accident. Next she told me about the teacher who had lost his wife to breast cancer only a month ago. I could only nod in silence. Would those two teachers have wanted me to know what Dianne was disclosing to me? I knew that sometimes people feel they have to protect the secrets and welfare of others. Dianne did say that she thought I should know something of their situation so that I could be sensitive to how difficult the notion of gratitude might be for some of my workshop participants. I thanked her sincerely. She had reminded me of something that I was mortified to have forgotten to say – a habitual prelude to all my workshop discussions. My own woes had so distracted me that I had neglected to fulfil one of my promises to myself – to *always* express the most important of caveats in a gratitude workshop: *Although gratitude for small everyday things, like what we can smell or see, may help in times of great adversity, there are some situations where it may be impossible, or even perhaps inappropriate, to expect ourselves to initially respond with gratitude!*

Respecting Dianne's confidence, I waited till later to weave those words of caution into the workshop. The moment I did, a woman lifted her head and her sad eyes met mine for the first time. Was she the grieving mother, I wondered? How could my many years of research and all the numerous scientific papers written on the topic of gratitude possibly offer her solace?

I presented my caveat along with the remarkable story of a Rawandanese refugee whom I had come to know during my work. His name was Joseph. Joseph had survived terrible atrocities against his people. He had been in and out of refugee camps. Recently during a local gathering of friends, Joseph relayed a very moving story and message. He had been in different refugee camps since he was four and came to Australia two years ago at the age of 35. He had witnessed unimaginable acts of violence and the greatest of losses. He had seen both his parents murdered and had lost his brothers and sisters in genocide in his country.

When he was twenty, he was in a camp with many others who had lost everything – their loved ones and homes and for some, their professional identity as teachers, doctors and accountants. All those incarcerated in the camp were very depressed; it was difficult to find a reason to continue living. Then one day at one of their regular community meetings they decided to try to dwell no longer on their losses, but focus instead on the fact that they had each other. During later meetings each person was asked to share a gift, a talent or skill with the community. Many camp dwellers began to feel relief from their suffering as they discovered great respect and gratitude for each other. Young and old attended regular meetings; each in turn shared what they knew. From there they started a school for the young children of the camp. Instead of spending many more years depressed about what they did not have, they learned to value the knowledge and skills they possessed. When Joseph had uttered his last sentence, "My suffering is my treasure", he had moved us all to tears. Joseph looked upon his life with gratitude.

Joseph's story inspired some teachers to share accounts of people who had "come out of the other side of adversity" and for whom gratitude was "the only response to life".

Empirical research: What a relief!

After a few moments' silence, I raked around in the box of resources I had brought along and held up the *The Psychology of Gratitude*[31], a large and formidable compilation of recent studies from various fields. I was moving on to the question 'Why gratitude?' The release of tension in some parts of the room was palpable. Those who had been wriggling in their chairs were perhaps uncomfortable or embarrassed – had the discussion so far been unwanted, intruding upon personal and private domains? Perhaps for them, 'appropriate' professional development might strictly relate to teaching techniques or curricula. Some teachers were animated, enjoying the focus on gratitude. Were others seeking a safer place to be, in the supposedly objective world of clinical, psychological research? For them was I, at last, stepping out of the 'airy fairy' into the real world of empiricism? I allowed a PowerPoint slide to slip onto the screen to show a list of some research findings.

Increased gratitude leads to:

- a greater sense of wellbeing
- increased optimism
- a tendency to exercise more often
- a decrease in depression
- a greater sense of connectedness
- a greater ability to deal with adversity
- improved relationships
- greater joy and satisfaction.[32]

This slide was to break the silence adopted by some teachers in the previous session.

They seemed to become increasingly alert when I shared the results of my own research into the effects of gratitude when addressing the vexed and perplexing issue of student disengagement. With another PowerPoint slide I displayed a quote from Johann, a first-year university student, who participated in a study-skills program where I introduced gratitude.

...thinking about things that I could be grateful for during the presentation itself, already increased my alertness in the class and my ability to learn. Often I feel lethargic during lectures, and although I am hearing what is being said, I am not properly listening to and taking in the content. I find that now, however, when I am grateful, that cloudiness in my head is gone and I can listen a whole lot better, without having to try so hard.

The workshop teachers were well acquainted with Johann's "cloudiness"; they saw it in some of their own students. Could they awaken now to the possibility that gratitude could 'clear the fog' for their students so they might be present in their learning?

I also referred to the "HeartMath" work of Rolin McCraty and Doc Childre, who demonstrate that concentrating on the emotion of appreciation for prolonged periods of time leads not only to improved health, but also to enhanced cognitive ability. During their research, they discovered that students of all ages and levels showed a significant increase in positive "emotional well-being, classroom behaviours, learning and academic performance." [33]

From the teachers' enthusiasm at the prospect of gratitude awakening a different kind of engagement in their students, I saw that I had found a way to reach into their hearts about the role of gratitude in education. They were interested in motivating their students to learn. If research could show positive outcomes, they could perhaps see the point of helping their students to practise gratitude. If there was one thing that I could share with Claire about the outcomes of this workshop it would be that her teachers were motivated to take up gratitude because of their concerns for their students' learning. This was far more important to them than Claire's agenda "to make the teachers more positive and less complaining".

Teachers' gratitude before students' gratitude?

Eager to teach their students the very next day to practise gratitude, the teachers were abuzz with creative ways of how they could do this. There were some activities that they had tried before with their students – and with quite impressive results: gifts and 'thankyou' cards to parents, librarians, parent helpers, the principal; placemats with pictures of all the things they were grateful for; students writing gratitude notes to each other.

I think the Eastgates teachers expected that my next move would be to further explore ideas of teaching gratitude. Instead, to intrigue them, I displayed on screen a photo of a massive waterfall in full flow. They caught my point immediately when I asked them to guess my aim. "Oh, so our gratitude flows down to our students", said one teacher.

As I had with the school leaders, I asked the teachers to consider how their students' ability to practise gratitude might be influenced by their own capacity to do so. I shared with them a time when I was trying to teach my pre-service teachers about the role of gratitude in the teaching and learning nexus, and received blank stares. On this memorable occasion the group of aspiring teachers did not seem to have a clue what I was talking about. I was trying to be passionate in teaching them about the power of their gratitude to influence their students' learning outcomes but they remained distracted, uneasy and uncooperative. Later, unbeknownst to them, I remembered that I had spoken ungraciously and negatively about a colleague behind her back – and took this attitude with me into class. I had missed the opportunity to turn away from backbiting and look for the good in that person, or at least change the discussion to something else. It was no wonder I found it hard to convey my own gratitude in that class, let alone teach about gratitude in ways my students could fully embrace.

To my surprise, over half of the Eastgates teachers signed up for the next stage of the project – to adopt gratitude practices and take note of their effects in their teaching context. Later, we would meet again to share ideas on how they could introduce gratitude practices to their students.

Finally I asked them to envisage what their school could be like if the practice of gratitude were truly active in the school community. They foresaw engaged students, co-operative classrooms, parents and school leaders who valued them, and harmony in their relationship with their peers.

Learning from parents

That evening, half an hour before the parents' gratitude workshop was due to begin, I was setting up at the back of the library when Claire arrived and advised me that twelve chairs would probably be enough. It was a wet evening and she did not expect a big turnout. Julie was more optimistic, saying that several parents had replied to her newsletter advertisement, headed *Gratitude in Education: Exploring the relevance for teachers and parents in assisting student learning.*

"Let's start with twenty", she insisted, "and we can always just move in a bit closer if not many turn up."

Soon nine parents arrived and warmed the room with the colours of their origin: one wore a lotus pink sari, one a sky blue taberna, and another a kuta sava flowing with yellow and orange hues. I sensed straightaway the air of respect and reverence that was filling the library as those parents sat down – this was in stark contrast to the feeling that took hold of me when the teachers had entered the same space earlier in the day. More parents from diverse cultures came into the circle of chairs. I could not help but ask about their countries of origin and found a father from Vietnam, a mother from Turkey, another from Iran, and a couple of Maori descent. A constant stream of parents continued to fill the room.

Claire seemed a little puzzled, but at the same time delighted, by the number of parents who were turning up for the workshop. She walked over to introduce herself to someone who sat alone between some empty places. Julie and another teacher flurried around to find extra chairs. Soon, thirty-five parents had arrived and there were still five minutes to go before the workshop was to begin.

Claire enthusiastically greeted the parents and thanked them for coming and taking time out of their busy lives. She talked proudly about the gratitude project that many of the Eastgates teachers had signed up for earlier that day, and of it being part of her strategic plan for the school.

When my turn came to begin the workshop, I asked the parents their reasons for coming. They shared rich cultural interpretations of gratitude and what it meant for them. We heard that in Islam there is a belief that one should be thankful and praise God in every circumstance. For example, Muslims answer the question, "How are you?" with the Arabic phrase, "Alhamdulillah", which means, "Praise and thanks be to God". The Koran teaches that God created human beings for the purpose of being grateful to him. We heard that in the Hindu religion, gratitude for everything, without expecting anything, is a very important principle, and one that is closely tied to the sacred texts that teach, "We should do all our duties in the spirit of service to the Lord". We heard from a Christian, who quoted from the books of the Corinthians, "It is all for your sake, so that as grace extends to more and more people it may increase thanksgiving, to the glory of God."

As these parents spoke passionately about why gratitude appealed to them and motivated them to come to the workshop to find out more, I could see that gratitude lay at the core of their faith. Their dialogue gave testimony to the view that gratitude is at the heart of many religions, a theme that commonly permeates religious cultures. Robert Emmons and Cheryl Crumpler state:

> …gratitude, like forgiveness and…love, bridges theological and psychological understandings of human nature…the roots of gratitude can be seen in many of the world's great religious traditions. In the great monotheistic religions of Judaism, Christianity, and Islam, the concept of gratitude permeates the texts, prayers, and the teachings. Worship with gratitude to God for the many gifts and mercies are common themes…[34]

These various interpretations sparked interest amongst those in the room, and presented an occasion for parents to learn more about the values and beliefs of others in their school community. Many of the parents seemed eager to take advantage of this forum, to see whether their sacred ways of expressing gratitude could fit the secular world of their children's education. Their experience and deep understanding was to provide a foundation for us to consider the meaning of gratitude and how to apply it as the workshop proceeded.

Most parents said they came along because they were intrigued by how their gratitude could assist their children's learning, and were eager to go straight home and teach their children how to be more grateful. I talked about the teachers' workshop where I had explained how the gratitude practice of teachers has an enormous influence on their students' gratitude. Similarly, the gratitude practice of parents and grandparents greatly strengthens this influence. Children find it easier to express gratitude if they see gratitude practices in their homes and feel their parents' gratitude for them.

I illustrated what I meant with an example in my own experience of parenting. Sometimes as parents we are tempted to empathise with our children's grievances about the school or their teachers. We support our children by joining in their negative complaint. This way we promote a negative attitude as being appropriate. An alternative approach might be to model gratitude to our children by speaking about what we are grateful for in their teachers or school, and expressing this often in tangible ways. Then our children are more likely to do the same.

One parent asked if all the teachers were going to be involved in this initiative, saying he could only envisage it working if all the school came on board. My response was to suggest that for the work on gratitude to have integrity, people must consciously and voluntarily choose to participate in the project.

"Just because teachers choose to not join the gratitude group doesn't mean they're not practising gratitude," I added, "and some have already told me that they prefer to practise gratitude individually and not in a group." I also assured the parents that the *quality* of the *practice* of gratitude from committed teachers – not the quantity – would be what would make the biggest difference.

As I shared some of the recent research on gratitude from positive psychology, I was acutely aware of a gap between the culturally rich stories that poured forth at the beginning of the workshop and the clinical, objective nature of these studies. One of the parents, Jane, a psychologist, questioned the validity of the research behind some of the claims of positive psychology. Brian, another parent replied to Jane that he, with other executives in his company, had attended a coaching seminar conducted by a "very skilled person", who based his whole approach to coaching and facilitation on values and strengths. Brian talked of the positive results he witnessed from this kind of coaching in his company. He was convinced that "there is something very powerful in all of this." I responded to Jane's query by recommending some of the experiences of counsellors and psychologists who practised gratitude in other educational contexts. I presented some words from Amy, a psychologist working in a university student services unit, who had joined a gratitude project:

> *...gratitude for me has come to be about the reciprocal nature of things, and the follow-through action, not just the thought. So how has it made a difference to my work? I suppose it's all in the attitude. Practising gratitude more consciously has enabled me to:*

– *step outside of complaint more often and therefore experience less suffering and be able to cope with the difficult situations (like overload) a bit better;*
– *appreciate more fully the positive experiences at work (e.g. with my counselling clients) and the positive benefits of just having a secure job with good pay;*
– *more fully appreciate the time I'm spending here at this workplace for what it is as I won't have it forever (e.g. the team support, the skills enhancement etc.);*
– *feel the solidarity and deep understanding of others;*
– *break into an unexpected smile or laugh during a tough day... .*

> *I continue to drift in and out of awareness of these issues, but I am always happy to gently guide myself back on the path of gratitude and become more aware, more conscious of it. I assume that practice can only make me get better and better at it over time!*

Amy's words seemed to appease Jane because she continued her involvement in our discussion.

Our consideration of the possible part gratitude could play in the role of school psychologists led to the idea of including everyone within the school community – librarians, counsellors, cleaners, and administrative staff. If we are to invite our students into gratitude, we need to work together as a community where gratitude can be natural for them.

We had already passed our allotted time for being together. It was time to close. Julie stood and asked the parents if they would like to join a parents' gratitude group where they could continue the discussion on the role of gratitude and share their experiences and challenges. Claire followed by thanking them again for coming, and voiced her pleasure at the turnout. Forty of the forty-five who attended registered their interest in joining the gratitude group.

The hope of gratitude

As we were stacking the chairs Julie told me how thrilled she was because many of the parents who had come that night had never before been to any school event or Parents and Citizens meeting. She said that her own understanding and respect for gratitude had been deepened by hearing how the tapestry of gratitude is so finely woven in the lives of parents. "The whole day has been uplifting," was her comment.

Julie was full of ideas of how she was going to promote gratitude in the school, starting with newsletters to parents and providing a forum where teachers and parents could share their experiences. She asked to read the list of teachers and parents who had registered for the gratitude group. Her face lit up as she read aloud some names and she declared, "The whole school could be transformed by this gratitude project!"

Before I left, I took time to read another quote posted on Julie's wall. This one was from Melody Beattie:

Gratitude unlocks the fullness of life.
It turns what we have into enough, and more.
It turns denial into acceptance,
chaos to order, confusion to clarity.
It can turn a meal into a feast, a house into a home,
a stranger into a friend.
Gratitude makes sense of our past, brings peace for today,
and creates a vision for tomorrow." [35]

I wondered if Julie's optimism was grounded simply in hope for a better world, or if it was a clear vision of a better life for teachers, a life where they feel deeply valued and appreciated. A candle in the dark lights a whole room. The candle was Julie's. Would she be able to keep the flame alight in the everyday struggles of the workplace?

Seeing the landscape with new eyes

My experience of introducing gratitude to the teachers and parents at Eastgates Primary School marked a significant turning point in my approach to gratitude and how best to share it with others. I had previously believed that gratitude was something that could be clearly defined in a way that everyone could, and *should* understand. I had spent many years trawling through academic papers and philosophical texts to find *the* ideal definition that would suit all educators and students. The idealistic notion that gratitude is something that everyone in education should wholeheartedly embrace had swept me away from reality. I had seen gratitude as an all-encompassing solution to many of the ills of education. And to help prove my point, I had welcomed the scientific findings about the positive effects of gratitude outlined in the burgeoning body of research in positive and social psychology.

Confronting my own inability to practise gratitude during recent times allowed me to listen more sincerely to the difficulties raised by the word 'gratitude', and the problems others have with putting it into practice. It seemed that at nearly every turn, life was reminding me of the saying that one needs to teach what one most needs to learn.

So for me, this primary school workshop heralded the adoption of a slightly more humble approach. As these teachers invited me back to explore their journey of gratitude in the course of that year, I began to follow the thinking of the Italian philosopher, Gemma Fiumara[36], and tried consciously to learn how to "dwell with" what was being said, rather than to know it and grasp it and control it in some way.[37] Shifting my stance from thinking of myself as something of an expert to that of fellow traveller with these teachers, I found that I was no longer able to take refuge in Henry Sedgewick's[38] notion of gratitude as a "truly universal intuition". I had moved into a world that speaks of gratitude with a multitude of different voices, feelings, opinions, beliefs and connotations.

I realised that for gratitude to have a wider presence in our lives, it had to appeal to and spread beyond the small group of already-converted practitioners who were radiant examples. If we are to deepen gratitude in our educational contexts, we need to find a compass to navigate around the abstract, inaccessible and, at times, inappropriate application of the word gratitude, in the hope that we might embrace its enormous power and importance in an age when disillusionment can so easily take hold. Again, in the wisdom of Marcel Proust, "The voyage of discovery is not in seeking new landscapes, but in having new eyes". When we invite greater consciousness of the power of gratitude into our educational workplaces, we need not change the landscape to fit with our notion of what gratitude is, but attend to what the landscape can teach us about gratitude. Then we are more able to respond to gratitude as a source of energy, a catalyst for developing harmonious relationships, and a wellspring for transforming negative events into positive moments for growth.

CAN'T WE CALL IT SOMETHING ELSE?

... everything is so different in every instance...it's not the same...it's not
something you can just put into a big large frame and go this is
gratitude...there you go...it's all very, it's so specific in every different thing.
It's so tiny...and sometimes it's hard to actually put it into words...
– Sarah, pre-service teacher, interview

Here I outline traditional and contemporary origins of the notion of gratitude and
its core elements, before considering the confusion that can occur when searching
for a meaning for the term 'gratitude' that works in an educational environment. I
illustrate the struggle that some educators have with its possible religious or new
age overtones, or associations with indebtedness. I postulate reasons why they
sometimes try to replace the concept of gratitude with other terms. An examination
follows of the complexities that arise when educators limit gratitude to being a
positive emotion or equate it with the notion of positive thinking. The chapter aims
for a deeper conceptualisation of gratitude by making finer distinctions between
gratitude and other terms, and by highlighting some of the difficulties that teachers
encounter when they use them synonymously. It thereby deepens our
understanding of the notion of gratitude when it is considered in a secular
educational environment.

Let's hide it

One day, John, who is a senior academic in my faculty, unexpectedly invited me to
lunch. I had recently won a national university teaching award "for outstanding
contributions to student learning". The award honoured my scholarship and
practice over fifteen years that contributed consistently to demonstrated positive
outcomes for students in their practice of gratitude in various teaching and learning
contexts. The recognition must have sparked John's newfound interest in me.

I remembered earlier years when my ideas had been shunned by many academics
for being "too radical" or "too removed from the main game of teaching". For me,
the award recognised much more than my own efforts. It signalled that academia was
prepared to acknowledge and reward one of its academics for a study of the
ontology of self as teacher and self as learner.

Was my lunch with John to be symbolic of this kind of change? I pinched myself several times during our discussion as John asked me to talk about how my work on gratitude might be relevant in the redesign of the faculty's new curriculum for our teacher education units. Although I had been invited to conduct seminars on the role of gratitude in other faculties in the university, there had not been much interest from my own.

As the conversation progressed, John named some people in our faculty whom he felt would have difficulty with the notion of gratitude and asked if we could use it, but hide it in some way. "Couldn't we put it under the umbrella of 'student engagement' and then just mention gratitude later?" he suggested, "Or could we just call it something else, not gratitude?"

I asked him what his concerns were with the notion of gratitude. He was quick to assure me that the apprehensions he brought to our conversation were not his own but those that he imagined others in the faculty would have. He named a few whom he believed would never embrace my topic of research or come along to any seminar I might present on gratitude. His eyes left mine when he mentioned that the term gratitude could evoke tones of religiosity for some people. He himself was not a religious person. He took a scientific view of the world. He could understand their position. He had also heard some of our colleagues label my work as "new age hype" and that I was a bit of a Pollyana trying to make everything in education cosy and nice.

John went on to tell me that I would have a hard time convincing others in the faculty that gratitude has anything to do with their educational goals, or to the content they were to teach. He wanted me to explain what it was about gratitude that made it relevant to the new curricula, and indeed whether its goals were just to make us feel good or feel positive. "Doesn't it fit more in the world of counselling or therapy?" he asked. John seemed untouched by the recognition that other colleagues had given me through my award, recognition from a governing body of university learning and teaching. Surely the educational imperative had to be at the heart of the decision-making of such an esteemed national organisation?

Before I had a chance to answer John's question, he proceeded to tell me the doubts he had about positive psychology, the field into which he had bundled my work. He warned me to be wary, as it was the new fad, but was "flaky" and lacking in rigour. "I understand that your students love learning about these things, so I'm interested. But can we work together to think of another word, one that could be more palatable to all academics in our faculty?"

I wondered from his questions and concerns if John conceived of gratitude as an 'it', an object to discuss as something separate from and external to us, that we can choose to possess or not. I knew already that for some, like some teachers who attended the Eastgates Primary School workshop, gratitude was a 'thing' that people can hold up as external to themselves and their relationship with others.

I moved immediately to assure John that although gratitude is linked to religion and spirituality, it has long been a topic for academic discussion in fields as diverse as anthropology, sociology, zoology, moral philosophy, political science and economics. Reaching for more secular currency, I asked John if he had read Adam Smith's *Theory of Moral Sentiments*, where he speaks of the societal role of gratitude in moderating our selfish interests.[39] John seemed to relax a little when I mentioned other thinkers who, throughout the ages, have discussed gratitude as a powerful transformative force both individually and in society: Seneca, Shakespeare, Kant, Rousseau, Einstein, Pufendorf, Chesterton, Merton, Cicero, Spinoza, Aquinas and Maslow, just to name a few.

John seemed less assured when I then added a few of the great modern thinkers who advocate for transformative learning – Edmund O'Sullivan[40], Tobin Hart[41], Parker J. Palmer[42] – some who hold that education should be driven by a vision of the celebration for the gift of life. John's seeming discomfort at the words "transformation" and "celebration" led me to refrain from suggesting that for those who follow a religious path, practising gratitude may allow them to more fully embrace their individual identities in their lives as teachers and learners. Cautious that the words I use to embrace gratitude might halt our discussion, I stopped myself from describing my own idea of gratitude as "bringing forth our higher consciousness" or "awakening our true selves".

He then quizzed me about my lack of empirical research, and asked if I had any way of measuring the successes my students reported with gratitude practices. In response to his question I wanted to summon my recent reading of *Revisioning Transpersonal Theory*, where Jorge Ferrer and Richard Tarnas[43] talk about "the unconscious holdover", where an old paradigm threatens to destroy the new thoughts, no matter how relevant, valuable or true they really are. Could John be accused of the unconscious holdover of a paradigm that says that the subjectivity of the teacher and learner is part of their private domain, and out of bounds for us to discuss as having influence on educational processes? My work is challenging this holdover and another one that runs alongside it, but also through it – and that is the one that says that we can only legitimate our pedagogy if its elements are robust in their research and concrete in their ability to be measured. I ventured to challenge John by saying that "Although there are many empirical studies of gratitude and this is a growing area of research, I suggest that the place of gratitude in education cannot be proven by scientific empirical research. Like many powerful aspects of teacher identity that exist only in the abstract and which cannot be measured or even clearly articulated, gratitude can only be acknowledged, deepened, widened, and unveiled."

I recalled the struggle I often encountered when I could not explain the inner dimension of self, the subjective nature of gratitude, in language that those who speak from a traditional positivist stance would embrace. I did not want to rob gratitude of its transcendental qualities, its potential to bring greater meaning to our lives. I was willing to admit there are vocabularies associated with gratitude that makes it appear quasi-religious. Yet I wondered if we, John and I, could find a common discourse in which we could discuss gratitude as a vehicle for restoring what is most important in education: transformation of self.

Perhaps sensing my awkwardness, John steered the conversation away from gratitude to other faculty matters. As we walked up the hill after our lunch, he confessed that his other big difficulty with the notion of gratitude was that it implies that we would owe something to others. "I think if we called it something other than gratitude, then people would not feel that they were somehow in a weaker position if someone expressed gratitude to them and they were not able to respond in a heartfelt way. I'm not sure if I'm explaining myself well here, but there is an uneasiness, an irksomeness about being beholden to someone else, that I feel others would try to avoid."

John's stance was not unfamiliar. I remembered again that Aristotle had proclaimed that we should avoid being grateful as it would force us to admit that we owe something to someone and this would take away from our human greatness. Gratitude to others would diminish our sense of being "self-made". Contemporary thinkers, such as Robert Solomon, problematise gratitude because of its overtones of indebtedness: "Gratitude presupposes so many judgements about debt and dependency that it is easy to see why supposedly self-reliant American males would feel queasy about even discussing it".[44]

Leaving the sandstone pillars of the science faculty, we were about to enter another old building that spoke to me of the tenets of individualism implied by Aristotle all those years ago: an individualism that was built on our own intellectual prowess, our separateness from the other. Individualism is often at the core of academic culture, which builds a tradition of affording status and position to the genius and hard work of the individual. Rarely is there an opportunity or acknowledgment that the individual is entirely dependent upon others for their success. Academia masks such dependency in the fierce competitive environment it creates and propagates. If I put my hand up for the meaning that I choose to give to gratitude – an expression of thanks as an acknowledgement of the debt owed to others – I challenge this traditional paradigm of 'self-made greatness' at its core.

John, and all those he believes he is representing with his request, may not be walking away from gratitude itself. They may be walking away from unresolved connotations with indebtedness if considered in the context of education, especially in situations of unhealthy power and control relations – a theme we will explore in later chapters. Gratitude nudges the truth inside. We are only here in this moment, and from moment to moment, because of the efforts of others – the country and society in which we live, the environment that gives us food, air, water, clothing and shelter, the parents who gave birth to us, the teachers who taught us what we know, the students who challenged our ideas, and the opportunities we are given. Questions Margaret Atwood asks us at the opening of her book, *Payback,* are pertinent here:

Are we in debt to anyone or anything for the bare fact of our existence? If so, what do we owe, and to whom or to what? And how shall we pay?[45]

I believe that gratitude and indebtedness are inextricably intertwined. May the celebration of our indebtedness live on! This is my catchcry and my reason for why we need to call 'it' gratitude, and not something else.

Isn't gratitude the same as being positive?

After my meeting with John, one of my honours students, Anastasia, came bouncing into my office to share some of her initial findings after transcribing her recordings of interviews and a focus group. Anastasia's project was to investigate the effects and challenges that six first year pre-service teachers experienced when practising gratitude during their in-school practicum. There was a particular quality of Anastasia's that I see in many other pre-service teachers: a certain humility that accompanies the learning of something new – especially something as fragile and tender as learning to teach young students. Many feel indebted to their lecturers and mentors as they themselves step into the daunting experience of standing in front of a class. This may be why many pre-service teachers embrace a sense of indebtedness that is associated with gratitude more easily than academic audiences. In the background of my mind I was still trying to see what I needed to learn from my encounter with John's scepticism, so I felt soothed and reassured by Anastasia's optimism about her project.

Anastasia handed me her iPod, enthusiastically wanting to share with me some of the words of a song called "Positivity" by young, local musician, Adam Cousens:

> ...Positivity will set you free
>
> Cos there's a lot of people that will try to bring you down
> but it's okay they're not as tough as they sound
> it's probably because they see something in you
> that they're lacking in themselves and they're trying to find it too
> so where there's no love pour love into
> and we can draw love out enough for me and you
> so count your blessings one, two, three
> positivity will set you free
>
> Positivity will set you free
>
> And many colours make a rainbow
> and the treasure at the end

is worth the same in every person's heart no matter what the colour of their skin
want to change the world must begin within
the hearts and minds of every kind of people through the actions that we bring[46]

As I listened to the lyrics I watched Anastasia's eyes willing me to acknowledge the message of hope released in this song; hope that positivity offers the world. She was wanting me to be encouraged by a similar message she felt that we are giving in our work on gratitude in education. When I returned the iPod to Anastasia, she eagerly shared with me that some of her research participants used words such as positive thinking to describe their gratitude practice.

I read some of the transcript of the interview between Anastasia and Harry. Harry was teaching History and Society to Year 10 students. He was distressed by the stories he heard about some of his students, many of whom struggle to get out of bed, battle with dysfunctional family issues and suffer many kinds of mental imbalances. His way of coping with this situation was to build his own resilience by determinedly holding on to positive thoughts. He told Anastasia that his gratitude practice consisted of starting each day with positive thoughts and then throughout the day, he would check for negative thoughts and turn them back into positive ones. For example, he tried to stop thinking negatively about the parents he thought were responsible for the terrible neglect he saw in one of his students.

Harry had not yet realised that expressing gratitude toward students or parents does not oblige him to think or feel positively about them. Practising gratitude and positive thinking are different and distinct ways of orienting ourselves to others and the world. Research has confirmed that gratitude is, as Michael McCullough and his colleagues say, "empirically distinct from constructs such as life satisfaction, vitality, happiness, hope, and optimism."[47] No matter how explicit I try to make the distinction between gratitude and positive thinking at the time of introducing my work, many teachers like Harry might be drawn to take up more gratitude as *the* answer to their negativity and the negativity they experience around them. They see the idea of gratitude as a technique that is as simple as replacing negative thoughts and feelings with grateful ones. They might think of gratitude as a 'feel-good' way out of anger, frustration, anxiety, or feelings of being overwhelmed by circumstances.

It is indeed true that a sense of celebration about the giftedness we feel might be a springboard for our gratitude, and it is also true that gratitude can lead us to have more positive thinking or positive emotions. The problem lies in equating gratitude with positivity or in making them synonymous. If this distinction is not clear, and unless we are particularly mindful and conscious, we may be mistaken for wanting to place a veneer over negative situations that are crying out for our attention and a more authentic response.

Barbara Erenreich [48] argues that positive thinking has become the "opiate of the masses". She issues fair warning about how the positivity agenda is causing many to step out of reality. She explores the example of how people with breast cancer, and/or their carers, can be left feeling guilty that they were not positive enough and so they did not survive as long as they had hoped. Erenreich also contends that the drive towards positivity is a means of social control – of keeping the masses in one state of mind so they do not question the status quo, or keeping them from complaining. Companies only want positive people, so the underlying position goes.

In a similar vein, Kathryn Ecclestone and Dennis Hayes lodge the same warning against therapeutic attempts of educators to coach students in certain positive emotions. They rightly question the educational imperative of such a move. If not understood, gratitude may also be mistaken to be a cure for negative emotions and be seen as a technique to make students and teachers feel good.

If we examine how gratitude is discussed in the positive psychology literature more broadly, and its application to education more specifically, it is easy to see why some applications could be labelled as therapeutic and open to the same kind of scrutiny and questioning. As Emmons and McCullough say in the introduction of their book, *The Psychology of Gratitude*: "Gratitude is an emotion, the core of which is pleasant feelings about the benefit received…It is important that gratitude has a positive valence: It feels good."[49]

A further look at some of the applications of such conceptions of gratitude to the field of education reveals that it is clear that gratitude has been equated with feeling positive. Gratitude is a cornerstone of the work of Martin Seligman and his colleagues' intervention of "positive education" at Geelong Grammar:

> After Signature Strengths, the next series of lessons for the 10th grade focused on building positive emotion. Students wrote gratitude letters to parents, learned how to savour good memories, how to overcome negativity bias, and how gratifying kindness is to the giver. The blessings journal, in which students nightly kept track of what went well (WWW) that day, is now a staple at GGS.[50]

While these strategies may well be wonderful ways of generating positive outcomes for students, my problem still lies with them being called gratitude practices. I am reminded of my concern at a recent conference where the word "gratitude" was thrown around by participants who seemed to not take sufficient account of its depth and complexity, as well as its qualitative differences from positive thinking. Gratitude was something that we could download onto our iPhone to be reminded to think of something we were grateful for at several intervals during the day. We were encouraged to complete an on-line survey, to tick boxes in a "strengths inventory". The sum of our ticks would measure if gratitude were part of our repertoire of strengths or not. We played a "gratitude game", where we stood in a large circle and shared with a stranger what we felt most grateful for right now. At the end of the game we ate our lunch as a "gratitude activity". Not one of the events mentioned that gratitude might be shown toward another. They all seemed to lead towards a solipsistic, self-absorbed notion of gratitude – one that, from my way of thinking, would not be gratitude. It would be something else.

Perhaps a key reason why gratitude is so easily conflated into positivity is because in most of the clinical studies of gratitude, it is defined narrowly as an emotion, mainly for ease of measurement and links with comparative studies. It is sometimes called a "positive emotion" a "forgotten emotion", a "pro-social emotion" or a "moral emotion"[51] – but an emotion nevertheless. Is this selection of gratitude as an emotion purposefully motivated by the need to universalise gratitude, to package it neatly so that it can be invoked, measured and clinically tested, its existence proven by contrasting reactions from members of one control group in whom gratitude is provoked with those in another amongst whom it is not?

My particular concern with this notion of gratitude as an emotion relates to how this is interpreted and lived out in the daily lives of students and teachers. Although participants in gratitude workshops start out very enthusiastically with wanting to practise gratitude, many report difficulty in continuing with this work because they find it "impossible to *feel* grateful *all the time*" or that it is impossible "to *feel positive* all the time". They equate gratitude with an emotion or a way of thinking that is associated with being continually positive.

A danger of perceiving gratitude as an emotion lies in the transitory nature of emotions. Attracted to a way of making them feel better about themselves and school life, teachers start out initially highly motivated to practise gratitude. Then they become disheartened when, just a few hours later, they are not feeling grateful in response to their coffee being cold or a student speaking rudely to them. They may start to feel that they are a failure, or that it is impossible to feel grateful all the time, and then give up. Their sense of failure may generate more negativity or self-doubt than if they had not engaged in the gratitude workshop. It may do more harm than good if these distinctions are not clear.

If a teacher or student loses the feeling of gratitude, they may think that they themselves are not grateful. What happens, for instance, when the student wakes up with the appreciation of being alive and then becomes overcome with another emotion associated with perhaps, the fear of going to school because of an exam that day, or dislike towards a particular teacher or subject? If gratitude is to be a virtue or a moral stance or a way of being in the world, it needs to be conceptualised in a broader way than an emotion that, by nature, comes and goes. As the etymology of the word 'emotion' demonstrates: e – motion, energy in motion. Emotions, by nature, are transient. They change from moment to moment or hour to hour.

When a teacher or student has feelings that are not grateful ones, they may take this to mean that they have somehow failed to apply gratitude. Equally as problematic is the idea that they should respond to all situations with an emotion of gratitude.

Another danger is that we might put certain conditions on times when we would be able to be grateful – that we need to be positive, or in a good mood, to summon gratitude. Our gratitude would then be conditional on our thoughts and feelings, and so very difficult to pin down as something we are enacting in our lives.

Although it might seem paradoxical, to be in a grateful state does not necessarily mean that we are going to feel positive or have positive thinking. When at first we open up to acknowledging what we have been given and decide to act on this by giving back in some way, we may stir inner feelings of regret or shame. A memory of the debt we owe our parents, for example, may lead us to feel inadequate because we can never express enough gratitude. Such regret may turn into remorse if our parents are deceased and we feel that we have missed our chance to express gratitude. In other words, gratitude does not necessarily involve instant happiness or gratification, as the feelings aroused may be ones of needing to give back in some way, and may be associated with emotions that are not so positive.

I needed to find a way to suggest to Anastasia that perhaps some of her research participants were not practising gratitude, but something else. They were practising positive thinking. I needed to choose my words carefully and not diminish the strong sense of resonance and hope she had found in the song 'Positivity'. I wanted to show her somehow, that gratitude, in its fully expressed form, is more than an emotion, and distinct from positive thinking. We returned to the words of Adam Cousens' song and explored together how the last two lines could build a bridge between gratitude and positivity:

want to change the world must begin within
the hearts and minds of every kind of people through the actions that we
bring

Gratitude holds the promise of personal freedom at the heart of this song, but it holds much more as it draws us into a world where, in giving and receiving, we are deeply connected, one to another.

The essence of gratitude

Some of the finer distinctions between gratitude and positivity help us to arrive at why these last two lines of the song are at the heart of gratitude. Positive thinking is often particular to one person, not connected to any other beyond the self. Individually, we can think positively for the sake of making ourselves feel better or our lives run more smoothly, or, in the words of the song, greater freedom. When we are thinking positively, there may be a reciprocal effect on others around us, but this is not necessarily the aim of thinking positively. Whereas positive thinking is possible without involving others, gratitude is "profoundly interpersonal"[52] and requires an interaction with the other, giving back and returning thanks. As Edward Harpham notes, "gratitude is always embedded in the relationship between two parties. The capacity to be grateful and generous develops in the context of a social relationship".[53]

In the Latin roots for gratitude, *gratia* means favour, and *gratus* means pleasing. Generally 'to please' would imply 'to please the other', not just ourselves.[54] As Robert Emmons notes, all derivatives from this Latin root "have to do with kindness, generousness, gifts, the beauty of giving and receiving."[55] Gratitude includes us in a particular kind of relationship with others – in giving, in returning thanks.

Gratitude encompasses an imperative force "that compels us to return the benefit we have received"[56] as anthropologist Afke Komter tells us. Gratitude is a moral force that connects us with something or someone outside self. It impels us to act in a certain positive way towards another. In this sense, gratitude is more than an emotion or way of thinking because it involves an action of some kind. Without this action, it is not gratitude but something else – perhaps appreciation or thankfulness.

In the literature there are two senses in which the term gratitude is generally used. A common coinage of the term gratitude is that of 'gratitude *for* someone or something': it does not necessarily involve reciprocity, in that it need not be an action focused on another person in direct return for something. Hence one can, for example, just feel grateful for being alive, or as the saying goes "count your blessings". Another way in which gratitude is discussed, particularly in relation to its ethical and moral dimensions, refers to 'gratitude *to* someone', inferring that it is actively expressed. Here the discussion is often steered towards such topics as obligation, duty, reciprocity and filial piety.[57] In the education context, both senses of the term are applicable. A pre-service teacher may be grateful *for* the ability to teach, and they may be grateful *to* their students.[58]

In following chapters we will explore how the elements of the dimensions of gratitude *for* are the basis of gratitude *to*, and often involve an interplay with each other. We will also discover how we need to move to true gratitude in order to more fully understand its place in transformational education. The following table outlines core distinctions between the two approaches – one highlighting a more 'therapeutic' notion of gratitude and the other lending itself more to what I call 'the essence of true gratitude'. However, this does not make one mutually exclusive of the other.

Gratitude for...	Gratitude to...
Internalised	*Externalised*
Emotion	*Action*
Receiving	*Giving*
Self	*Other*
Solipsistic	*Altruistic*
Materialistic	*Transcendent*
Therapy	*Transformation*

Figure 1. Distinctions between 'gratitude for' and 'gratitude to'.

By seeing both the contrast and the interplay between the elements of these two approaches, we can gain a closer glimpse at the essence of gratitude. My purpose here is to clarify the term rather than give the impression that gratitude is easy to define. A wide array of definitions of gratitude appears in different texts, having their own grammar and rules of usage[59], depending on the context. Writers discuss gratitude as a way of thinking, a belief, a sense of appreciation, a disposition, an emotion, a philosophical emotion, a virtue, a habit, a value system, a celebration, a ritual, a short-term state, an economy of exchange, a character trait, an attitude, a passionate and transformative force, a quality, an emotional core of reciprocity, an interior depth, a way of being, and a character strength.

Are any of these definitions more suitable than others for discussing the place of gratitude in teaching and learning? The answer to this question is both intricate and multi-layered, having particular consequences when applying gratitude in the education context – as our previous discussion on the differences between gratitude and positivity disclosed. Complexities lie in the need to have a definition of gratitude that respects difference, is suitable to the modern day, is secular, is adaptable to students and teachers, but is not confused with other concepts.

Another important question in determining which of these definitions might be relevant to our deepening relationship with the term, is whether or not it is *useful* to our understanding of the place of gratitude in education. Using this criterion, my search within the context of education has helped me shape the following way of describing gratitude[60], and this will be further explored in other chapters:

Gratitude goes beyond an emotion or thought to be something that is actualised in one's daily life through the heartfelt active practice of giving thanks. Gratitude is usually expressed towards someone or something. It is also an inner attitude that can be understood as the opposite of resentment or complaint.

Figure 2. Definition of gratitude in education.

We may also ask if gratitude can stand on its own as a concept, or rather needs to be embedded within other concepts to make its meaning clear. Indeed, many workshop participants want it to link to their value system or moral stance. For example, does gratitude embody trust or generosity or respect or altruistic love or transcendence? We saw that the Eastgates teachers wanted to connect gratitude with praise and care – cornerstones of their approach to teaching and their teaching identity. Some of the teachers and parents wanted to connect gratitude to their religion. This question of where gratitude links to other concepts is discussed at length in the literature. According to Ross Buck[61], Aquinas saw gratitude as a component of justice, whereas Spinoza viewed gratitude as the reciprocation of love with love. The social anthropologist Margaret Visser[62] explores how, depending on the culture, humility, reciprocity, loyalty, freedom and equality, are at the heart of expressions of gratitude. Andre Comte-Sponville[63] believes that gratitude "borders on charity".

My own personal resonances are sparked by the work of Charles Taylor[64] in his epic, *Sources of the self: The making of modern identity* where he narrates a convincing argument as to why an underlying value, or "good", at the source of every human encounter, and indeed at the heart of our language and means of communication, is the worthiness of human beings. For me, without this underlying value, gratitude makes less sense, or holds less importance. I believe that gratitude is an important way of honouring this worthiness, of acknowledging and recognising it in the other. This is my motivation to express gratitude in my life.

Objectifying gratitude

After Anastasia left my office with a deeper understanding of gratitude versus positive thinking, I looked to my bookshelf and reached for Maxine Greene's *The Dialectic of Freedom.*[65] I imagined her chastising me for thinking I could place John, the academic with whom I had earlier discussed the place of gratitude in our faculty's new curriculum, and myself at opposite ends of a spectrum. Instead of seeing the objective world so highly prized above our subjective ways of experiencing it, Maxine Greene would say, "Find a way to speak to each other!" Within minutes of skimming the pages I was reading again the power of engaging in a dialectic:

> ...to objectify...to separate oneself as 'subject' from an independently existing 'object' is to sacrifice the possibility of becoming the author of one's world; and the consciousness of authorship has much to do with the consciousness of freedom.[66]

The word 'gratitude' invites us to contemplate our relationship with ourselves, with our ethics, morality, religion or culture. Subjective overtones may leave some of us doubting that gratitude could be present in environments where disinterestedness and disengagement are the preferred ways of being. Maxine Greene reminded me of my purpose in advocating gratitude in education: to discover how gratitude can *influence* analytical and objective thinking. Rather than presenting gratitude as a radical alternative to traditional notions of 'higher' education, one that might live outside it, my ongoing journey in the world of academia is to probe into this question: in what ways can gratitude enable us to function better, think better, research better, in fact learn and be better, even *in* that world of analysis and objectivism?

I wondered why I lost my sense of purpose when John was challenging me. Was it that gratitude is so dear to my values, to my sense of self, that I find it difficult to enter a dialectic with the objective world? As Margaret Sommerville says in her book *Ethical Imagination,* "language is fundamental to being human – fundamental to becoming fully our 'self', relating to others, experiencing our world, and finding meaning in life...we must take great care in using it..."[67] I felt gratitude is something so fundamental to our sense of self. I perceived John to be saying that we would be better off without it. But was John saying that we would be better off without the word, or without gratitude itself? Would the chasm between us close if I were able to demonstrate to him how gratitude is crucial to our world of teaching and learning, or would it be pointless to try?

I went to my computer to compose an email to John to attempt a possible way forward to come to a shared understanding of gratitude. Then as I scrolled through my inbox I came to a message entitled "Gratitude project", an email from Jenny, a teacher in the gratitude project at Eastgates primary school. Hoping to find solace and encouragement, I opened Jenny's email:

Kerry, I'm writing to apologise for the fact that I can't continue with the gratitude project. I have so many extracurricular activities to attend to, that I just don't feel that I have the time to take on another thing at present.

I did try practising gratitude for the first week and noticed that I felt more positive and calm when I remembered to practise. But then I found myself reverting to my old habits again and couldn't keep up having grateful feelings all the time. I kept forgetting to do it and then found myself going back to feeling negative when I knew that I should be responding with gratitude. Sorry.

P.S. I think that a few of the others in the gratitude project feel the same, and now we're not quite sure what gratitude is anymore.

I picked up the phone to call Julie, the assistant principal. With her usual unflinching optimism, she told me that people often withdraw when participation in projects is voluntary. Julie was right, in fact a month on from when they had originally signed up, only ten out of the eighteen teachers would remain on the project. Julie assured me: "It's nothing to do with the importance of gratitude, but more about the busy schedule and pressure that people are under as report-writing time and parent-teacher nights are approaching. Some teachers are telling me that as they just could not stick to their goals to be more grateful, it was best for them to drop out of the project."

As I placed the phone back in its cradle, I remembered many instances where teachers in other contexts had withdrawn from the project of gratitude for similar reasons – "not enough time", "cannot feel positive all the time", "started out well but couldn't sustain it all of the time", and "the concept of gratitude isn't clear". I needed to think deeply about what I could have done differently to help the Eastgates Primary School teachers see that gratitude is not something we must feel all of the time. Although I had emphasised this impossibility several times during the workshop, this point had not taken hold.

Part of my disappointment was that I thought that I had pre-empted all of the issues mentioned by Jenny and Julie. This was why I had spent so long on the "What is gratitude?" part of the workshop and invited teachers to explore their own meanings and challenges raised by the term.

I thought long and hard about what I could have done differently, and then the thought slowly dawned on me: I was doing exactly what John had done! By putting all my stakes on a definition – that I had left each of them with on beautifully embossed cards – I too was objectifying gratitude. I had identified and defined it as a thing, named it as an object, an "it", outside ourselves, possibly separate from our daily lives. No wonder Jenny reported that she could not take "it" on as another "thing to do" in her busy schedule. No wonder gratitude had been externalised to such an extent that she, like John, also believed gratitude to be a thing that we would have to work hard to access, and to be clear about.

Ruefully, I arrived at the thought: by calling gratitude a "project", I had cemented it within an objectivist tradition. In an environment where teachers often have so many associations with "projects" that have a clear beginning and end, my choice of the word 'project' could very well have further cemented the notion that gratitude is a 'thing' outside of themselves – to be managed, achieved, conquered, completed, or put on their ever-growing (and often annoying) 'to do list'. I ought to have led them towards a journey where awakening to the meaning of gratitude from within could reveal itself in their everyday life. I wanted to shout in my email to the Eastgates teachers, "Throw away those cards!" "Throw out the word project!" "Let's call it something else!"

Gratitude as autobiography

Recently, an aboriginal football player, Liam Jurrah had been noted in the press and amongst his peers for not engaging in the rituals of thanks in the same way in which Westerners are accustomed. This was misinterpreted as rudeness or lack of appreciation, until it was pointed out in a recent biography that:

> In Warlpiri culture, it's all about reciprocity. Giving and receiving is the Warlpiri way, a reflection of their complex notion of obligation. Your teammate, like your brother, has an obligation to help you, so there is no reason to say 'please' or 'thankyou'.[68]

In other words, our individual expressions of gratitude are inextricably linked to our culture and sense of etiquette and politeness. We cannot expect everyone to abide by the same rules, or to value expressions of gratitude in a similar way.[69]

In trying to grasp the essence of gratitude and box it in clear boundaries, so that it was not used synonymously with other terms like positive thinking, my custodianship had ignored this very personal dimension. It is no wonder Jenny and some of the other teachers found it to be something else once they started to live gratitude more consciously in their daily lives.

On one level, to use a word and expect others to know what it means, in its entirety or 'true' sense, as I had been trying to do, is absurd. The meaning I attribute to the word, for example, will reflect the experience of my life world and no one else's. Does gratitude need to be defined at all? If we give way to naming and defining things, are we obliged to mould them to the name we bestow upon them?

We have already explored how gratitude cannot be a complete individual internal state. It lives and breathes in relation to the other. As the following chapters reveal, teachers' experiences with gratitude uncover it to be complex, messy, hermeneutic, vague, individual, and incomplete – particularly as they enter the territory of associations of gratitude with indebtedness, involuntary participation, reciprocity, giving, and the possible implications of feeling further burdened by a greater degree of accountability and civic debt.

In order to grasp the full potential of gratitude we need an expansive notion of what it is to understand.

Tobin Hart offers an insightful interpretation of the notion of "understanding" which is to "stand amongst", and is the opposite of objectification which is about distancing us from the other, or "standing against". Understanding requires "connection, relatedness, intimacy, even oneness".[70] He says:

> Understanding requires a fundamental shift in the way we know. Whether an idea, a rock, or a person, understanding meets and accommodates the other directly instead of manipulating or categorising it, and the result can be appreciation, awe, and even reverence.[71]

In his enlightened text, *The Untethered Soul*, Michael Singer shows us how *consciousness* is one of the greatest words that ever existed: "Consciousness is the highest word you will ever utter"[72]. Our attention to gratitude awakens our consciousness to our connectedness to the other, and also to what happens to this connection when we do not have gratitude, or worse still, when we express ingratitude (a topic to be dealt with in later chapters). So when we try to live with more gratitude in our daily lives as educators, we recognise as much about the hidden depths of gratitude as we do about ourselves. I believe this is why so many teachers, school leaders, academics, pre-service teachers and students immediately resonate with the word gratitude – because, although complex and embedded in different cultural meanings, it awakens them to something deep inside themselves and highlights the presence or absence of something fundamental to who they are.

Coming to a shared understanding of what gratitude means in a school or other educational institution adds further contextual dimensions. If we have a community of teachers gathering together to encourage each other to practise gratitude, the unfolding nature of gratitude in such a context is a very powerful way to understand its meaning – amongst the struggles people have with those who do not value gratitude or who are negative, the judgements teachers lay on themselves when they forget to practise gratitude, the pain when others are ungrateful towards them, the shared stories of transformation from increased gratitude that generate both celebration and a sense of shame if each person's gratitude does not measure up, and the power play that can go on if the intent to practise gratitude is one of manipulation or blind ritual. If our gratitude can help us stand amongst others with greater integrity, acknowledgment and recognition in the midst of such complexities, it gains greater meaning and pedagogical significance than if only considered in relationship between two people – which is how most other studies have considered it.

Through all of this, I resolved that no longer would my intention be to argue that one definition is more valid than another. The more important question for me would be whether or not a certain way of distinguishing gratitude from other terms is *useful*. As Mugerauer notes, Heidegger advises us that we think best not by objectifying, defining or describing, but by "letting ourselves into the meaning which hides itself."[73] However, through all this, I remained certain that we cannot call it something else.

GRATITUDE AS A PRACTICE

To speak gratitude is courteous and pleasant, to enact gratitude is generous and noble, but to live gratitude is to touch heaven.
– Johannes A. Gaertner

This chapter highlights some of the quandaries raised by educators as they grapple with applying the concept of gratitude as an action. We explore that a way forward may be to distinguish between an action and a practice, which requires a different kind of consciousness, one where our intention and attention are purposefully directed. In this chapter I also examine the aspects of giving that characterise a gratitude practice and investigate some of the ambiguities when gratitude is associated with reciprocity and altruism. The chapter highlights some of the giving practices that teachers have adopted and strategies they use to remind themselves to practise gratitude on a regular basis.

From the ideal to the real

On my way to Eastgates Primary School to meet with the ten teachers who remained in the 'gratitude project', I felt fired up more than ever before to protect gratitude from being an object external to us. My first aim was to confess to them my folly in inviting them into a 'gratitude project'. I needed to find a way of authentically representing my revised thinking on gratitude since our time together at the first workshop. It needed to be one that symbolised its deeper form, a form diminished by my usual PowerPoint slide, with its definition of 'gratitude' written in yellow letters on a blue screen. I also used my flying time to think through how I was going to respond to these teachers' unrealistic expectations of the need to "be grateful all the time".

When I arrived at the school office, Julie greeted me warmly. She told me that all of the teachers were excited about my visit, and would meet me in the staff room shortly. They were released from their classes to attend our meeting for the last hour of their teaching day. Some came in happily, but some seemed ambivalent. Julie opened the session with certain outcomes in mind. She told the group that I had come to set up the next stage of the project and she hoped that my visit would also clear up any difficulties that people were experiencing.

Stella took this as her cue to speak on behalf of the group: "I think I can talk for all of us in saying that when we started practising gratitude, we just realised how little we actually do it every day."

Responses chorused: "It's hard to keep it up", "It's hard to be grateful all the time", "I often don't feel in the mood to be grateful". Gratitude was a 'thing' to be 'applied' or something to 'be' or 'do', – 'all the time', and this was unattainable for them. I shared with them my own difficulties concerning my inability to feel grateful all the time. Two of the other teachers present then admitted that they felt like impostors, as they had "not done much" since the week after beginning the project. Although they had felt a renewed sense of calm when they tried gratitude for the first week, they found it hard to sustain their practice. Various nods came from around the room.

Some teachers were eager for me to clarify if what they were doing was gratitude or if it was something else. They gave examples of greeting their students more consciously, of thanking parents more frequently, of using paper more preciously. When I affirmed their acts as wonderful instances of gratitude, they seemed wary of it being so simple, and thought there must be something else to it. How could just a few extra acts make them grateful people, especially when they were conscious of many more times when they were not grateful?

Sam, another teacher, proclaimed that I was not telling them anything new, and that most of the teachers in this school already practise gratitude. The only difference my work with them was making was bringing a different language and framework, a different kind of consciousness to gratitude. He was taken aback when I agreed with him wholeheartedly. Sam's comments were followed by a few of the teachers proudly telling me how they had facilitated their students' practices of gratitude. I wondered if they had skipped over the process where we focus on teachers' gratitude before students, but decided not to say anything at that point.

Some also expressed apprehension because they did not get the results they were looking for from their expression of gratitude. They went back to the research and examples I gave in the workshop that I had presented to the whole staff, and lamented that they could not see it made any difference to their students' behaviour or to their own happiness. They were after quick results, a quick fix.

I suggested that workshops on any topic, particularly those that concern our state of being, our inner life, have the potential of transforming our attitudes or behaviour in the first week or so. If we have a profound awakening about something we feel is going to make an important difference in our way of being, it can seem so important and true and real to us at the time. We think it would only be natural to immediately put it into practice and expect ourselves to be different from that point onwards. However, the awakening is often not enough to sustain a permanent change. Our enthusiasm can start to quickly fade, especially when 'busyness' hijacks our heightening consciousness. We can become despondent when we find ourselves returning to old habits. I shared that this was my main reason for implementing a structure of support and ongoing reflection beyond the initial gratitude workshop.

We might feel shame and a sense of failure if we do not get our new focus on gratitude right the first time. Competitive, high-pressure environments – which we find in many educational institutions – might contribute to our sense of ineptness when we are not able to gain immediate competency in a new area of learning. We also might be more accustomed to professional development opportunities that are packaged in such a way that, if we follow a list of instructions to perfect a new skill or new part of teaching the curriculum, immediate positive outcomes are assured. Implementing more gratitude, on the other hand, requires a different kind of approach. By its very nature, gratitude calls upon us to accept that we are far from being perfect practitioners and to see that just when we have gained a closer grasp of gratitude in one situation or relationship, another pops up to stretch us and help us more deeply reflect on both gratitude and ourselves. Although starting out with good intentions and clarity of what it is we are practising, gratitude looks, feels, and sounds different every time we express it. There will inevitably be some situations and times where we are closer to our ideal 'grateful self' than others.

Because we have already expressed gratitude many times in our lives, we may think we are grateful people. After being reminded of its potential in a workshop, we may think we will instantly know *how to do it* because of past experience. However, the ephemeral, ever-changing nature of gratitude can catch us by surprise and humble us when we are not able to apply it to a new situation. We may need to adopt a "beginner's mind". As the great Zen Master, Shinryu Suzuki tells us, this is where the mind is "empty, free of the habits of the expert, ready to accept, to doubt, to open to all the possibilities."[74] If we approach our new attempts to be grateful with this mind, we might be more forgiving of ourselves and others.

Perhaps our discussion of these complexities made some teachers wonder whether it was worth proceeding. I started to tell them of my realisations about the folly of calling this focused work on gratitude a "project", and how I wanted to move beyond the clear, neat definition I had left them with on the embossed cards. But these teachers did not want me to be as spontaneous and open to interpreting gratitude differently in every situation as I had hoped. They expected me to be a sturdy and unyielding rock, a foundation against which they could measure their own understandings. If I did not have it all worked out about what gratitude means, what right did I have to come and recommend them to "do it"? They were happy with the clearer meaning of gratitude I had left them with. Some said perhaps it could be grounded in practical examples where they did not have to feel grateful all the time.

My way forward with these teachers was to remind them that gratitude needed to be *acted upon* in some way in order for it to reach its full expression. I was hoping that this distinction would at least help them to see that they did not need to think grateful thoughts all the time, or feel grateful, they just needed to take action in one of the areas where they felt grateful. I rummaged through my notes to read to them what Charles Shelton says about gratitude, and stressed his recommendation that gratitude be a "purposeful action":

> ...when truly grateful, we are led to experience and interpret life situations in ways that call forth from us an openness to and engagement with the world through purposeful actions, to share and increase the very good we have received...[75]

I gave them the example of being grateful for warm water. When we stand under the shower we can think of how wonderful it is to have water, to feel grateful for all the things that have brought this water to us, where the water comes from, and all the efforts of both nature and humans to warm the water. Perhaps this could extend to our loved ones and our homes and those who have provided us with our material blessings. This would be a way of awakening our gratitude. When we move to expressing gratitude for water, by trying to preserve it and having a shorter shower, it becomes gratitude in the truer sense of the word.

What is a practice?

In response to my example, Stella interjected in what seemed to be a tone of frustration, "Yes, but as we have been saying, even though we *know* gratitude needs to be deeper than our thoughts or feelings, that it needs to be an action of some kind," she said with a use of 'we' that indicated she was again speaking for the whole group, "We might do it once or twice, but then we forget. We lose our motivation and focus very quickly because we get busy, or we're tired or exhausted or not in the mood. We can take action one day, but lose motivation the next!" Again, this showed me that an intellectual understanding of gratitude as an action did not go far enough. As our discussion had revealed, to act out of gratitude once or twice did not make one a more grateful person, nor did it necessarily make it easier to be grateful in that same situation the next time it came around.

Stella's words also touched on the difficulty of putting conditions on our acts of gratitude. We may feel that we can only practise gratitude when we are in the mood, or when we feel grateful, or feel positive. There needs to be something more to this process, so that our acts of gratitude are sustainable, so they are consistent and ongoing, and not dependent upon how we feel. One of the biggest challenges teachers report about putting gratitude into practice is that it is difficult to be grateful when others around them are so negative.

I suggested a way forward might be to distinguish between an *action* and a *practice*, as up to this point we had been using the two notions interchangeably. Perhaps Shelton was hinting at this distinction in his description of gratitude actions as being actions that are "purposeful". The Oxford Dictionary says an action is "the state of doing something"; and a practice is a "repeated performance or systematic exercise for the purpose of acquiring skill or proficiency". Returning to my example of expressing gratitude for warm water, this would become a practice if I consciously developed the habit of having shorter showers and did this on a regular and consistent basis. My practice would be purposeful as it would be done with the heart of expressing gratitude for water.

The famous music teacher, Shinichi Suzuki, placed great value on the notion of practice and, no matter what it is we are practising, he saw repeated practice as essential to developing our character. He argued that there is "a special relationship between a human being and ability", and "...the development of ability cannot be accompanied by mere thinking and theorising, but must be accompanied by practice."[76] In his teaching of music using the Suzuki method, he encouraged his students to gain joy from the very practice itself, and to build their character through steady, consistent practice, regardless of whether they felt like it. Similarly, our gratitude practice could help us develop our character if we adopted it as a means in itself, not looking for outcomes beyond the practice.

In the same way that a violin player needs to improve his or her proficiency by practising, regardless of how they feel, we also need to make our practice of gratitude independent of being motivated by our feelings or the right conditions. If we want to continue in our practice, it is important that we do not rely on whether or not we are in the mood or if the conditions are right or if others around us are grateful. In fact, in many ways we need to rise above our feelings in order to continue in a consistent way in our practice. The concept of 'practice' reminds us that we need to be involved in some conscious act rather than leaving it to chance or when we feel like practising. We acquire the consistency of our practice as we direct our attention to our practice rather than our emotions surrounding it.

I suggested to these teachers that the notion of 'practice' invites us to consider that we are 'trying out' something, or training in it in order to become better skilled. If we decide to practise something, like learning how to play the violin or to play tennis or to teach, we are not considering ourselves to be experts. Otherwise we would not need to be practising. As the saying goes, "practise makes perfect", but this does not mean that our practice *is* perfect. If it was, we would not need to practise any more.

When we conceive of gratitude as a practice, we are able to rid ourselves of the notion that we need to be grateful "all the time". We can be living gratitude by taking up just one or two practices in a steady and consistent manner. A violinist practises regularly but not all the time. His attention to violin practise and his growing awareness of how to play the violin lead to his identity as a violinist. In the same way, we can think of ourselves as grateful if we steadily and consistently train ourselves and develop our character through the practice of gratitude.

I had noticed that Kathryn had been smiling but quiet during our earlier discussion. However, at Julie's invitation she told us that she had been attracted to this notion of gratitude as a practice when she first heard of it in the workshop and decided to try it with one of her difficult students. Kathryn had been so run-down by the behaviour of this student that she took every opportunity to off-load her emotions whenever her colleagues or friends asked her how she was going. It was hard for her to find anything that she liked about this child. However, after the first gratitude workshop Kathryn could see that her attitude toward the child might have been contributing to the problem. She then decided that her practice would be to concentrate on any effort that this student made in class, notice it and praise her for it. Kathryn did not do this in a forced way as she felt it needed to come naturally. She was able to achieve this by focusing on what the child was giving her rather than being dissatisfied with what she was not receiving. Every time she thought of this child, Kathryn would utter to herself (or aloud if no one else was around), "thank you". She knew that just being grateful once was not going to bring about any results. She needed to consistently praise and thank this child.

At first things started to get worse and she questioned the wisdom in this method. But as she continued to practise looking for the good in this child, Kathryn noticed that the anxiety in her interactions with this troublesome student diminished remarkably and day-by-day the student became more cooperative. Unexpectedly, she felt calmer and like a teacher with more self-control. She had started out with the practice of looking for just one act of the child she could give thanks for. Gradually she spotted more to give thanks for, characteristics that were imperceptible to her previously. Her constant words of "thank you" seemed to stop her from having negative thoughts about this child. The wonderful changes in the student's behaviour inspired Kathryn to practise in the same way with other students.

Identifying our practices

After listening to Kathryn, the mood of those in the room seemed to be more optimistic. I thought of John Dewey's[77] great wisdom that an idea needs to be revealed in action, in experience, for its truth to come alive for us. The teachers were able to see that just choosing one or two practices was achievable and powerful. But some were still at a loss as to where to start.

A few teachers reached for their pens and paper as I invited them into an activity where we could more clearly articulate our practices. They wanted to write down my reference to the philosopher, Patrick Fitzgerald and the three components of gratitude that he identifies: "1) A warm sense of appreciation for somebody or something; 2) a sense of goodwill toward that person or thing; and 3) a disposition to act that flows from appreciation and goodwill."[78] In order to capture the first of these components I suggested that we take inspiration from Brother David Steindl-Rast's notion that "Gratefulness is always whole-hearted"[79], and can be accessed by being open to what takes us by surprise, "…and whatever causes us to look with amazement opens 'the eyes of our eyes'. We begin to see everything as a gift. An inch of surprise can lead to a mile of gratefulness."[80] In his delightful book,

Gratefulness, the Heart of Prayer, Steindl-Rast takes us through exercises such as taking nothing for granted, looking for surprise, and seeing life as a gift – to experience which he calls "a celebration".

Most commonly, amongst the groups with whom I work, members initially link gratitude with phrases that evoke these dimensions. They say gratitude is a "beautiful sunset", "a child's smile", "a warm meal around the family table", "a feeling of peace and oneness with the world", "a feeling of joy about just being alive". Many writers conceive of gratitude as an emotional response to the joys of life, or to "one's blessings".

Thomas Merton, for instance, said of gratitude that it "takes nothing for granted, is never unresponsive, and is constantly awakening to new joy." In "uncovering astonishment" or "setting the groundwork", we are "developing the capacity to see with fresh eyes an infinite array of everyday wonders".[81] This is how Alan Jones and John O'Neill in *Seasons of Grace* describe the emotions associated with gratitude. We might consciously bring our emotions of appreciation to the fore as teachers, by seeing our students and our school "with fresh eyes". This in turn might lead to an expanded appreciation of the goodwill and efforts of others. We might, for example, acknowledge that if it were not for the parents of these students or, indeed our own parents, we would not be able to gain all the benefits from the present situation.

To engage the Eastgates teachers in the first two of Fitzgerald's steps, I suggested that if we are to invoke a state of surprise or awe, it is best to be spontaneous, to not over-intellectualise or rationalise our reactions. As Steindl-Rast recommends, truehearted thankfulness does require our conscious use of intellect "in order to recognise the given world as truly a given."[82] Yet, to fully capture this giftedness requires us to engage with the specific details of how we have been gifted. Rather than thinking of "students", for instance, we might think of a particular student for whom we felt much appreciation.

Three teachers agreed to share some of their specific thoughts which I then wrote on the board:

- Isabel making an effort not to talk.

- Simon, a parent who came to thank me when his child had done well in a maths test.

- The fact that I walk into a clean classroom every morning.

- The help I was given by two parents on a recent excursion.

- Getting help with my photocopying from an administrative assistant.

- The materials that enable me to teach and my students to learn – like paper, paints, computers, a nice classroom.

- My colleague with whom I share my resources and ideas.

- My healthy body and the fact that I am well enough to teach in a job I love and earn money so I can provide for my children.

Our next step in enlisting the third suggestion from Fitzgerald was to write actions we might take to show our gratitude. Together we thought of examples of actions for the list on the whiteboard:

- Isobel making an effort not to talk. *Praise Isobel and thank her often.*

- Simon, a parent who came to thank me when his child had done well in a maths test. *Send him a card to thank him for his acknowledgement and appreciation.*

- The fact that I walk into a clean classroom every morning. *Leave the cleaners a box of chocolates and a thankyou note.*

- The help I was given by two parents on a recent excursion. *Publicly thank these parents at the next school assembly, if that's okay with them.*

- Getting help with my photocopying from an administrative assistant. *Thank her often, and send her a thankyou note, even when she is not doing something for me.*

- The materials that enable me to teach and my students to learn – like paper, paints, computers, a nice classroom. *Treat these materials preciously and with respect.*

- My colleague with whom I share my resources and ideas. *Acknowledge her efforts and praise her often. Make time for the relationship.*

- My healthy body and the fact that I am well enough to teach in a job I love and earn money so I can provide for my children. *Look after my health and teach to the best of my ability.*

Some of the things on this list lent themselves to becoming a gratitude practice more than others. In order to become a practice, it needed to be more than a one-off action, and something that could be developed steadily and consistently over a period of time. If we consider Suzuki's point about practice for learning an instrument, it also needed to be something that helped to develop character. We then generated the following list of gratitude practices that could be used in a variety of situations, but with the awareness that to be effective and achievable, we might just take one or two of these and apply them in one or two situations – consistently.

- Express gratitude to particular students, for small things, without wanting anything in return.

- Send thankyou notes home to parents and find ways of thanking them for the opportunity to teach their child.
- Acknowledge the behind-the-scenes work of admin staff and non-teaching staff in the school and give spontaneous gestures of thanks when things are going well, not just when we need their help.
- Make efforts to meet parents at the gate in the mornings to thank them.
- Teach with a sense of appreciation for the opportunity to teach in this school.
- Thank the principal and school leaders often.
- Look for the good in others and tell them what you see.
- Give priority to relationships rather than tasks.
- Publicly acknowledge the help and inspiration you have received from colleagues.
- Treat materials such as water, paper, books, computers and food, preciously.
- Eat food more slowly and with greater consciousness and appreciation of where it comes from.
- Give warm and positive greetings.
- Regularly tell our students what we are grateful for.
- Express gratitude to our bodies and senses by treating them preciously and maintaining our health.
- At the end of each day, write down five things for which you are grateful, and one way you will express this the next day.

If time had permitted we could have kept going, as this list is by no means exhaustive. The practices these teachers were embracing were solving the dilemma which we had started with at this meeting: how to capture the individual nature of gratitude as well as its essence of returning thanks for what we have received? As we discussed this list, we could see that although two people might choose the same practice, it would be expressed in their own individual way and look different according to the context and personalities involved. Barbara Fredrickson captures some of the creativity involved in generating ways of expressing gratitude when she writes that gratitude "appears to broaden people's modes of thinking as they creatively consider a wide array of actions that might benefit others."[83] No one individual expression of gratitude can be the same as any other. The teachers were also encouraged by the realisation that a gratitude practice could be a verbal expression, and did not have to necessarily involve a physical action beyond speaking to others.

Gratitude as a practice of giving and receiving

After the listing exercise, Bill eventually voiced his concerns. Although he was listening to the other teachers, he had seemed fairly uninvolved up to this point, looking out the window or at his watch while the others were writing their list of gratitude practices.

"Honestly", he said, "I don't see what the big deal is! Most of these are just examples of what good teaching is: caring for our students and those who are looking after them. Greeting our students, praising our students and colleagues, looking after the school environment, is just part of our everyday teaching practice. We should be doing this as a matter of course, as part of our professionalism, and most of us do, well I do. I don't see anything new here." Bill continued, "This all seems very basic to me."

Like Bill, many teachers think that gratitude is the same as praise or care. I tried to explain to Bill that these are two of the many ways of expressing gratitude, but where the difference lies is in our *intention*. The practice of gratitude is one that arises from our motivation to *give back* out of acknowledgement for what we have received. For example, we might be greeting our students as part of our everyday ritual but this would not be a gratitude practice. It would only become so if we did this with the purposeful intention of expressing our gratitude to them for coming to school and for the ability to teach them. As the philosopher Robert Roberts says, gratitude is about "...givers, gifts, recipients, and the attitudes of giver and recipient toward one another."[84] We can care for or praise another, but a sense of giftedness does not necessarily lie behind such actions.

Bill's heartfelt reply was, "Isn't the teaching profession so full of giving anyway? Isn't it all about us giving and giving until there's nothing left to give so we get burnout and leave?"

The resignation in Bill's voice matched the tiredness in his eyes and the worry lines across his face. He then admitted, "To tell you the absolute truth, I'm clinging on to this project as my last hope. When I heard you in the workshop talk about the research that said that people felt calmer and more energised when they practised gratitude, I thought that this was my answer. But when you talk about giving more, it just makes me want to get up and walk out. I feel safe enough in this group to say that I'm sorry but I have nothing more to give!"

The hope that Bill was reaching towards is one of my primary justifications for discussing the role of increased gratitude in education. When we consider how Western institutions construct education, we find the teacher is bestowed as the giver of education; the student, the recipient. It is a one-way street. Hence we can observe that students are not encouraged to think of what they can give to their teachers or the learning situation, only what they can receive; and teachers do not know how to look at what they receive from their students, as to be a 'good teacher' is to be imparting their knowledge and expertise to their students, to give of themselves in their passion and enthusiasm for the subject. When students are fee-paying or positioned as a 'client', they are even more fully entrenched as the receiver, and they often approach their education from a position of entitlement. Perhaps more than any other time in history we are teaching students who, from a very young age, approach their education with a continuous orientation to what they are getting and evaluating the worthiness of their time spent. Many teachers report that they receive less and less from their students, who expect it all to be given to them. Some say that it is a feature of the 'me generation', which characterises 'Generation Y'. The slightest deviation from their expectations generates complaints. As most teachers come from a generation where they were not allowed to complain, this is a constant source of bewilderment and, in some cases, stress. Christopher Peterson and Martin Seligman issue a warning about the consequences of an attitude of entitlement:

> The absence of gratitude marks those people who are belligerently entitled, who proclaim themselves as self-made men and rugged individuals, who see no need to say please or thank you because – after all – they deserve everything they have.[85]

Katie, a younger teacher, admitted taking this position as a university student. "Oh, yes, I can see now that this is exactly how I and many of my friends carried on while at uni, " she affirmed. "We thought that as we were paying such high fees, we should be given the very best by every teacher and we were constantly complaining that we were being ripped off. One of my friends would whisper to me in a lecture how much per hour this was costing us."

For positions of giver and receiver to be less entrenched, we as educators need to be open to possibilities for seeking, acknowledging and receiving gifts. Gratitude gathers together and entwines giver, receiver and gift and so has the potential to restore education to a true dynamic, where there is a healthy flow of giving and receiving. As we will explore in future chapters, gratitude invites us into a cyclical process: the more we are open to receive, the more students will give; the more students give, the more energy we feel for giving back. There is no doubt that we need to educate students to become givers rather than just receivers. This is a crucial part of our inquiry into the place of increased gratitude in education. But we need to model this for them first and also reflect on our potential to be open to receiving from them. As Brother Steindl-Rast reminds us, "...the circle of gratefulness is incomplete until the giver of the gift becomes the receiver."

Bill moved into our conversation with greater enthusiasm, and said, "So if I look for what I receive from my students, instead of expecting them to directly give to me in ways that I want them to, I might be able to feel more replenished and not so empty." This realisation helped Bill to nominate his gratitude practice: "Look for what I receive from my students".

Deepening our practice

Our memories of when we have taken up practices in the past might help us to recall that we need vigilance in order to be consistent and sincere. As we enter the dynamic of giving and receiving, motivation to continue our practice comes to us easily because we gain strength as we feel the effects. This will help us to have the willpower to withstand the pressures of other demands and be less distracted.

But we also need to ensure that our practice does not become overly ritualised, or robotic, or even empty after a period of time.

To deepen our practice over time, is it enough to be motivated by our intention to give back, or is there something more that is needed? In their book, *Living Deeply: The Art and Science of Transformation in Everyday Life,* Marilyn Schiltz and her colleagues explore a distinction between a practice and a *transformative* practice.

> ...Most commonly, practice is thought of as the act of repeating something over and over for the purpose of learning and gaining experience... transformative practice is any set of internal or external activities you engage in with the intention of fostering long-lasting shifts in the way you experience and relate to yourself and others...[86]

Our intention, which they describe as "the will to change...the determination to act in a certain way"[87], needs to be "deep, strong, pure" in order to stop our commitment from wavering. For our intention to foster the long-lasting shifts they are recommending here, we need to focus on *both* our practice and ourselves. In other words, we should not see our practice of gratitude as something that is external to who we are, to our own personal development. We need to have our eye on both if we wish to deepen our gratitude and become a more grateful person, or to "live gratitude" and "touch heaven" as the quote at the beginning of this chapter says.

To engage with our authenticity and integrity in our intention to practise gratitude, it is important to constantly ask ourselves *why am I practising gratitude?* Our intention may be weakened if it does not come from deep within ourselves; if we practise gratitude because we were asked to; or if others were suggesting it would be a good idea. This is why initiatives to practise more gratitude in educational contexts need to be voluntary. We may also need to renew and revise our intention often. As we grow and change we may find different reasons for why we are practising gratitude.

From where do we get this intention, this motivation and will to aspire to approach our practice in this way? Some draw their intention from their religious or spiritual beliefs, and some from their personal ethics or culture or upbringing. Schiltz and her colleagues point out, "...a practice is both the act of performing a set of exercises and the form, philosophy, or worldview underlying these exercises."[88] I suggested to the group that we might also draw our intention from our experiences of the changes we see within and around us as a result of our practice, perhaps in how we are growing, becoming a better teacher and person, feeling more in integrity, calmer and clearer. We can also be motivated by our vision of what our classroom or school or community would look like if more people were practising gratitude.

Gratitude has its own inbuilt motivations to act. Michael McCullough and his colleagues propose that gratitude serves as a "moral barometer", a "moral motivator", and a "moral reinforcer".[89] It motivates the receiver of our gratitude to reciprocate and thus encourages moral behaviour. In his *Theory of Moral Sentiments*, Adam Smith wrote, "The sentiment that most immediately prompts us to reward is gratitude." The philosopher Emmanuel Kant held that gratitude is one of the "passions and affections" that "prompts to action" in order to "make acknowledgements and requite the favour".[90] Afke Komter carries this argument further in stating that gratitude goes beyond the nice feeling that one has received something of benefit, to encompassing an imperative force "that compels us to return the benefit we have received".[91]

I invited the teachers to consider this notion of moral motivation from their own experience if they neglect or forget to act on their feelings of appreciation toward another. A gift received from another stirs within us a need to act with gratitude: we tend to feel a sense of incompleteness, or to use the term coined by Paulo Friere, an "unfinishedness",[92] if we do not take this action. In Western culture such action often needs to be overt and immediate. In other cultures, it may be a given that some time in the future this acknowledgement of what has been received needs to be lived out in some way. Our lack of action resides within us as regret, remorse, a sense of something not quite finished, easy to ignore in the midst of our busyness or preoccupations – a common excuse for not expressing gratitude.

A deepening of our practice of gratitude also calls for an awareness of the *purity* behind our practice of gratitude. The intention and the giving need to be part of a functional and equal relationship. As Harpham cites Seneca "for gratitude to be adequately expressed in the world, a gift must be properly given."[93] For gratitude to be genuine it involves, according to Ross Buck, "reciprocity and mutual respect, and the perception that the rules are being followed fairly and equitably."[94] There is therefore an important distinction between what Buck describes as a gratitude of exchange and gratitude of caring. We may think we are being grateful but, unless we are vigilant about our intention, we might be expressing gratitude so that we receive something back in return or to hold someone in our debt.

As alluded to in the previous chapter, the dimensions of gratitude that involve reciprocity can take an ugly turn if teachers make their students beholden to them in some way. Perhaps unknowingly a teacher may manipulate the dynamics of a giving and receiving situation so that students give back in the teacher's currency – of what they value and look for rather than what the students are wanting and able to give. Unhealthy relations stemming from the power of the teacher over the student can diminish the purity of the intention. Brother Steindl-Rast issues a similar warning about our *will* to express gratitude: "Our will must stay clear of both compulsive self-sufficiency and slavish dependence in order to freely acknowledge the bond that the gift establishes."[95]

However, it might be impossible to escape the exchange aspect of gratitude: all of our actions are driven by a desire for something in return. Much of our modern Western society is built on a paradigm of exchange, where we see giving as a way of receiving, and education is no exception to this.

Patricia White suggests that we can overcome the *quid pro quo* interpretation of gratitude by seeing it more as a response "by which the beneficiary honours and celebrates the benefactor's goodwill".[96] This is a case of a mutual relationship, not of one person having a hold over another. When we express gratitude, it is a natural aspect that is an integral part of our everyday life. Teachers may express gratitude to their students as they become increasingly aware of everything they have received from them – without a planned exchange in mind. No "norm of reciprocity" needs to be at play here. If we view the situation in this way, we could untangle ourselves from the exchange aspect of gratitude because we would also need to focus on ways of making the situation one of mutual respect and understanding. These would be crucial conditions for healthy expressions of gratitude in education.

Another useful distinction is made by Vaughan and Estola who identify two paradigms – the exchange paradigm and the gift paradigm. Each has its own distinct values and logic, and each is diametrically opposed to and cancels the other out. Vaughan and Estola stress that the exchange paradigm involves equal payment and is ego-oriented, while the gift paradigm is directed towards satisfying others' needs and is other-oriented. Our practice of gratitude requires us to be conscious of our act of giving, our gift, and to focus our giving on the other and not upon ourselves and our own rewards. This same distinction is characterised by Harpham like this:

> A person does not provide another with a benefit because he or she expects something in return. That would be exchange in the marketplace, subject to different sorts of sanctions. A gift is given freely because of a desire, in and of itself, to assist another person. Similarly, a person does not simply respond to a benefit with an equal benefit, not more, not less, in return. That would be to treat gratitude as a commodity exchanged between individuals for an equal benefit.[97]

According to Schlitz and her colleagues, another important component of a transformative practice is repetition. Brother Stendl-Rast says, "…by practising gratitude you are, at that very moment, doing what you hope to do after your practice…"[98] Our challenge is to withstand everyday pressures that entice us to continually move on to something new, and to stay with one thing, one practice, just for the sake of the act of repeating it and what it can teach us about both gratitude and ourselves.

Our time together at Eastgates helped us discover that to develop our gratitude practices requires our strong intention, our vigilant attention and our repeated action. I wanted to leave the teachers with some inspiration from the effect that just one practice could make. I read a story recently sent to me from a semi-retired high school teacher who had participated in a gratitude workshop:

Over forty years ago I was teaching at a boys' boarding school, at Maritzburg College in Pietermaritzburg (Natal) South Africa. I had just started teaching and was assigned a very well-loved and respected teacher as my mentor. He was the most popular teacher in the school and his reputation spread far and wide. Before every lesson, he would pause outside the classroom before going in to teach. He would close his eyes almost as if in prayer. When I asked the teacher what and why he was doing this he told me it was a ritual he had followed all his teaching career. He paused to be thankful for the opportunity to teach, reminding himself he was about to enter a class where there would be students brighter and more articulate than he was and who would be going on to achieve greater things in their lives than he ever would. He felt privileged to share the learning experience with them and paused to prepare himself to give of his best in this coming opportunity.

Thankfulness has to be learnt by constant repetition. That was the lesson I learnt from my mentor. I felt that I never taught as successfully as he did but learning thankfulness made my own teaching experience much more enjoyable.

LITTLE PRACTICE, BIG EFFECTS

...each sight or incident scores upon the consciousness. Let us not take it for granted that life exists more fully in what is commonly thought big than in what is commonly thought small.[99]
– Virginia Woolf

Sometimes it is difficult to know where to start in our gratitude practice. Everywhere we look, there can seem to be a need to express gratitude and we may feel overwhelmed and perhaps ineffective if we take up just one or two gratitude practices. A sense of personal inadequacy could also be felt if we compare ourselves with others who may appear to practise gratitude more naturally or more easily than we do. Chapter 5 offers ways of setting realistic expectations and overcoming perfectionist tendencies when practising gratitude. It emphasises the need to feel comfortable with one's own starting point and the use of 'little gratitude practices', which can be adopted in a step-by-step way to great effect. The chapter draws on Barbara Fredrickson's 'broadening and building' theory to show how, when applied to gratitude as a practice, just one extra attempt to express gratitude on a regular basis can lead to a teacher's increased creativity, enhanced relationships, and individual transformation.

Gratitude lives in a context

Rose, an education student who was doing her honours project on gratitude, accompanied me to Millbrook Primary School, which had the potential to be a site for her research project. I had recently been invited by Natalie, the principal at Millbrook, to present a gratitude workshop to the teachers. There were many points of contrast between Millbrook and Eastgates. Millbrook was a smaller school, relatively mono-cultural, and situated in a low socio-economic district.

During my workshop, Natalie and all fifteen of the school's teachers seemed to respond confidently to the possibility of gratitude to promote more giving and valuing within the school. Their initial thoughts were that they were good at expressing gratitude to each other and to their students, and had started thinking about how gratitude could influence and improve their pedagogical practices in rewarding ways. To many of the staff, Natalie radiated gratitude. She was a strong and respected leader who, since her arrival two years ago, had made many beneficial changes at the school. She placed a high value on relationships and would go out of her way to ensure that she was understanding others' points of view and not just imposing her own. These teachers gave instances of where Natalie's gratitude had helped change the school culture to make them feel valued. Very often she gave particular attention to the good points of individuals, both teachers and students.

When I came to the point in the workshop where I talked about parents' involvement in the gratitude work, and how excited I had been that so many parents had turned up for a parents' gratitude workshop at Eastgates, the mood in the room changed – dramatically. The teachers had to alert me to the stark differences between Eastgates' parent group and Millbrook's. The participation rate by parents in school activities or events was very low, with only twenty or so regularly helping out on canteen duty, reading activities or excursions. Many children were in the third generation of welfare dependency and often their parents had not been successful at school themselves. In the school district a higher than average crime, drug and alcohol-abuse rate was recorded, as well as a high incidence of abuse and neglect of children.

I agreed that involvement of parents might not be initially possible. "Perhaps we could consider the impact of teachers' gratitude towards these parents." Regretting that I uttered these words as soon as I said them, I looked over at Rose, who winced in disbelief. I was asked how I could possibly think that gratitude could have a place with parents who neglected and abused their children, and on the whole, resented schools and teachers. Many students came to school without having breakfast and with no food to sustain them during the day. Sometimes teachers had to withstand verbal abuse from some parents.

I had failed to apply one of my guiding principles when offering workshops: *gratitude lives and breathes in a context*. If I had remembered the importance of this, I would have recognised that the *context needs to speak of where gratitude is most needed and most appropriate*. I acknowledged to the teachers that my work on gratitude in other schools did not articulate with the language or culture at Millbrook. But I had the sense that they now labelled me as one of the many who come along offering some form of professional development, which often alienates them by its unrealistic expectations and lack of awareness of the reality in their classrooms and their community.

The Millbrook teachers wanted me to know what they go through on a daily basis. One teacher related a conversation she had just that morning with her Year 5 students about their future. One girl had said that her mother wanted her to "get out of school as soon as she could", and that her mother was 15 when she gave birth to her. Another girl said that her mother left school at the end of Grade 8. Where could gratitude fit in the lives of students who have low expectations of themselves and have a narrow perspective on what their future can hold?

"Is gratitude a middle-class, elitist concept?" Heath, one of the other teachers, challenged me. "Is it something that's the privilege of the few who are lucky enough to have attained a place on the top of Maslow's hierarchy of needs[100] –

those who have the luxury of aiming for self-actualisation?" Heath clearly thought my ideas were lofty abstractions for this community. "Many Millbrook parents find it difficult to get out of bed in the morning," Heath continued, "or to put food on the table. All they can think about from day to day is survival."

Emily, another teacher, remarked, "If a parent can leave her child at the school until 7pm or can arrive here drunk, even early in the morning, how can we possibly respond with gratitude?" All the other teachers seemed to know the parent Emily was speaking of, and agreed that the idea of expressing gratitude to this parent was "criminal" and "immoral". Emily's question prompted a tirade of stories of neglect and abuse and the feeling that they were left to pick up the pieces by dealing with 'damaged' students in their classroom.

The teachers redirected their conversation to the high schools in their district where many of the students were "crawling off the walls" and were so determinedly disrespectful to parents, teachers or other authority figures that their teachers could find no more energy to confront them. Many of these high school teachers were totally cynical and despondent. "How on earth could you believe that gratitude has a place in such out of control, so-called education?" Heath asked.

Fortunately, Natalie jumped in at this point, and spoke of her belief that gratitude *could* make a difference. She told the group that since she had initially met with me about the gratitude work, she had started practising it more consciously with one of the difficult parents. Before she was to see him, she would think grateful thoughts towards him and his child. When face-to-face with him, she thanked him for taking the time to come and see her, and thanked him again at the end of their meeting, pointing out the good things she saw in his child.

"I might have just been wanting it to work," Natalie told them, "but I believe my gratitude really made a difference. I was expecting a nasty confrontation, but he was unusually calm and we were able to discuss the issue without him getting angry."

I looked around the room and saw that the teachers' respect for their principal helped most of them stay open to the rest of the workshop. Some confessed that their difficulties with many of the parents in the school had often caused them to be judgmental and to not bother communicating with them when they came to collect their children from school. Natalie impressed upon them the possibility that gratitude could bridge the gap that divided teachers from parents. She was all too aware of the different behavioural problems the teachers were dealing with moment-to-moment with the children, yet she also had compassion for the parents.

"Looking at things from their perspective, I'm concerned that recurring data from surveys of our parents tell us many are not happy with the way they are treated by the school or with the communication processes that some teachers use. I'm proud of the gratitude we have for each other and for most of our students," she went on. "However, sometimes, our own relatively middle-class values differ so greatly from the values of our parent community. Perhaps this difference is what stops us from seeing what's really going on for them: we're too quick to judge. It's important for us to appreciate what the parents do, even small things."

Chelsea expressed her concern, "but some parents never show gratitude to us, even though we do so much for their children. They never thank us because they think it's our job – even to do more than teaching, to babysit and care for their children."

Natalie responded, "Perhaps they feel that we're expecting something in return and are intimidated and don't have the confidence to relate to us as real people. Perhaps they have not had much gratitude expressed to them in their own life. Ever. But, I'm not saying they want our pity. They would feel patronised."

One teacher, Maddy, shared that she already thanks parents for their support and will ring them at home for that purpose. She said the personal contact was powerful and appropriate, and made an impact, especially when made at night, because parents often commented they could not believe she was still working.

"Just a little effort goes a long way," Maddy said. "I hadn't really thought of this as a gratitude practice, but when I think about it, I'm wanting to acknowledge any efforts these parents are making and to thank them for helping with their children's homework. When they spend time speaking with me on the phone, I'm so grateful! Perhaps I should tell them this more often."

As I was finishing the workshop, Natalie expressed her vision, "We have a new building and great new facilities. But we must not let the resentment that's existed between teachers and parents for the last three decades, ever since the school started, infuse the new building of our school". Although she acknowledged what she was expecting was a big ask, Natalie shared her hope that all the teachers could increase their gratitude to parents. The only way to move forward as a school, she believed, was to work together to find a way to be more inclusive of the difficult parents at Millbrook.

In the shoes of others

Natalie sent me an email at the end of that week, saying that all of her teachers had agreed to participate in the gratitude work. As it was her policy to only proceed with any new initiative if all of her teachers were on board, she was pleased that all had recognised the need to focus on gratitude to parents at Millbrook. Concerned about having started so incompetently, I wondered whether this was more about their allegiance and loyalty to Natalie and less about their true feelings about the potential of gratitude. However, Natalie also said that she was delighted to discover that many of her teachers had realised their gratitude to the parents, particularly the difficult ones, needed to be made more conscious. Gratitude to parents was to be the focus of this school's gratitude practice.

In my next few meetings with Natalie and the other teachers, I could see that some were assimilating the suggestion of taking up gratitude practices; others seemed only half-heartedly attentive to it. I consciously tried to say as little as I could, while I posed questions and attempted to clarify different dimensions of gratitude. Mostly, I listened to their challenges and their stories of how they had consciously practised gratitude since we last met. Given the difficulties with many of the parents, each small step towards gratitude was a major move in a positive direction. When listening to their struggles, I wondered how I would express gratitude if I were working in a similar community.

The teachers became attuned to the notion that gratitude to parents could, in turn, have a flow-on effect to the students, and thus to the need to treasure the role of parent more fully. They said "thank you" to the parents who came to the classroom or the school car park. In an initial response to the parents' complaints, they would thank them for taking the time to come and tell them their concerns. Following the lovely example set by Maddy in the first workshop, some teachers rang parents to thank them for their efforts if they noticed something good in their child. Overall, they noticed changes that were occurring in the school: more parents were coming more regularly and staying around the school for longer than usual.

Maria excitedly shared her story of sending a note home to a parent of a very difficult child, Tim, who was in her Year 6 class. She decided to look for something she valued in this boy and then wrote this in his diary. Afraid that the parents might not read Tim's diary entry, she also phoned them. She felt ashamed that this was the first time she had made contact with these parents and was surprised how nice they had been on the phone. They were overjoyed to hear from her as they had only ever had bad news from Tim's teachers all the way through his schooling. Tim came to class the next day, telling all his classmates and Maria that his parents had taken him out to dinner the night before to congratulate him for making more efforts at school. At lunchtime that day, Tim stayed back and asked Maria what he could do so that she would send another note home to his parents. Maria told us that Tim was more engaged and cooperative in class from that point onwards.

Elise seemed to be annoyed as these teachers shared their stories. Hers was one of disappointment. She took a lot of time to send letters of thanks to her students' parents, but complained to the group that she felt disheartened because she did not receive any in return. "Not one parent responded! So it doesn't always work!" Elise proclaimed, seeming to think that she was a failure.

I could see her mental struggle. Her intention behind her gratitude had been to receive something in return. I did not see it as my place at this point to clarify this for her. One invaluable lesson I had learned from working with other groups was that we needed to come to an understanding of gratitude at our own pace, through our own practice, reflection and discussion. It would be antithetical to the spirit of gratitude if a person were made to feel wrong or inadequate in their practice or understanding of gratitude.

Our discussion so far caused me to reflect on how my place amongst these educators at Millbrook was different to that at Eastgates. This was partly from my learning at Eastgates, and partly because of the stark differences in context and what each group required of me. At Millbrook I was a facilitator of the wisdom from the group, allowing Natalie and some of the others to take the lead in what gratitude means and its rightful place in their community. At Eastgates I had assumed more of a leadership role and brought stories in from outside, taking people in the direction I had wanted to go.

Natalie suggested they think of creative ways of expressing gratitude, something "behind the scenes" that would work for their school community. They took inspiration from the stories shared so far and some said they wanted to send home messages of gratitude to parents, or call them, noticing the good points in their children. They agreed they could send postcards made by the children, or themselves, with 'thankyou' messages to the parents, for reading with their child at home, or for ensuring their child wear a uniform in accordance with school guidelines, or for getting their children to school on time every morning.

Rose spoke up at this point. She jumped out of her role as researcher to share gratitude gestures from teachers that had moved her as a parent of three children – one of whom has autism. Although positive communication was rare, Rose shared how much she valued teachers commenting on the joy they found in teaching her son. Rose often felt inadequate and out of her depth when dealing with teachers who were not able to handle her son's idiosyncratic behaviour. Rather than wanting acknowledgment of the difficulties in raising such a child, most of all she valued any teacher who looked for the good in him and told her what they saw.

Rose's enthusiastic recollection prompted others to acknowledge similar experiences, and to relay how the gratitude of their children's teachers had made them feel more connected to the school community and more confident that they were doing something right as a parent. Some regretted the fact that they never received any such acknowledgement in all the years of their children's schooling, and the difference it would have made if they did. Then Angela shared, "This is showing me how judgmental I've been of the parents in this school. I had put them into a separate category from myself as a parent and didn't see that their needs for acknowledgment are the same as mine or any other parent, and perhaps more so."

As I was leaving, I saw Heath and Chelsea shaking their heads. I had noted their silence and glances at each other throughout our discussion. Natalie invited me into her office and began our conversation by saying that she was happy with how the teachers were progressing with the idea of expressing gratitude to parents. She was concerned though that Heath and Chelsea might undermine the gratitude and unity amongst the others with their cynicism, a kind of scornful doubting that she felt she could almost touch.

"They're just not happy about some recent decisions I had to make about staff changes", Natalie confided. "I have to admit that they're the most difficult to shift in their attitude towards this gratitude work. I think I can see why. They're the ones who have been the most hurt by some of the parents' abusive behaviour."

Natalie and I discussed that it is not our place to shift Heath's and Chelsea's attitude or change them in any way. The health of gratitude initiatives in a school can be heard in the open and honest dialogue that engages and does not exclude those who are unimpressed by an increased focus on gratitude. The only point of change that should concern us is what is going on inside ourselves. Our own growing confidence about the discourse and potential of gratitude can lead others in our community to feel judged by us if they are not grateful. We need to be ever vigilant of not setting up an 'us and them' mentality. If we take time to listen to others' concerns and dilemmas about gratitude, we might enlighten ourselves with a deeper understanding of their thinking, and of gratitude itself. If we put ourselves in the shoes of those who are opposed to practising gratitude and truly listen to them, we can help them open up and speak to us about other underlying issues. Then with empathy and open-mindedness, knowing something of what it must be like to wear their shoes, we might be able to help them speak to us openly about how they are feeling.

The folly of comparisons

Rose interviewed some of the teachers two months after the second workshop. She was particularly interested in the kinds of gratitude practices that the teachers adopted with parents and results they had experienced.

Later, when Rose came to see me in my office about her project, I recognised the expression on her face. It was the same when she had tried to hide her disappointment in something before. At first, I thought she had lost confidence in writing the fifth version of one of her thesis chapters. I had already expressed my view that her second version was nearly there, but hid my bewilderment that she felt the need to keep writing draft after draft until it was perfect.

"I don't think this gratitude is making much of an impact at all," Rose complained. "Here's the transcript of the interview I've done with Emily. Except for the beginning, she hardly mentions gratitude at all. Look at all the gratitude practices that Natalie has given me. Emily and the others I interviewed didn't do anything like that," she continued, giving me the list of Natalie's practices, with her look of disappointment growing.

- *Handing out merit certificates to parent helpers.*

- *Holding a gratitude breakfast for all parents, where the teachers would cook the breakfast out of appreciation for parents.*

- *Making a point to get in early to thank the parents as they leave their children at the school.*

- *Looking for what I appreciate in a parent and their child in readiness for a meeting between them, especially when I am going to discuss difficult matters.*

- *Thanking teachers regularly and finding many ways to acknowledge their efforts.*

When I read the transcript of Rose's interview with Emily, I gently questioned Rose about her disappointment with Emily's gratitude practice. Was she using Natalie's example as a yardstick to compare with Emily's practice of gratitude? Admittedly much of Rose's transcript was full of the difficulties that Emily had with Jill, a mother of one of her troublesome students, before she started to practise gratitude towards her. There were descriptions such as:

I found that she could be fairly negative towards teachers on the whole and things that happened in the school and...she always came across as being just not satisfied with what the school did. Nothing you did was enough.

Emily had decided to show compassion for Jill, and invite her into her classroom to read with the children. Given the resentment she had felt towards this parent, to invite the parent into her classroom was a huge gesture of gratitude on Emily's part.

When I invited Rose to consider this as significant, she admitted that before the interview had even started, Emily had told her that she often felt "way out of my comfort zone" with the gratitude practice, and that she felt that other teachers in the school probably thought that she was being overly optimistic about thinking that she could make a difference. As she was sharing this with me, Rose realised that Emily was trying something not only out of her own comfort zone, but also out of the comfort zone of the predominant culture of the whole school.

Rose went on to disclose that underlying her response of disappointment in Emily's gratitude were her own feelings about how she felt her gratitude was inferior to Natalie's. With tears in her eyes, she confided that she was thinking of giving up her honours project because she thought her writing was not good enough and she could not feel grateful enough. "When I look at my life", she said, "I can see so many situations where I'm failing in my gratitude. I can't be grateful when my little boy is misbehaving, or when I'm struggling to pay the mortgage at the end of the month, or when I don't have the energy to do my honours project."

In Rose, I could see so much of myself. We both judge ourselves when we see we are not perfect. We are both writing about gratitude. This could make us feel that we *should* be there, at the top of the mountain as grateful people or as shining examples. Our intense concentration on gratitude could cause us to focus on our deficiencies. I would so often have to shake myself out of feeling unworthy even to approach the subject of gratitude. Hoping to encourage Rose, I shared with her that gratitude for everything is next to impossible for any of us to achieve. That is why we call an initiative of increased gratitude in education a *practice*, where we choose only one thing to practise and become better and better at that before moving on to something else. The notion of practice implies that we are not perfect.

The butterfly effect

I reminded Rose about some of the 'small gratitude practices' of teachers who say thank you, greet others by smiling or waving to them, look for the good in others, send notes of thanks, or reflect on what they are grateful for in their students on the way to work. They noticed outcomes such as increased engagement, greater bonding with students, a calmer and more harmonious classroom, and the students saying thank you in return.

"But how can such a small action bring about such a big effect?" Rose inquired. "There's something there that's just stopping me from truly believing all of this. I can understand how Natalie's gratitude is having such a big effect, but with these other teachers, I wonder if it's just what they want to happen or what they think is going to happen because of the research, or other people's examples. Perhaps there were many other variables that could have led to these outcomes." Her scepticism echoed the views of some of the teachers in gratitude groups in other schools, who also questioned the simplicity of these practices.

Was it the simplicity of the practices that Rose and others were questioning or was it something else? Could it be that it is often more difficult for us to own the power and significance of our actions, words and thoughts – to, in fact, own our great innate potential and what we are truly capable of? To do so would mean that we would have to take far more responsibility than we normally do on a moment-to-moment level – both for our positive and the negative impact. I asked Rose if she had heard the famous saying by Marianne Williamson:

> Our deepest fear is not that we are inadequate. Our deepest fear is that we are powerful beyond measure. It is our light, not our darkness that most frightens us.[101]

I suggested that perhaps the principle of 'the butterfly effect' could come into play here. Rose was familiar with Edward Lorenzo's chaos theory, first published in 1963, of how a small change in the initial conditions in one place can result in a large change somewhere else. Lorenzo's findings proposed that a flap of a butterfly's wings could set off a chain of events that creates a minute change in the atmosphere that might eventually alter the course of a tornado.

Most of the time, however, we miss this long-term effect of our actions, and do not allow ourselves to reflect on it or own it to any great degree. I experienced this recently while conducting a focus group with high school teachers who had come together to share their effects of practising gratitude. One of these teachers, Andre, shared how astonished he had been by the dramatic effect of focusing his gratitude on one particular Year 11 student, Temerley, whom he had found to be very disruptive and disengaged. He spoke proudly of how Temerley's behaviour had completely turned around once he focused on thanking her often. He also spoke sadly of how Temerley commented that she had never been thanked before by any other teacher at any school she had attended.

As the effects of Andre's gratitude practice had been so profound and he had reported them so publicly, I was quite surprised to read of his comments on a follow-up questionnaire where he said that it was unlikely that he would continue to focus on gratitude because he saw this as a one-off example that probably would not have long-lasting effects.

Rose and I speculated how the principle of the butterfly effect might come into play in Andre's one action with that student – the gratitude practice of saying thank you to her. What chain of events could that initial gratitude practice have sparked that perhaps could have affected that student's direction in life forever? Through Andre expressing gratitude to Temerley, her behaviour improved and she became more engaged in class. This may have helped other students in the class and Temerley's other teachers might notice a lessening in Temerley's disruptive behaviour – both of which might influence the capacity for all students in the class to learn in a more settled environment. This in turn might have a positive effect on Temerley feeling more accepted by her peers and therefore more confident to participate in classroom activities. Perhaps the connection Temerley felt to this one teacher would also help her feel more connected to the school and her studies, enabling her to finish her school work successfully and then go on to do further study and pursue a fulfilling career?

Our speculation is not so far-fetched when we consider the many documented examples of how much just a few words from a teacher can alter the course of the life of a student. In her book, *Teaching Outside the Box*, LouAnne Johnson[102] captures this fact as she relates the story of a person who had a private detective agency and was asked about the most common reason people hire private detectives. After interviewing over 150 detectives in his agency, the most common request by people is not for matrimonial surveillance, but to gain help in finding a former teacher so that they can thank them. We also witness this in the many sayings about the impact of teachers, like the one by Henry Adams: "A teacher affects eternity; he can never tell where his influence stops"; or Helen Caldicott: "Teachers I believe are the most responsible and important members of society because their professional efforts affect the fate of the earth;" or Victor Hugo: "He who opens a school door closes a prison".

Still, our effect as teachers is something very difficult to grasp. Caught in the grip of the exchange paradigm, we are more able or conditioned to measure our impact in terms of tangibles that are going to be quantified and reported on or be checked against in our performance management. It is much easier to look at our successes in terms of students' grades increasing or, in the case of academics, the number of papers we have written or how our teaching has been evaluated. Rarely do we measure our success by the impact of aspects that are less tangible, like the consciousness we bring to our words and actions. Whatever we are held accountable for by those around us is generally where our attention goes. We judge our greatness in other people's terms and this is too often based on how well we perform a task or on external quantifiable results. These are usually measured in terms of the short-term effects – we want to see the results now.

"But that amount of consciousness and the responsibility implied here would be far too intense for most of us", Rose responded, "by the end of just a few minutes we would be too overwhelmed. And we might also see how imperfect we are at getting it right. We would need to take responsibility for the negative impact our words and actions, our lack of gratitude or ingratitude, has on others as well." My reply was that perhaps for us to take on this amount of responsibility we would need to not judge ourselves if we do not say the right thing or take the correct action.

A way forward out of our perfectionist tendencies is to recognise that gratitude calls us into a beautiful humility – one of the nets that holds gratitude in place. This is a gentle humility that accepts that we are not perfect, and so we have no right to judge or criticise others or, importantly, ourselves. It is a humility that leads to self-love and acceptance. It can often be found amongst people who radiate gratitude most of the time, who, though not conscious of themselves as grateful people, constantly look for ways in which they can express gratitude.

"Perhaps we need to start with being grateful to ourselves so that we can build the resilience we need to accept the enormous impact our words and actions can have on those we teach," I suggested to Rose. "And a big part of this would be to love ourselves and not judge ourselves for our imperfections." In the same way as we practise gratitude towards people we do not like, we can practise gratitude for aspects of ourselves that we do not like. Both require our compassion and willingness to accept imperfections, and both are very important for our state of being. In our discussion about our perfectionist tendencies, we were also uncovering something very important about the nature of gratitude itself. To get close to what it means in our lives as teachers requires us to fail often, so that we can see how we need to grow and change.

Our conversation then returned to the power of thinking about gratitude as a practice. The focus need not be on all our thoughts and actions all the time, but perhaps on just one or two actions. If we do not acknowledge the butterfly effect of these actions, and the potential for great impact – not immediately visible – we are not able to embrace or envision the full power and capacity of gratitude. To stand tall and accept the large impact our small acts of gratitude can make on others' lives, can lead to greater love of ourselves and a greater motivation to continue with our practice. If we accept the effect just one small gratitude practice can have, we can perhaps take on this practice with greater pride and determination.

It often helps to start with gratitude in areas where it is easy to practise, and then build upon our practice to approach the more difficult challenges we find in life.

If we start with the most difficult, we can become disillusioned or disappointed. We might think that we are not able to respond with gratitude. In Chapter 8, we will see that there is an art to expressing gratitude in times of adversity and part of this is to start with things that are unrelated to the challenging event or person. For example, if we are experiencing conflict with a colleague and the situation is so painful that it is difficult to see anything we can be grateful for in this person or this situation, we might be better to look at building our gratitude by expressing it towards something or someone outside this situation. It is important to start with small steps.

Gratitude broadens and builds

Rose still questioned the speculative nature of our exploration of the butterfly effect. "How would this all stand up in a research paper?" she asked. "How would you be able to prove that just one practice had such a large effect? It just doesn't seem academic or scientific enough for me. It's more like popular science than real research."

This was one of many discussions I had with Rose in which I so appreciated her honest scepticism. An openly ardent atheist, she would question anything that smacked of faith or belief in something that could not be scientifically proven. Her first degree was in environmental science, and her motivation to take up the topic of gratitude was her deep love of nature. Rose believed that gratitude was a missing link in environmental education. However, she would often struggle with the claims made about gratitude in the 'new science' that underpins positive psychology.[103] Her concerns resonated with others who had questioned the research evidence, deeming it to be unworthy of being called "empirical proof".

I understood Rose's issues and knew that the work she respected the most, and which for her was "the easiest to digest" because of what she named as "good science and academic rigour", was the broaden-and-build theory of Barbara Fredrickson.[104] I went to my bookshelf and took down my well-worn copy of *The Psychology of Gratitude* and together Rose and I searched for possible answers the chapter contributed by Fredrickson could give to our question of how we might scientifically explain why little practices of gratitude have such big effects.

A basic tenet of Fredrickson's broaden-and-build theory is that positive emotions appear to *broaden* "people's momentary thought-action" by "widening the array of the thoughts and actions that come to mind".[105] On the other hand, negative emotions lead to narrow, survival-oriented behaviours. She has mounted her theory on both the findings of studies on the effects of positive emotions, and her own randomised control studies, where participants watch films that arouse particular emotions – both positive and negative. She has shown that joy creates the urge to play and be creative, hence to "take in new information and experiences, and expand the self in the process."[106] Contentment can broaden thought-action by "creating the urge to take time to savour current life circumstances and integrate these circumstances into new views of self and the world." [107]

Positive emotions, like joy and contentment, broaden their impact by *building* "enduring personal resources". Fredrickson shows that the urge to play arising from joy, for example, builds both physical and social resources, as well as intellectual resources, because it fuels brain development. Contentment, according to this theory "produces self-insight and alters world views"[108]. Importantly, Fredrickson also notes that personal resources that increase as a result of positive emotions, "outlast the transient emotional states that led to their acquisition."[109]

Fredrickson's empirical work on these positive emotions holds great potential in answering our question about the wide-reaching impact of gratitude. Relating her broaden-and-build theory to gratitude, Fredrickson describes gratitude as arising when "an individual perceives that another person (benefactor) or source (for example, God, luck, fate) has intentionally acted to improve the beneficiary's well-being".[110] She illustrates the broadening capacity of gratitude:

> ...grateful individuals appear to creatively consider a wide range of prosocial actions as possible reflections of their gratitude. Perhaps reflecting the creativity in returning gifts... [111]

The broadening capacity of gratitude as an emotion leads to individual transformation as people continually grow in "an upward spiral toward optimal functioning and enhanced emotional well-being".[112] As people become more grateful they are "more creative, knowledgeable, resilient, socially integrated, and healthy" and better at "dealing with stress and adversity."[113]

Gratitude's building capacity is discussed by other researchers who attest to its capacity to build social and psychological resources, by building and strengthening bonds of friendship and because, as Fredrickson says, it often "fuels reciprocal altruism".[114] Fredrickson notes that gratitude can build the social resources of communities: it links individuals to society and strengthens one's spirituality. Gratitude builds people's skills for loving and showing appreciation in that "it prompts them to stretch themselves to think creatively about how to return kindnesses."[115]

Rose and I returned to the transcript of the interview with Emily to see if Emily's gratitude practice broadened and built in ways Fredrickson had suggested to us. Emily had expanded her mental resources by creatively thinking about how she could express gratitude to this mother, Jill. She not only invited her into her classroom to read with the students, but also reached out to Jill when she looked sad, and bought her a card that said, "If you ever need anything, let me know". We were delighted that Fredrickson's theory helped us to see that Emily was extending her ability to love and express kindness with an inner attitude of giving. Since giving this parent the card, Emily said that the mother comes in every day to say hello, "Every day she talks to me in the corridor. Like when we've gone to the Association meeting, she'll sit there and she'll say things like 'I love what Mrs X has done in her class with this group of kids.' It's just amazing!"

We speculated on the many ways that Emily broadened her resources. First, she created a more harmonious relationship with this parent. Now this mother was supporting her. Emily's acts of gratitude had increased harmony and possibly accelerated this process by decreasing disharmony, in the sense that Jill may have continued to feel angry and alienated if no gratitude was expressed to her. In turn, the increased harmony had a positive impact on Emily's confidence and resilience.

We also noticed that Emily might well have broadened the resources of other teachers who observed her behaviour toward this mother. In Rose's interview with her, Emily related some changes in her colleagues in this way:

There are two teachers in this school who openly despise this woman as she has spoken rudely and not very nicely to teachers in the past. So when I mentioned that I was doing the gratitude with this parent, they weren't offended but they were a little bit upset because they felt that I wasn't supporting them. So I've had to explain why I'm doing it and just by making that extra effort to be open and honest with them that they will hopefully probably change their behaviour. One teacher who is quite loud and out there and who gets easily offended, she's starting to notice what I'm doing and how it's working and I've noticed she'll walk past her in the corridor now and say (to the mother) 'Good morning Jill, how are you today?' Whereas before she wouldn't even look at her. It does work.

"So," Rose proclaimed, "Emily's little gratitude practice has already affected so many people – and we haven't even started to scratch the surface of the impact on this mother's child!" We were excited at the possibility of going back to that data to explore how these emotions arising from gratitude gave life to the application of Fredrickson's theory to educational contexts. Emily had inspired both of us. The impact of her gratitude was perhaps greater than she would ever know!

THE CHARISMA OF GRATITUDE

... every major thread of one's life experience is honoured, creating a weave of such coherence and strength that it can hold students and subject as well as self. Such a self, inwardly integrated, is able to make the outward connections on which good teaching depends...[116]
– Parker J. Palmer

This chapter draws together the principles and dilemmas explored so far, and positions these in a wider theoretical framework of teaching pedagogy. I propose that contemporary constructs of 'teacher identity' and 'teacher reflection' can be enriched by attending to the ontological domain. Following the principle of Parker J. Palmer's notion that "We teach who we are", the chapter explores how educators can best prepare their 'inner attitudes' in ways that are an effective form of teacher preparation. I demonstrate how teachers' gratitude practices are highly relevant to this process. The chapter also considers the challenges of engaging in this kind of reflection when there are large amounts of content to cover and a perceived lack of time. It advocates a way of achieving a higher level of consciousness of one's inner attitude rather than a new technique that requires more time, effort and skill development. I introduce a new approach to teacher reflection that I call, 'A State of Preparedness', or 'reflection *before* action'. This approach challenges traditional paradigms that separate a teacher's personal life from their teaching life.

Sophie and her "ratbag" students

In my professional studies tutorial, I asked my first-year pre-service teachers to share their most important learning after their first visit to a school. As they went from class to class in their assigned high school they had made observational notes. One of my students, Jason, related his experience. He noted what many of us witness in our schools today. While teachers in the staffroom praised the students who were doing well, they wished that more of the other students would either act the same, or "go somewhere else". One complaint had a continual echo: having to deal with difficult "out of control" students who were not there to learn. It seemed easy, Jason noted, for many teachers to talk negatively about students in public.

Jason's assigned mentoring-teacher, Rory, described the students in the Year 8 class that Jason was to observe throughout that day. There were students that Rory expected to conform and stay on task, and there were those who he said would be impossible to teach. Rory's tone changed to exasperation as he described "the ratbags" of the class – a group of three boys who were "beyond help and would never learn". He told Jason that it was not really their fault as they came from "ratbag parents" who drank to excess, who had been unemployed most of their lives, and who never visited the school. Rory shared with Jason his "strategy" for "dealing" with the boys: he ignored the bad behaviour and used backup plans for serious punishment if they went too far. He recited all the rules that he had established for them to follow and the consequences if they broke them.

As Rory predicted, and as Jason watched, the three so-called "ratbags" misbehaved. They did not keep to the task they were to follow and found numerous ways to distract others, constantly soaking up Rory's attention. They broke Rory's rules and he delivered the 'relevant' punishment that was the consequence of their bad behaviour. This seemed to increase their defiance and make them even more unsettled. As Jason followed the students to other classes, he observed the same patterns of behaviour between these students and the other teachers.

Jason had expected the last class of the day to be the worst. A Grade 8 maths class would surely be the time when the three boys would be at the peak of their disruptive behaviour. But as the boys approached this class, Jason noticed that their walking was different. Their defiance and boisterousness had dramatically diminished. When the "ratbags" entered the room, they were as calm as their teacher, Sophie, who greeted them and everyone else with a smile and a genuine "Thank you for coming today". Even from a distance, Jason could see that this teacher had a certain presence that the boys responded to, with something almost approaching respect.

Jason thought that this teacher "exuded gratitude" – for her subject, for the school, and for her students. As far as he could see Sophie was not using any special teaching techniques or being any more creative in introducing content than the other teachers he had observed that day. The main difference was that throughout the lesson, Sophie praised the boys often and thanked them for little things they did, making a special effort to notice and acknowledge their efforts. Jason also talked about Sophie's presence as being one that deeply connected with each of her students, and he described the class as having an atmosphere of joy and enthusiasm.

At the end of the lesson, Sophie stood at the door of the classroom, and thanked everyone again, and the three boys filed out in an orderly and settled manner that amazed Jason. He was shocked by the difference in the boys' behaviour and attitude. Why were these "out of control" students calm and attentive in Sophie's class and not so in the others? Could a teacher have that much impact on students' behaviour?

Jason told us that after the class when he talked to Sophie, she related that she was so proud of these students for having the courage to get up in the morning and come to school, in spite of their difficulties. She pointed out many of the good points she could see in each of the boys, and Jason noticed that her way of speaking about them revealed her genuine respect for them. Sophie also talked of what she received from these boys – she liked the challenge they gave her as a teacher to create ways of keeping them engaged. She also liked the challenge of noticing something she could say to other teachers who could not appreciate any of the boys' strengths.

Jason had provided our class with a wonderful example of the transformative power of one teacher's approach. The context was the same, as perhaps was the quality of instruction and materials. Each teacher was following the curriculum. The "ratbag boys" were moving from class to class with the same group of students. All of the other teachers followed Rory's lead of trying to control the behaviour of these students with rules and punishment.

This was an opportunity for us to explore the question: What part did gratitude play in bringing about the change in Sophie's students?

Gratitude as 'recognition'

Insights offered by the social anthropologist, Margaret Visser, are helpful here. She tells us that the French word for gratitude is *reconnaissance*, which contains the meaning 'recognition'. Gratitude is a way of *recognising* the other: "giving is itself a voluntary sign of recognition. And returning out of gratitude *(reconnaissance),* is a gift that echoes the first giver's recognition *(reconnaissance).*"[117] Moreover, "there is in human beings a powerful longing to be recognised."[118] Visser sees this need for recognition as a "fundamental struggle for identity, relationship, and belonging"[119]. Importantly also, "Recognition is not something one inherently has, it must be given."[120]

In our tutorial we explored how we could bring Margaret Visser's insights to life, assisting us to deepen our understanding of how Sophie brought about such a change through her gratitude. As Sophie greeted the boys by thanking them for coming, she was giving them the gift of recognition, a gift that satisfied a need, a deeply felt human need, that might not have been met in any of their other classes. Perhaps before our students can be present and attentive in our classes, we need to recognise them somehow. This may be why so many teachers relate stories of transformation in their students, and a calmness in the class atmosphere, when they engage in the simple act of greeting them from a heart full of gratitude. Their greetings are bringing about *reconnaissance.*

Sophie did not just recognise her students by name. She recognised their qualities as human beings. She saw how their qualities disclosed themselves to her as gifts from which she could learn, and which impelled her to return in kind, with gratitude. The more we identify and articulate what we receive from our students, the more our students perceive their own gifts. Often it takes someone else to recognise our gifts before we can recognise them in ourselves.

Sophie recognised the boys for who they are, rather than imposing a set list of behaviours of how she wanted them to be. Her gratitude revealed another kind of recognition. Gratitude helps us to respect difference in the other – a point that is made clear, again through Margaret Visser's profound insights:

> ...the process of linking through giving, receiving, being grateful and giving back preserves the fact that she is Another – one who also deserves the distancing effect of respect for her difference.[121]

I took this opportunity to share with the class another example of recognition through gratitude that an ex-student, Adam, recently shared with me. Adam is now teaching secondary students in one of the most difficult and challenging schools in the state. This was only his third year out teaching, and I had heard from others who taught in the school that Adam's reputation as an outstanding teacher was spreading far and wide. He wanted to relay this story to me, as the most profound moment he had experienced so far.

Adam had been perplexed about what to do with a group of his Year 8 female students who had been involved in cyber-bullying and nasty behaviour towards each other. He tried to talk sense to the girls individually and as a group, spent time trying to understand them and listen to them, showed them the consequences of this behaviour, but none of his strategies was working. He saw that the girls had very little regard or respect for themselves or anyone else. Nothing seemed to matter. This situation was impacting on everyone else in the class and on Adam's capacity to teach. Quite spontaneously in one of his classes he went around the class telling each student what he valued in them. He started out by saying that the only real ways of judging yourself or others is by the way we treat each other and ourselves. He spoke from his heart about what he was grateful for in each student, the gifts these students gave to him, and made each statement very particular to the student. For example, "Max – You help keep me young. You play hard but fair in everything you do, this makes you an incredibly fun person to be around."; "Brie – "You're witty, funny and are able to keep me on my toes in a way that I find challenging yet entertaining at the same time." "Chloe – Thank you so much for the courage you show in persevering and remaining strong, even though your sister has a poor reputation in the school and you often feel labelled as being bad because of this." Adam said that when it came to some of the students' turns, they looked away, as if to say that he would find it impossible to see anything nice in them or perhaps they could not accept the praise.

As Adam went around the class, some students started to cry, others settled more than they had in a few weeks, and a certain reverence, a gentleness that had been lost, returned. After he told the last Year 8 student what he valued in him, that student spontaneously said, "Right, now we'll go back around and say what we value about having Mr Tilford as a teacher." Adam was moved, and surprised, at hearing what he meant to these students, as he heard statements such as "Mr Tilford, thank you for being the first teacher who has accepted me for who I am and for thanking me when I make an effort"; "Mr Tilford, thanks for being totally with us when you are with us and not being distracted by anything else"; "Mr Tilford, thank you for being there for me when I need to speak about my problems and no one else understands;" "Mr Tilford, thanks for encouraging us to do better, not just with our work, but as people as well." From that point onwards, the girls stopped their bullying behaviour. A deep need for recognition and to recognise had been met. The classroom was now a place where students and teacher felt comfortable and supported, safe to speak about what they value in each other.

Adam's example illustrated a beautiful point made by Visser that "…gratitude causes the receiver to look beyond the gift to the giver. This movement in itself transcends the object or favour given; it 'opens' the receiver to the person of the other…" It is also a lovely way of extending our notion of recognition to what Martin Buber calls "confirmation", a quality described by the ethical philosopher Nell Noddings:

> When we confirm someone, we identify a better self and encourage its development. To do this we must know the other reasonably well. Otherwise we cannot see what the other is really striving for, what ideal he or she may long to make real. Formulas and slogans have no place in confirmation. We do not posit a single ideal for everyone and then announce 'high expectations for all'. Rather we recognize something admirable, or at least acceptable, struggling to emerge in each person we encounter. The goal or attribute must be seen as worthy both by the person trying to achieve it and by us. We do not confirm people in ways we judge to be wrong.[122]

Similar to this is Patricia White's notion of the reciprocal nature of gratitude – a relationship she encapsulates as 'the beneficent circle of gratitude'.[123] The benefactor offers a gift or help and the beneficiary accepts such help and recognises the good intentions of the benefactor and gives in return. As a result, the benefactor can also be grateful, "… thus the beneficent circle of gratitude is created."[124]

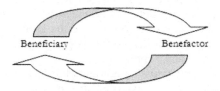

Figure 3. The beneficent circle of gratitude involving two people.

When Adam acknowledged the gifts in his students, when he recognised them, they could not help but reciprocate. They intuitively sensed that the circle was not complete unless they returned their thanks. When Sophie recognised her students in her greetings and words of thanks, they could not help but reciprocate with giving her their gift of attention during her lesson. In these powerful examples we can see that gratitude, by its nature, encourages reciprocity.

It is our recognition of our connectedness with the other that, as Thomas Merton describes, is at the core of compassion, and which many other writers, such as Martin Buber[125], Carl Jung[126], Charles Taylor[127], Margaret Sommerville[128], and Sooren Kierkergaard[129], have argued is at the heart of our relating, and of enriching our lives. Indeed, discussion of the role of our sense of inter-subjectivity is at the centre of many philosophical texts. Some writers embrace what I call a "radical interconnectedness", which is at the core of many spiritual and religious philosophies and teachings.[130] It proposes a oneness, a "universal consciousness" that weaves a common thread through all of humanity, and for some, all of existence.

Teacher ethic

In a later class we moved on to other ways in which we could bring the power of *reconnaissance* to our relations with others in our school community – by warmly and genuinely greeting colleagues, parents and administrative staff, and actively going out of our way to acknowledge their good points. As many teachers in the Eastgates group had reported, if we make our recognition of others our gratitude practice, we can move from a functional relationship where our greetings are overlaid with a need to get something from the other – like a timetable, a student report, an idea for a lesson – to one where we value the person for who they are, not what we need from them.

"But what happens if we just don't like some of our students or their parents or some of our colleagues?" Brett asked. (Brett had previously been a teacher for about a decade and had entered the course to update his qualifications and skills.) "I can think of many students for whom I can't think of one thing I like. They gave me hell from the beginning of the year to the end."

Brett's question was important as it highlighted one the biggest obstacles to practising gratitude, and has the potential to undermine our attempts to even try. It raised the larger question which I then posed to the group: Are we obliged in our role as teachers to move past our dislike for others, and move towards recognising them in the way that Adam and Sophie had?

The mutuality of *reconnaissance* highlights the interconnectedness embedded in our acts of gratitude. As was explored in our discussion of the meaning of gratitude in Chapter 3, true gratitude moves away from an individualised, internal sense of gratitude to one of giving to the other: it necessitates the involvement of at least two people. Visser notes, "Gratitude is always a matter of paying attention, deliberately beholding and appreciating the other."[131] Is there something about our interconnectedness with the other that is so inherent in who we are as human beings that we need to acknowledge this in some way, regardless of our feelings towards them? Can our gratitude, through our recognition of others, facilitate a deepening sense of interconnectedness?

As was already mentioned, the philosopher Charles Taylor holds that if we pay attention to the strong evaluations and frameworks of meaning in our lives, we will find that the highest good, that is at the root of our being and our language, is not freedom, but "the worth of every human being". Taylor sees the redemption of meaning in our lives as the finding of our moral source in the "divine affirmation of the human"[132]. In this same sense Margaret Sommerville calls us into a "shared ethics", of a "secular-sacred" kind, where we have "deep respect for all life and a profound respect for the human spirit."[133]

In stark contrast to interconnectedness, Taylor explores the impact of disengagement on the identity of the individual and how we have arrived, through "disengagement from embodied agency and social embedding", at a "monological consciousness" which leads to methodological individualism. As a result, "Each of us is called upon to become a responsible, thinking mind, self-reliant for his/her judgments".[134] However, we have tended to take this as part of our human condition rather than as the ideal of "the reification of the disengaged first-person-singular self" which is propounded by modern epistemology. As Taylor[135] points out, our understanding is seen to happen in mental representation rather than through action. However, such a position excludes consciousness of the body and the other, as well as the unarticulated and unformulated aspects of our actions.

According to Taylor, the common stance of disengagement, enforced as the preferred position of many higher educational practices, could be a large contributor to the overriding sense of meaninglessness that many experience in today's world. Taylor shapes an alternative theory in which the essence of the self must be seen as dialogical, rather than monological, "because a great deal of human action only happens insofar as the agent understands and constitutes himself as part of a 'we'.[136] The mutuality of giving and receiving through gratitude strengthens the dialogical, and builds the interconnectedness that is crucial for Sommerville's profound respect for the human spirit.

The sociologist Georg Simmel calls gratitude the "moral cohesion" of human relations and society, and speaks of gratitude as a "bridge" that enables us to come closer to the other. He famously said that "If every grateful action, which lingers on from good turns received in the past, were suddenly eliminated, society, (at least as we know it) would break apart".[137] Here Simmel is drawing our attention to the special part gratitude in particular might play in enabling us to reach past self-interest in order to acknowledge our inherent interconnectedness with the other.[138] He says: "...it gives human actions a unique modification or intensity; it connects them with what has gone before, it enriches them with the element of personality, it gives them continuity of interactional life."[139] Gratitude, according to Simmel, not only holds society together, but it also "forms it." In Simmel's work we see the offer of a real answer to Brett's question of how we practise gratitude to those whom we do not like:

> we do not thank somebody only for what he does: the feeling with which we often react to the mere existence of a person, must itself be designated as gratitude. We are grateful to him only because he exists, because we experience him...It is independent of any particular act of receiving; it offers our whole personality to the other, as if from a duty of gratitude, to *his* whole personality.[140]

Although this was a nice ideal, I could relate to Brett and some of the other students who were still finding it hard to be grateful for students whom they found difficult. They wanted a more practical way forward. Margaret Sommerville acknowledges how complex it may be to conceptualise our connectedness with others in a world where rampant individualism has overtaken our sense of this. She recommends a certain kind of "ethical imagining" for this to occur. John Ralston Saul also holds imagination to be at the heart of our ethics. "Transcending the self is about imagining the other, not to weaken the self, but to be capable of reaching beyond it. No convincing argument has yet been made which limits you or myself to our self-interest".[141] To assist this process of ethical imagining in relation to gratitude I drew students back to a lecture I gave a few weeks beforehand on 'Teacher Love', where I introduced Nell Noddings[142] work, *The challenge to care in schools*. I invited them to explore how we might be able to draw parallels between an ethic of care and an ethic of gratitude.

Noddings argues that "ethical caring", which she describes as "a state of being in relation, characterised by receptivity, relatedness and engrossment,"[143] should be at the heart of our ethical decision-making. Through our experiences and increased consciousness of what Noddings calls "natural caring" or "all-caring", of the kind we find in a mother's relationship with her child, we can summon ethical caring. Although we may not be able to be "all-caring" to all people, we can, and should, "care about" them by imagining and summoning the qualities of caring we have experienced in natural caring relationships where we care for and are cared for. In this sense the underlying principle is "descriptive, not prescriptive". Here she says that "Ethical caring's great contribution is to guide action long enough for natural caring to be restored and for people once again to interact with mutual and spontaneous regard". [144]

I asked the students if they could draw from their experiences of expressing gratitude and having gratitude expressed towards them, in situations where it was easy to do so. In returning to the points made by some of the great thinkers we had discussed, could they use this ethical imagining to at least appreciate the humanness or 'worthiness' in the students, and to acknowledge, to recognise, this interconnectedness through their gratitude towards them? Most could see the wisdom in taking on gratitude as part of being ethical and professional in their role as teacher. Regardless of how they think or feel about the other, their interconnectedness was inherent and not something they could choose to ignore. From this belief came an obligation to, at the very least, value and appreciate the essence of the other.

Finding gratitude within

"So, was it Sophie's sense of interconnectedness with these boys that gave her the charisma that Jason talked about, or was it her gratitude?" Rita, another student asked. "Surely it was more than the words of thanks she used? I'm keen to know how I can have that quality where my presence calms students and makes them feel valued."

Rita's questions prompted Jason to recall for the class the qualities that Sophie displayed that seemed to be absent in the other teachers at the school. He had described it earlier as a charisma, a light, a presence. As others chimed in with words that describe teachers they knew who had these qualities, I wrote these words up on the board – an aura, aliveness, centredness, charm, magnetism, gift, power, exuding something special from within, lighting up the room with their presence. We also drew from some of the statements that Adam's students used to describe him – that he is "totally there for us", "when I think of you, I feel warm and safe."

I referred back to the article we had studied earlier in the semester on 'Teacher Presence' by Carol Rodgers and Miriam Raider-Roth, where they describe teacher presence as:

> ...a state of alert awareness, receptivity, and connectedness to the mental, emotional, and physical workings of both the individual and the group in the context of their learning environments, and the ability to respond with a considered and compassionate best next step.[145]

To be able to respond to their students with a "considered and compassionate best next step", we agreed that teachers like Adam and Sophie would need to keep hold of a sense of interconnectedness and mutuality. Indeed, Rodgers and Raider-Roth make note of the qualities of a teacher that engender "relationship authenticity" crucial to teacher presence – qualities of self-knowledge, trust, relationship and compassion. Importantly, they also emphasise the importance of *recognition*: "The person needs to both recognise the other in all her complexity as well as sense that her self is also seen and accepted."[146]

Teachers are able to acquire this kind of presence by "bringing our whole self to full attention so as to perceive what is happening in the moment"– a state that other thinkers have labelled as "aliveness", "wide-awakeness", "mindfulness".

As Rodgers and Raider-Roth note, such presence was at the heart of Nell Noddings' ethic of care, as cited:

> 'I do not need to establish a lasting, time-consuming personal relationship with every student...What I must do is to be totally and non-selectively present to the student – to each student – as he addresses me. The time interval may be brief but the encounter is total.'[147]

If gratitude assists teachers to have better relationships with themselves, their students and society, and it can help them bring more of their whole self to the teaching process, then it also enhances teacher presence.

Our discussion brought us back to the core text for this unit, Parker J. Palmer's, *The courage to teach: Exploring the inner landscape of a teacher's life.* We had already explored his notion of "We teach who we are" and his premise that: "good teaching cannot be reduced to technique; good teaching comes from the identity and integrity of the teacher."[148]

"But what does it mean to bring our whole self to our teaching, and what does Palmer mean when he talks about identity? I've read that text several times and find it really inspiring, but I need more practical ways of knowing how to do this," Emma sighed. Her question was followed by a comment from Felicity, "I never get what they're talking about when theorists discuss about our 'being', it's far too ethereal for me. I just want to know what it is I have to change, and go 'right, I can understand' and then just do it. When I hear all these terms I just get overwhelmed and don't even try." A few of the other students joined in saying that they were aware that our character influences our teaching, and that we need to be good role-models, but they just didn't know where and how to start.

"Well, I just don't want to change myself. I'm happy with the way I am, and the way my parents brought me up," Anna said. "And besides, we're too early in our teaching career to be able to look inside ourselves that critically".

Then Ali challenged Palmer's notion of "We teach who we are" by raising a question common amongst many educators, "But I heard most teachers say how glad they were to get away from school on the weekend and forget about their students and their work. Isn't that the time to relax and unwind and not be a teacher at all? Surely our partners or children don't want us to be a teacher to them, they just want us to be our normal selves?"

I could understand that it was difficult for these students, and for many teachers. When we say "I teach who *I* am", what aspects of this *I* are we talking about here? What aspects of self do we bring our attention to? Are we expected to attend to our thoughts, emotions, actions, beliefs, or values? And if so, do we focus on all of these or just one aspect? A similar question needs to be asked about our gratitude practice. If it is not only our practice we are attending to, but also ourselves as we do this practice, who is this self? It is important to find answers to these questions because the language associated with self-transformation – such as 'way of being', or 'identity', or 'self' – can appear to many teachers as too abstract or vague to be practical.

These students' questions were also highlighting how concepts such as "we teach who we are" and "bringing our whole self to our teaching", challenge the traditional divide between the public and private domains of the teacher. Most teachers approach their work by becoming 'a teacher' when they enter the school gates, and leaving that identity behind when they depart. Indeed they would say that this is what gives them their sanity and resilience, by being able to switch off being a teacher at the end of the day and on the weekend. However, an alternative view to this is that we take our self to the teaching *role*. There is not a separate teaching self. We ditch the teaching role before we walk into our home, but our self stays the same.

If we consider that who we are, wherever we are, has an influence on how we teach and interact with our students, we are being called to move past a fixed notion of self, and to embrace a sense of what I call 'self-in-continuum'. This is the self that Rodgers and Raider-Roth describe as an "evolving entity, continuously constructed and reconstructed in relationship to the contexts, experiences and people with which the self lives and functions."[149] It is the 'undivided self' articulated by Parker J. Palmer:

> ...every major thread of one's life experience is honoured, creating a weave of such coherence and strength that it can hold students and subject as well as self. Such a self, inwardly integrated, is able to make the outward connections on which good teaching depends.[150]

In answer to the students' inquiry of 'who is this *I*?' I suggested that an aspect of self to be attended to with great power and focus is a dimension I call 'inner attitude', and which others might call our schema or overall outlook. Our inner attitudes lie securely behind our thoughts, feelings, and actions, and constantly influence them. We might imagine our inner attitudes as sending out inner energy, vibrating to all other aspects of our being. Ernest Holmes captures the impact of our attitudes: "One may have an optimistic or completely negative attitude in his approach to life, which makes for his success or failure. All man's experiences come out of his mental attitude."[151]

Attitude is a kind of lens we look through to orientate ourselves in the world. The attitude we take determines the positive and negative responses we have to people and events. Attitudes act less on a conscious level than belief or opinion, which we often can express clearly in words. I like to refer to 'inner attitude' to protect the term 'attitude' from usages we might commonly hear in educational settings – "that child has the wrong attitude"; "she needs to improve her attitude to maths"; "the wrong attitude will get you nowhere". Inner attitudes are often concealed. We may need to reflect deeply to identify them. "Attitudes are rooted in our being", says the philosopher Mary Midgley, "they are to do with our inner understanding, not external possessions."[152]

We can gain a clearer grasp of this dimension when we examine what happens when we change our inner attitude. To demonstrate this I offered the example of Emily, the teacher in Rose's gratitude practice, who saw deep change in a parent she had been having conflict with, once she changed her inner attitude towards her. I then asked the students to contemplate instances where situations were not able to change, no matter what external strategies they used, or changes they tried to make that were external to themselves, until they changed their inner attitude.

We were able to see that it was neither just Sophie's greetings and words that gave her the presence she had with these students, nor just Adam's words of valuing his students; it was the inner attitude, or spirit, behind these actions and words. Of course, there are many different kinds of inner attitude, many different lenses through which we are able to view the world. There may be an inner attitude of humility, just as there may be an inner attitude of pride. One can have a positive or negative inner attitude, for example. When a person has developed a habitual way of seeing the world through this outlook, where they have this inner attitude over a period of time, this can also be a way of describing a person's character traits.

By understanding this notion of inner attitude, we are able to gain a practical way forward in realising an integrated self, a self-in-continuum. We always have an inner attitude of some kind and we bring this to our teaching all the time, because it is part of who we are, whether we are conscious of it or not. It is not something we can switch on or off when we please. Importantly, the inner attitude that we have when we wake up in the morning before we go to work, when we are driving or walking to work, when we are marking our students' work on the weekend, when we are preparing our lessons, when we are playing with our children, all have an impact on the outcomes of the activity. To have the effect she had on those students, Sophie would not just have thought grateful thoughts in the time immediately before they arrived. She would more likely have brought that inner attitude of gratitude with her at the beginning of the day.

Margaret Visser links the meaning of gratitude with attitude. "The word *gratitude*", she says, "stands for the process – freely undertaken and therefore hard to pin down with definitions and generalised explanations – by which a person's attitude changes."[153] Robert Emmons and Charles Shelton suggest the type and level of reflection we require. To attend to our gratitude requires personal commitment to examine our daily life and "...to invest psychic energy in developing a personal schema, outlook, or world view of one's life as a 'gift' or one's very self as being 'gifted'."[154]

In returning to the notion of 'transformative practice' we are reminded that in order to be effective, our focus needs to be on both the practice and ourselves. We have learned that the impact of our gratitude practice does not only flow from the practice itself, but the attention and intention behind it. Where this dimension of attention and intention lives, is in our inner attitude.

In his introduction to *Words of Gratitude*, Stendl-Rast alludes to the essence of gratitude as being an inner attitude. It is "…more than a feeling, a virtue or an experience; gratitude emerges as an attitude that we can freely choose in order to create a better life for ourselves and for others."[155] To achieve this would require us to invest our practices with an inner attitude of gratitude, inscribing them with determination, imagination and inventiveness, with intention to give back, without wanting anything in return.

Attention to our inner attitude also gives us access to the aspect of teacher presence where we are aware of the impact of our thoughts and actions on those we teach. There is a dynamic interplay between our inner attitude and our thoughts, feelings, words, behaviour and self-talk; changing our inner attitude changes everything else. Rose's interview with Emily, as discussed in the previous chapter, showed that when Emily changed her attitude to the difficult parent, she spoke more kindly to her and changed the way she spoke about her to her colleagues. She changed her behaviour by inviting her into her class and by buying her a card. Emily then noticed that her feelings toward the parent were more empathic and appreciative.

I invited the class to explore how this model may have worked in the case of Adam's Year 8 students who were displaying bullying behaviour. When Adam recognised what he appreciated in each student, they may have changed their inner attitude towards themselves and each other. This in turn may have led to a change in their emotions, the way they spoke to each other and their behaviour.

We can examine our thoughts, feelings and words at the end of the day, or throughout the day – to reflect on the kind of inner attitude they are projecting. For example, we might start with an inner attitude of gratitude towards a particular student, but find ourselves complaining about this student when having morning tea in the staff room. We might ask ourselves about the level of sincerity with which we were approaching this student, and indeed whether or not we were able to move past our resentment and towards engaging in ethical imagining of our connectedness to them, human to human.

One of the advantages of being able to reflect on inner attitudes is that we can imagine inner attitudes that would render gratitude difficult. Although not discussing these as inner attitudes, Bono and McCullough[156] summarise the characteristics that are the antithesis of gratitude as: perceptions of victimhood; narcissism; an inability to admit shortcomings; a sense of entitlement; envy and resentment; and an over-emphasis on materialistic values.[157] In the following chapter we will examine the impact of some of these.

In our reflection on our inner attitude we also need to observe the particular influence this dimension has because of our role as teachers. Just as our passion, enthusiasm and knowledge of our content flows to our students, so also does our inner attitude.

A State of Preparedness

"But how can we focus on ourselves at the same time as the content?" Rita challenged me. "How can we do all of this reflection when we haven't even mastered the curriculum? Wouldn't we be better off learning all this after we've been teaching for a few years, and we know how schools work, and how to teach our subject matter?"

A similar issue was raised recently in a research project I was doing in a high school, Palmwood College, where we were exploring the effects of practising gratitude toward students during pastoral care time. Initially the teachers were very excited about greeting the students at the door, thanking them for coming to class, noticing and valuing what they gave to the school, and their practices had a good effect. However, after a few weeks, some reported that they felt overwhelmed by tasks and administration, and had to get too much done, so they abandoned the gratitude practice as they felt they could not practise it at the same time.

It needs repeating that whether we are conscious of it or not, we always have an inner attitude of some kind. To attend to our gratitude is to heighten our awareness of the consciousness we bring to our tasks, not to perform another separate task. We *can* focus on both content *and* our being at the same time. Donald Schon[158] brings to light how we do this in his theory on "reflection in action". He says that experienced teachers are able to think, almost subconsciously, while teaching. They can reflect in action by deliberately witnessing what is going on both inside and around them, and at the same time engage in acts of teaching.

One reason we may feel that we cannot concentrate on both the content and our being at the same time, or that we think that we do not have enough time to do both, is that we are locked into fixed notions of time, or as Charles Taylor would say, a fixed "punctual" self where there is no narrative of past or future. We may neglect to see that the self doing the task is of equal importance in our orientation as the task itself. One cannot be separated from the other. In returning to Palmer's philosophy, who we are when we teach is influencing the way the task is performed.

Insights in the literature from phenomenology offer a view of the self which is continuously in the process of 'emerging'. Rather than seeing consciousness as fixed and individual, the educative process involves a consciousness which is continuously impacting on the self-making process. Understanding is thus a "self-constituting process", which has reflexivity of consciousness as its basis. As Burch[159] argues, when we become conscious of our "lived experience" we at the same time establish our self-identity. Furthermore, without this "phenomenological reflexivity", there would be no "self-identity". Maxine Greene[160] has articulated this as the notion of a self which is continuously being formed as "more perspectives are taken, more texts are opened, more friendships are made."[161] This is essential to imagination, creativity, and most importantly, freedom. The concept of 'the emerging self' is paramount to be able to "to look at things as if they could be otherwise".[162]

"Reflection *on* action", Schon says, is a more common kind of teacher reflection that occurs *after* the teaching event. This is the time when we might give thought to how our attitude, words, thoughts, strategies might have been different and to reflect on implications for the next lesson. Such reflection may be less effective if we only focus on the outcomes of activities and not the self, the inner attitude, with which we performed them.

We can overcome some of the complexities involved in focusing on both our task and our selves at the same time, if we give more attention to the time *before* we go into the teaching or learning activity. In other words, we can place ourselves at the centre of our day or lesson ahead of time, not just when we are actually there. Our traditional notion of teacher preparedness is usually associated with preparation and planning of content, resources, teaching strategies or student activities. In an approach I call 'A State of Preparedness', I propose that our focus be also on preparing the state of being we bring to teaching. To practise this, we examine our inner attitude as we imagine our day ahead, and then choose an inner attitude of gratitude. Margaret Visser captures this notion of preparedness when she writes, "Gratitude…springs from a cultivated disposition to be grateful; one is in some sense grateful in advance of any gift or favour, because one is *prepared* to recognise goodness and be grateful for it" (my italics).[163] If we prepare our inner attitude before we teach, we can have considerable influence on the actual time that we spend in the classroom with our students, or when we are doing any other tasks.

Often we do not start our day with a consciousness of our inner attitude or invite this in advance to be one of gratitude, so we need to practise our State of Preparedness by thinking about the day ahead, reflecting honestly on the outlook we are bringing to various situations – to our interactions with our students and colleagues, our meetings, our lesson planning, our time in the staff room – and thinking of the gifts we receive from each of these. If doing academic work, we might like to prepare our inner attitude before writing a paper or doing research, contemplating all that we have been given that enables us to be able to partake in such an activity. We might like to start with just one student or staff member, or one situation, and focus on changing our inner attitude to one of gratitude. In preparing our inner attitude in this way, we prepare the ground for the kind of growth from seeds that are planted. Whether we are conscious of it or not, our inner attitudes before the event set the tone of what is to lie ahead.

Rather than taking up more time, or competing with other tasks, preparing for practising gratitude would take only a small portion of time. As we experiment with and witness the positive effects of this kind of preparation, we gain confidence and motivation to take up A State of Preparedness as a gratitude practice.

We see the underlying principle of A State of Preparedness at play in many examples, such as that of sport. A swimmer prepares for Olympic events with visualisations of how they want to be during the race. We can prepare for our day ahead by spending time walking in nature or writing, nurturing our inner attitude of gratitude and gaining inspiration for our sense of giftedness.[164]

In a gratitude workshop recently, Phillip, a high school teacher of social sciences inspired participants when he told us how he started his day. Phillip is a vibrant young man whose aliveness captured my attention the moment I met him. He lived near the sea. He would start his day at dawn and paddle out on his surf ski with a few mates. Rain, hail or shine they bathed in a "heavenly trail of beauty", of different hues depending on the weather, the time of year, and the energy of the surf. That was when Phillip felt at one with the world and himself before he faced the students in his classroom.

During one of my visits to the school after the first workshop, Phillip told me that he had always seen this morning ritual as a way of maintaining himself for teaching and for his role as head of department; a position, he admitted, that challenged his inner resources. His morning ritual prepared him to feel whole in his work, and brought him immovable joy. However, until then, he had not thought of contemplating what he had been given and the conscious ways he could give back. He had not given much thought to appreciating his students or preparing his being with gratitude. After engaging in the gratitude work, Phillip extended his communion with the sea to think about the qualities that he valued in his students and the many gifts he received from his work. After a few weeks of doing this, Phillip sent me this email:

I realised what a great job I had and how lucky I was in general compared to the majority of people on the planet and was determined to make the best out of the situation. This was reflected in the classroom through a number of small changes that have resulted in a much better learning environment. My first priority was to learn the names of ALL the students I taught and use their names as often as possible. I have always loved my subject matter (Legal Studies, Society and Culture, Geography and Commerce) and decided that I had to make everything I taught relevant to them. To do this I applied all my examples in class to them and became a lot more grateful/appreciative of all the students in my classes. I make an effort in class to welcome everyone into the room, smile, acknowledge the good points of students, thank them and wish them a great day. Not surprisingly, the students have responded in the best way possible, a genuine increase in the general engagement with all my students. I must admit, I was a little surprised as to how a change in attitude could have such positive results. I know the students are appreciating my efforts!

Some of my students with children of their own reacted negatively to Philip's example. "Yes, well I could focus on my inner attitude of gratitude too if I could kayak on the ocean every morning. Get real!" I agreed, and invited them to capture the essence of this story, to see how they could take even a few moments to reflect on their State of Preparedness before they started teaching. Then Rita said, "There's a tree I love looking up into as I walk into school," and another student commented that he liked to check what the sky was doing before he disappeared inside. We can all use our travelling time to school to reflect on the gifts we are about to receive when we meet our students or colleagues. We might only have time to take a few conscious breaths to prepare our inner attitude before we walk into our classroom. Remember this is about the quality, not the quantity of time.

Many teachers report practising A State of Preparedness in relation to areas outside of teaching – in preparation for being with their children or loved ones, for example – with positive effect. They begin to notice and absorb the characteristics of gratitude in those around them. The impact of the greater harmony this gratitude engenders has a positive effect on their State of Preparedness for their teaching. This is the potential of A State of Preparedness.

IN TOXIC WATERS...

...gratitude tends to bind us together in relationships of friendly reciprocity, whereas resentment tends to repel us from one another, or to bind us in relationships of bitter and hostile reciprocity...[165]
– Robert Roberts

A return to Eastgates Primary School sets the scene here. Six months on, the principal faces issue that divides the teacher and parent community and causes much disharmony and disunity. The culture of resentment and complaint is characteristic of that which is encountered in many other educational communities. This is where gratitude is most under threat as many teachers report that it is difficult to practise gratitude when others near them are negative. Teachers who use gratitude as a way of reaching beyond an habitual response of complaint give examples of their actions. Such gratitude requires empathy but can also lead to it. The chapter reveals how choices to express gratitude direct teachers towards a more proactive response. It also draws on theoretical insights that see gratitude as symmetrically opposite to resentment. This is not to suggest that gratitude should be used to put a positive veneer over a negative situation, but rather that it can be a point on the compass by which we can navigate our way if we are in a culture of resentment and complaint. Some important conceptual distinctions are made between negative and proactive complaint.

Ingratitude

I felt the tension in the atmosphere as I entered the gates of Eastgates Primary School. I was about to join the gratitude participants six weeks after we had last met. Several of them had sent emails about a conflict in the school that seemed to be escalating daily. Although their gratitude practices had been reaping rewards, some were thrown by their sense of powerlessness as the negativity of others surged. A few also reported battling with their own despondence in response to the situation.

Apparently Claire, the principal, had decided without much consultation to cut a very popular music program. She needed Glen, the teacher who was in charge of the program, to return to teaching full-time in the classroom. Although her key arguments for this related to funding, she had underlying issues with the way Glen was conducting the music program. She feared that it was turning into an "elitist music ensemble" – one that favoured students who were confident musicians and excluded some children who were not as able. Angry with her actions, Glen called a meeting with some of the parents and teachers to lobby for the program to continue. He did this without any consultation with Claire. At the meeting he publicly protested about Claire's leadership style and provoked dissent amongst some of the Eastgates staff and parents about Claire's competence. This was dividing the school and causing factions for and against both the program and Claire.

On my way to the staff room, I walked past Claire's office. She turned her head away from a parent she was talking to, and signalled for me to wait a moment. As I was waiting, I noticed that gratitude posters were still hanging in Julie's office, the next room along the corridor from Claire's. A new saying had appeared, chosen from the *Psychology of Gratitude* book.

> People who are regarded as ungrateful incur the risk of becoming isolated and estranged because of their inability to contribute to the essential symbolic nourishment human relationships are fed on, that is, the mutual exchange of gifts connecting people by the bonds of gratitude.[166] – Afke Komter

As I read this quote, I could see the great wisdom in it, but wondered if it could be seen as punitive in this present disharmonious situation. Because of Julie's position as assistant principal it could come across to some as a threat. Those opposing Claire could be deemed to be "ungrateful".

The parent stormed out of Claire's office. "He's the third father I've seen this afternoon who has insisted that the music program is vital to his son's performance progress," Claire said, with an exasperated tone in her voice. "He doesn't want to hear my side of the story. Each parent tells me that they should have been consulted. I never thought that I would find myself longing for the parent body of my previous school! They'd come in with *real* problems – not having enough money for food, let alone school uniforms. Music lessons were considered a real bonus. They were too busy surviving to care about what their kids did or didn't get." Claire continued, "Where has all the goodwill gone?"

It seemed to me that since I had last met Claire six weeks ago, she was more defensive and less positive. She told me she believed that her decision was just and fair and that the matter had been blown out of all proportion.

"I'm trying to believe that they just want the best for their kids," Claire continued, "but that's the problem – this is all about their own child. And the way they complain! I never hear what's going right, or what I've done for the school already – all that extra funding I gained to build the school hall. They don't know the sacrifices I make for this school!" She went on to name two of the teachers who were opposing her decision, saying that they seemed to forget that it was because of her support that they were able to gain permanent jobs at the school. Now she felt they were undermining her. She expected their loyalty and felt betrayed. She was shocked and disappointed by their ingratitude.

Claire's feelings of betrayal echo a sentiment familiar to many teachers. Students may write negative comments on their teaching evaluations, even though the teachers have helped them a lot and tried their very best to teach them well. In primary school, parents may complain about teachers not caring enough about their child's learning, even when they have stayed on after school to find resources that can help them. Pain can become stronger when people to whom we are giving feel they are entitled to our gifts, and so do not see the need to give thanks in return. This pain teaches us how much of a human need gratitude is – something deep inside is broken when we are not thanked, or indeed, when our good deeds are ignored.

One of the primary reasons why we need to be more vigilant with our gratitude in the context of education is that there is so much about the way we work that causes us to forget our gratitude and ignore relationships in our workplaces. Driven by a constant flow of deadlines and performance targets, as well as pressure from teachers or parents to show outcomes, our attention is drawn towards the task ahead and there is little time to reflect on what we have received in the past. Visser laments that ingratitude is symptomatic of our modern times with our "speed-driven, unthinking separation from one another, each ignoring the interests of others in order to pursue his or her own. People forget that favours have been done for them, or have no time to respond."[167]

Many teachers who take up the gratitude practice of placing priority on relationships rather than tasks, report a vital transformation in their teaching and their social wellbeing. It is important to remember that gratitude is embedded in the relationships between people, it is an expression of thanks *towards* another. Afke Komter's words placed on Julie's wall remind us that bonds of gratitude feed "the essential symbolic nourishment" of human relationships. For it to achieve this we need to attend to both the relationship *and* gratitude. A healthy relationship is primary or foundational to our expressions of gratitude, but relationships cannot live on gratitude alone. They need our honesty, authenticity, and awareness if they are to thrive.

If Glen and the other Eastgates teachers and parents were able to voice their opposition to Claire's actions in ways that placed the preservation of their relationship with her as central, perhaps they would have done things differently. Rather than undermining Claire, they might first seek her understanding or try to see things more from her point of view. Similarly, if Claire valued her relationship with Glen and the parents and other teachers more fully, perhaps she would have also found ways of understanding and being open to their grievances. She would almost certainly have consulted them more fully before cancelling the program.

We also need to be aware of the particular aspects of gratitude that can make relationships difficult. As we explored in Chapter 4, a deepening of our practice of gratitude requires awareness of the *purity* of our gratitude so that our intention behind our giving involves both a functional and equal relationship. Ross Buck reminds us that for gratitude to be genuine, it involves "reciprocity and mutual respect, and the perception that the rules are being followed fairly and equitably."[168]

To achieve this purity of intention, and to investigate Claire's perception of teachers' and parents' ingratitude, we need to unravel what I call the "sticky web of ingratitude" – a web of misunderstandings, power dynamics, and inability to put ourselves in the shoes of others.

Is it possible for our gratitude to be so pure that we give without wanting anything in return, and therefore others' ingratitude is irrelevant? If so, do our feelings of pain when others forget what we have given them require us to examine the purity of our original intention? We can find a radical answer to these questions in the philosopher Fitzgerald's exploration of "gratitude and justice". He says, "If giving to those in need enriches one's life, then one owes a debt of gratitude to those who needed the gift".[169] He further argues that such acknowledgement is essential to one's own sense of fulfilment, self-awareness and personal happiness. We cannot give unless there is someone to whom we can give, and who is willing to receive our gifts. In accepting what we give, the receiver is automatically giving back to us.

Claire may have been conscious of her own efforts and what she was giving to the teachers and parents, but may not have been aware of what they were giving to her and the school. The teachers and parents who were defying Claire may well have felt that what they received from Claire was their due and right, because they were already giving to her.

Had the teachers and parents whom Claire thought had betrayed her forgotten the debt of gratitude they owed her? Or were they exercising their freedom to not express gratitude, and their right to respond in an authentic way, unburdened by that debt? The web becomes sticky at this point, because we fear that the person on the receiving end of our grievance may interpret our action as one of ingratitude. This may cause us to sacrifice our authenticity, our truth, in order not to hurt the other person. One of the ways we may stay too long in a difficult situation without speaking up is because we feel the need to continually act out of gratitude. We may allow ourselves to be bullied or undervalued by our employer or colleague for the same reason. But if we stay too long and do not act, our original gratitude is soured and becomes something else – guilt or shame or resentment. This sticky web can often be a reason why people are reluctant to become indebted to others in the first place.

Often, we cannot arrive at a place of authenticity in our relationships without going through times of conflict and disagreement. We need to find a place where gratitude can co-exist with conflict, as sometimes expressing our concerns is the only way we can clear the air enough for relationships to thrive. Our attempt to move the relationship to a more authentic place by expressing our grievances can be an act of gratitude in itself. In the midst of conflict we might be wise to ask these crucial questions: what am I trying to preserve here? Is it my relationship with this person or is it my own rights or ego?

The web becomes stickier and more entangled in situations where we have a strong need to have a sense of belonging. Perhaps the teachers and parents who opposed Claire were motivated by their need to be a part of that opposing group? Equally, those who swore their allegiance to Claire may not be acting out of their authentic position on the matter of the music program, but rather because they have a strong need to be in Claire's favour.

Claire's use of the word "goodwill" is important in relation to gratitude. In Chapter 4, we explored Fitzgerald's three components of gratitude, and noted that the third is "a disposition to act that flows from appreciation and goodwill".[170] Philosopher Emmanuel Kant[171] argued that the highest form of good is goodwill. He believed that goodwill is to perform our duty, not out of self-interest but for the duty itself. Our modern-day interpretation of Kant's theory may be that our duty as teachers is to be motivated by whatever that duty requires of us – even if it does mean giving more than what we feel we should. However, to keep the beneficent circle of gratitude going, there needs to be a cycle of giving and receiving, otherwise our goodwill will dry up. When we feel appreciated for our efforts, we tend to want to do more than what is asked. When teachers' efforts are met with ingratitude, they tend to move from a gift paradigm to an exchange paradigm, where everything is "a bargain across the counter".

Had some of the goodwill at Eastgates dried up due to ingratitude? The gift needs to be offered in ways that can be seen and felt by the receiver, not on the giver's terms. One of the most important qualities of a good school leader is their ability to perceive how best to give thanks to those in their school community, for it is their thanks that resound the loudest and the longest. Perhaps some of the teachers at Eastgates did not experience Claire's gratitude because she did not thank them in ways they could hear. Claire might have thanked them in the way she thanked her teachers and parents at her previous school, but our gratitude needs to be fitting for each different context. Eastgates teachers may have been expecting gratitude to be offered in the same way as their previous principal had expressed it, and were disappointed when Claire did not express it in the same way.

Gratitude and trust

Claire wanted to tell me more about the injustices she felt were inflicted upon her and the unprofessional way she thought that some of her teachers were behaving. However, she was also keen to find a way forward. At that point, Julie came by to announce that all the teachers had arrived for our meeting to further explore their experiences with gratitude. Claire asked me to drop in again at the end of our discussion.

Expecting a sombre greeting from the gratitude group, I was surprised when some rose to thank me for coming, and one cheerily proclaimed the timeliness of my visit. Julie was as radiant and positive as ever. She explained to the group that she had already told me about some of the things that had been going on at the school so that I could have some background to prepare for this meeting. Others reported that they had also written to me.

First they talked of the spin-off effects of their participation in the group during this time of conflict. They had gathered regularly since we last met, to discuss their practices and support each other with their challenges. They spoke of experiencing a deepening understanding of each other's situation, and closer relationships with each other. There was solace to be found in talking about how difficult it was to move from an intellectual grasp of gratitude to putting it into practice. It was safe to pour out words, to "go blah" when gratitude was too hard; when children argued; when tension rose as they tried to leave the house to go to work; when the task of balancing work and home life seemed impossible and they felt overcome by feelings of guilt because they were not spending enough time with their children; when it was impossible to practise gratitude with some of their students when there was a negative situation around them such as this music program business. Their sharing with each other assisted them to see they were not alone when they found it hard to show gratitude.

They also discussed how complex it was at times to be part of this gratitude group. When they were not able to respond positively to the situation of conflict, some other staff members would say, "Aren't you supposed to be practising gratitude?" They felt the pressure of putting themselves up so publicly to be advocates of gratitude when they were not necessarily agreeing with Claire's approach. "Aren't we being just as bad as the others by talking about how we find the complaint in the school demoralising? Aren't we just being negative about the complainers?" Katie asked.

"Surely we aren't supposed to be grateful to Claire?" Bill questioned. "She's come in here making these very unpopular decisions like a bull in a china shop. How are we supposed to be grateful? What's worse," he lamented, "is that when I express my complaint to her directly, all she does is get hurt and defensive. Before I know it I'm in her bad books and she's telling everyone that I'm against her."

Tipene then spoke on behalf of the group about what they hoped to gain from this meeting. They sought a deeper grasp of how they could practise gratitude amidst so much anger and division in their school. What kinds of gratitude practices could they adopt to protect themselves from the resentment and negativity they sensed amongst those around them, and the similar feelings they had towards some in their school community?

"Most people in the school were behaving like this long before any of this blew up!" Bill proclaimed. "This conflict between those who support Claire and those who back Glen has just brought all the hidden negativity to the surface. To tell you the truth, there are very few people in this school whom I trust. But it's the same in every school I've worked in."

"Yes, it was the same in the school where I taught in England," admitted Sam, one of the younger male teachers. "There was the in-group and the out-group. Just to be part of the in-group when they first arrived at the school, people would join in with the negative culture of the school. It felt like it was the only way a person could survive."

Stacey offered the following comment. "I love my students and I love my teaching, but I walk into school knowing that I'm targeted as the topic of some of the other teachers' gossip and ridicule, just because I don't bond with them. I've stopped going to the staff room if I can avoid it. That's one of the main reasons why I've joined this group – to find out how I can be grateful when they ridicule me."

I remembered Claire's original intention for bringing the gratitude work into Eastgates Primary, as she feared that teacher complaint would dominate the school culture. I agreed with Sam and Bill's point that the phenomena of resentment and negative complaint is ever-present in many of the university and school environments where I have worked. I shared with them that I found these conditions amongst the most challenging in which to practise gratitude. Our discussion highlighted what I call the '*malaise* of the education system'. In the Cambridge dictionary, 'malaise' is defined as "a general feeling of being ill or having no energy, or an uncomfortable feeling that something is wrong, especially with society, and that you cannot change the situation."

In his book, *The speed of trust: The one thing that changes everything*, Stephen Covey (Jnr)[172] proposes that we have a "crisis of trust" in many of our workplaces. He gives examples of situations that exemplify this crisis, many of which had been mentioned by the Eastgates gratitude group: politics; feeling sabotaged by peers; contributions not being recognised; "walking on eggshells" because of the fear of being fired; being micromanaged; and not knowing who to trust."[173]

Megan Tschannen-Moran's[174] work, *Trust Matters: Leadership for Successful Schools*, discusses the key elements of trust and distrust as they play themselves out in schools. Her description of trust relates directly to gratitude: "Trust is manifest in situations in which we must rely on the competence of others and their willingness to look after what is precious to us..."[175] Trust, she argues, is essential to fostering relationships and communication, and, most importantly, student learning. Trust plays a vital role in helping our students feel orientated to their studies. As Tschannen-Moran notes:

> Students who do not trust their teachers or fellow students cannot learn efficiently because they invest their energy in calculating ways to protect themselves instead of engaging in the learning process.[176]

When I put it to the Eastgates group that their and other teachers' mistrust of each other might be flowing on to their students and affecting their ability to be present enough to learn, they seemed motivated to explore how their gratitude could help restore trust. Tschannen-Moran documents research that shows that trust between staff has a significant impact on student achievement.

> A study of trust and achievement demonstrated that the greater the trust in students and parents, the higher the level of school achievement in reading and mathematics, even when the impact of socio-economic status was held constant.[177]

Tschannen-Moran's research also showed that the single most mentioned dimension of trust amongst colleagues was that of 'benevolence'. She documented acts of gratitude as being seen as one of the most important ways to express this behaviour.

I asked the group how they had been practising gratitude in the midst of their difficulties. "I've made it part of my gratitude practice to stay away from those people who gossip and who are always negative," Katie, the youngest teacher in the group, responded. Katie had begun her first teaching job at this school a year and a half ago. She had become disillusioned by the behaviour of many of the older teachers. "Too many of these teachers who are nearing retirement spend most of their time moaning and groaning about everyone and everything. So a group of us younger teachers has decided to stay away from the influence of their negativity to protect ourselves!"

Although this may well have been Katie's way of dealing with the difficulty, I did not feel that it could be considered a gratitude practice. To stay away from our colleagues means that we are not entering into the symbiotic relationship of giving and receiving that is inherent to gratitude. However, I kept silent at this point.

Next, Dianne shared the power she gained from her gratitude practice of looking for the good in others. She spoke of gratitude being the only thing that had worked in her many months of conflict with another teacher. Everyone seemed to know who that was.

"Actually, I've noticed that there's more harmony between you two lately. Can you tell us what you did?" Julie asked.

"Well at first I was just grinning and bearing the situation, while trying to have as little contact with this person as possible. When I could see that this wasn't getting me very far, I made it my gratitude practice to do my best to avoid talking negatively about her to others. But then I kept on failing, as it was really hard to not join in when others would sympathise with me. All I could say was that we all have bad points, but it was difficult for me to hide my pain. Then I remembered another gratitude practice on our list: looking for the good in others. I decided to find five good things in this teacher and focus on these whenever she did or said anything that upset me. That made it so much easier for me to face her in the mornings – something I used to dread – and then after about two weeks of doing this, we were much more harmonious. The best thing about this was that when others came and complained about this teacher, I was able to automatically respond with her good points. I didn't need to fake it or try too hard – it just flowed naturally out of my mouth!"

Dianne's example spoke of the power of gratitude to build a healthier relationship. When we look for the good in the other or the gifts we receive from them, we open ourselves up to the other in a positive way. Again, as Visser notes, "...gratitude causes the receiver to look beyond the gift to the giver. This movement in itself transcends the object or favour given; it opens the receiver to the person of the other."[178]

Gratitude and its opposite

When we are feeling disempowered, or feeling like victims in unjust or inequitable situations, we tend to blame others for our plight. Resentment then becomes our (default) state of being and can be a major contributor to mistrust in schools, or in any group situation. It is often our resentment that prohibits us from remembering what we have received. It inhibits our harmonious relationships and festers in time-poor environments, because it takes time to notice what we have received from others and to consciously make relationships count. When we are full of resentment, we make mistakes, get sick and stressed, and the quality of our work and the inspiration behind it suffers tremendously. We can also get stuck and become unmotivated, waiting for someone else to take away our pain or rescue us from the situation. Although intellectually we may have grasped that this is not a healthy way of being, the hurt we feel can dominate our response, and immobilise us. We go over and over our grievance with whoever wants to listen because we think that it makes us feel stronger – and that doing so will take away our pain and make right the intense wrong we feel.

When two or more teachers share their grievances without awareness of their part in where this resentment comes from, the toxic impact on their school community and the undermining of trust rises exponentially. So too a self-righteous attitude can cement a resentful inner self. Unless we take time out to reflect on the impact of this toxicity, we may not recognise that our resentment is generating toxic thoughts, feelings, behaviour, and words. Moreover, we are attracting this vibration of resentment from those around us, and so tend to be surrounded by others who have a similar inner attitude.

Resentment robs us of our gratitude. It makes us forget what we have been given and clouds over the goodwill and gifts we may have received. It stops us from remembering these gifts, and others could interpret the actions that arise from our attitude of resentment as ingratitude. As the word 'resentment' implies, we send it on. Gifts may come our way or we may be in a situation where we have much to be grateful for, but resentment might cause us to repel this or not notice it. We poison the gift, as Margaret Visser would say.

Our resentment can also often cause us to view things in a distorted way, to interpret other's intentions or actions incorrectly, or to mistakenly feel that others have wronged us or are doing things against us. We may read things into situations through this lens of resentment, though in reality there may have been no intention on behalf of the other to hurt us or cause us pain.

How aware are we of the degree that the resentment we hold impacts on our teaching and our students' learning? If our inner attitude and practice of gratitude are integral to our interconnectedness with others and our teacher presence, what might be the impact of states that are the antithesis of gratitude? Importantly, Rodgers and Raider-Roth argue that in order to understand teacher presence, we also need to reflect on what robs us of this, as "a key learning moment in the teacher-student relationship occurs when the connection falls apart":

> It is important to ask what causes a teacher to fall out of connection with her students. What pulls her away from being present to their experiences and their learning? What are the consequences of this retreat? How does she re-enter after a disconnection? How does she notice that she has fallen out of connection at all?[179]

If we return to the case of Jason and Sophie in the previous chapter, we can see that Rory and many of the other Year 8 teachers had held resentment towards the "ratbag boys" – and perhaps towards their parents. As Jason observed, the boys responded accordingly with their rebellious and rude behaviour. As our inner attitude of gratitude flows to our students, so too does our inner attitude of resentment. We may be working on the premise that we can hide our resentment, or push it aside or bury it, when we are in front of our students. However, if they feel our resentment they will not be able to have a sense of trust and therefore will not be able to be settled enough to learn.

If we attempt to *replace* our inner attitude of resentment with that of gratitude, we may well stand in danger of repressing negative emotions or not addressing the situation in a proactive way. It can, however, be helpful to consider the *symmetrical nature* of the relationship between gratitude and resentment. The philosopher Robert Roberts says that there is "a remarkable symmetry between resentment and gratitude. Resentment and gratitude seem to be mirror opposites of one another."[180] In other words, resentment cannot live where there is gratitude and gratitude cannot live where there is resentment. Gratitude is considered to be a virtue, because as Roberts says, it is "a readiness or predisposition to respond to the actions of others by seeing the goodness or benevolence in them."[181] Resentment, on the other hand is considered to be a vice because, according to Roberts, one is "quick to notice offences and to find people to blame for them, looks for things to resent, and has a hair-trigger readiness to notice offences and take offence at them..."[182]

Our expressions of gratitude unite us with others by causing us to acknowledge, recognise, celebrate, become calm and connect. On the other hand, resentment divides, rejects, ignores, laments, disquiets and disconnects.

I like to use the analogy of a cave when I picture this symmetrical relationship between resentment and gratitude. Resentment lives in the dark depths of the cave, where it is impossible for gratitude to survive. Gratitude lives at the edge of the cave where it is bathed in light and sunshine. When resentment comes into the light it dies. The warmth of gratitude melts resentment. Each time we step away from resentment, even by identifying it within ourselves, we step towards gratitude, towards the light.

As Dianne showed in her example, when she looked for the good in the person whom she felt resentful towards, gratitude had the power to melt her resentment so that harmony could be restored. When two people are in conflict, it takes one of the parties to move towards a more harmonious direction. Our gratitude for what we have received from the other can direct, or focus this move, and give it meaning and intention.

Our acts of giving back out of gratitude are not just about 'nice' reciprocal relationships that speak of immediate love and harmony. They can, perhaps more powerfully, also be acts of repairing pain, restoring bonds that have been broken, and looking for what needs to be repaired. We can give back by for*giving* or asking for forgiveness. This may be a long and painful process where past pain needs to be acknowledged and dealt with in a healthy way. If our purpose is to move away from resentment, this can be more powerful in its impact than other practices that may have positive associations with gratitude – practices such as smiling or expressing thanks to our colleagues or students.

Understanding that the relationship between gratitude and resentment can be viewed as a symmetrical one assists us to deepen our State of Preparedness. An effective way of gaining this state before we teach is to reflect on the gratitude-resentment symmetry and whether we have an inner attitude of gratitude or one of resentment. Recognising an inner attitude of resentment, manifested in negative complaint, can alert us to the power of this to cancel out our attempts to practise gratitude. We can witness the impact of this phenomenon when we reflect at the end of our day and honestly ask ourselves if our inner attitude was one of resentment, and what were the consequences. We can engage in action learning by taking note of the effects that a resentful or grateful attitude have on our teaching, and making changes accordingly.

We can also extend this practice of A State of Preparedness to our relationships with others. As Dianne's example showed, she developed her State of Preparedness by thinking of the other teacher's good points in the time leading up to her encounters with her. In other words, it is helpful to extend our notion of reflection *before* action, to encompass the time leading into relationships with others – meetings, our time in the staffroom, our parent-teacher interviews. By consciously choosing to start our day with gratitude, we are creating the conditions to ward off resentment. If we do this regularly and with clear intent, we are simultaneously adopting a powerful gratitude practice. Our gratitude can also help us become more resilient to the resentment in others around us, as it diminishes that which is its opposite.

Isn't complaining a good thing?

In what ways might we show resentment when we find ourselves in conflict with our colleagues? "Moaning, grumbling, blaming, backbiting", the members of the group said, "also fault-finding, cynicism, whinging, bickering, disparaging, belittling".

"But isn't complaining a good thing?" Katie asked. "At university we were taught to use critical thinking, to be sceptical and doubtful and find fault with arguments and others' ideas or practices. We were graded in terms of how skilled we were at criticising others." She then told us of her best friend Gemma, who was studying for her PhD in environmental science. In Katie's view, Gemma's complaint about the current environmental policy was the force that was driving her to get up early in the morning and work hard on her research into the depths of night.

So for Katie, it seemed, to complain eloquently and intelligently is a hallmark of critical thinking and reflects one's prowess in the academic world. A dissatisfied mind will provoke us to make changes to circumstances so that they can become better. Katie challenged the notion that gratitude, in presenting a positive spin, might rob us of this great asset that has brought about much needed change.

Katie's question led our discussion to 'complaint and critique', in which we perceived a number of illuminating differences. In critique, we weigh up good and bad to make some kind of assessment to act upon in some way. Our motivation is to find fault in ideas for the sake of reaching a truth or better answer than someone else's. In complaint, we have no desire to change or improve our circumstances, rather we seek consolation and support, and we resent attempts to correct us for what we do and say. We apply a great deal of consciousness to critique, as it is a skill. However we often complain unthinkingly, and without reflecting on the consequences of our words or actions. There are also some instances where complaint is consciously used to undermine others, without bringing the benefits of critique to advance the situation in a more positive way.

I then presented another perspective in answer to Katie's objections. If we consider the power of A State of Preparedness, resentment and anger may not be the best states of being from within which we approach research. History speaks of many minds motivated by awe, wonder, joy or delight, as sources for creative inspiration in their work. Albert Einstein[183] held the mystery of the universe in awe. Carl Jung[184] said that the mind plays with objects it loves. Fritjof Capra observed that when the mind is relaxed, "...after concentrated intellectual activity, the intuitive mind seems to take over and can produce the sudden clarifying insights which give so much joy and delight."[185] If gratitude helps to give rise to these states of mind, we could well abandon complaint as a conscious state while doing research, or for that matter, any intellectual endeavour.

There was another distinction to observe: that between negative complaint and proactive complaint. As we had explored in our previous discussion, negative complaint usually arises from resentment.

On the other hand, when we complain proactively, we consciously address the conflict: we *act upon* rather than *react to* the situation. We take responsibility. A good starting point is to ask what the lessons are for our personal growth and self-development, our part in the situation. Such actions can take us out of feeling that we are victims. Then perhaps we are more able to go directly to the person whom we feel has wronged us, and express our complaint by seeking to understand and be understood, rather than accuse or attack. This often requires us to speak frankly and honestly and to open up possibilities so that the other person can also be proactive and speak their truth in return. To adopt this kind of complaint calls for courage, trust and skill. Sometimes it seems that we risk hurting the other with our honesty, and we might feel the need to retreat to avoid causing them pain. However, we may hurt them more if we are not direct and honest with them.

"It's not the people who get me down in this school so much. It's the systems that aren't working!" Stacey said. "The toilets are often blocked, the photocopier breaks down, we have to fill in loads of forms, reporting takes forever, and now the league tables are putting further pressure on us! What are we to do with our complaints about all this?"

"I was able to respond more positively to the situation about the toilets recently," Katie answered. "When I was at the last parents meeting, there was a lot of negative complaint about the inadequacy of the toilets. I asked if we could all get together and do something about it, rather than leave it to someone else to fix. Now we've started a fund-raiser and it's made us closer, given us a common goal."

The need to belong

Some members of the group admitted they were still struggling with how to refrain from negative complaint in their response to the situation over Claire's management style regarding the music program. Returning to my cave analogy, I put to the group that as we develop a heightened consciousness of which part of the cave we choose to inhabit, we also shine a light on our integrity. Talking together and struggling with how we can move away from resentment towards gratitude, or even identifying that we have lost gratitude, is a mark of our integrity: it is a step into the light. To take this step is a gratitude practice in itself. Importantly, we need to see that changes within ourselves are a measure of success, not changes in Claire's behaviour.

"What do we do when people come to complain about Claire to us? Doesn't our gratitude just push them away and make them feel that we are different or distant?" Sam protested. "What do we say to them? Do we say that they should feel grateful? They might say, 'oh yeh, peace, love man. Thanks for not supporting me.' "

Sam's questions were met enthusiastically. We were getting down to one of the group's core difficulties. Was responding with gratitude when others were full of resentment a threat to their sense of belonging? They neither wanted to make their colleagues feel uncomfortable nor did they feel good about changing in ways that would make them stand out as different from them. Sam talked of feeling strange and uneasy. He felt he had to become a different person. Joining in with the negative complaint was often an easier way to be with people.

I related how I experienced many of my student teachers as being particularly vulnerable to the overpowering force of the need to belong. They saw their practicum as the chance to impress their mentoring teacher so that they could do well in their results and be considered for employment at the school in the future. They wanted to fit in with the culture at the school, and to be accepted by the other teachers. Before embarking on their practicum, most were convinced that gratitude was an important aspect of their teacher identity and pedagogy. Intellectually they had grasped the wisdom of the gratitude-resentment spectrum and the need to engage in critique or proactive complaint, instead of negative complaint, as a way of practising gratitude. However they often reported how difficult it was to practise when negative complaint was the cultural norm. They were driven by strong forces – to survive, fit in, and make a mark.

I put to the group that perhaps we can gain the willpower to refrain from negative complaint when we raise our awareness of the long-term positive impact this can have on a toxic culture, and the difference this can make to our State of Preparedness and our students' engagement.

"Kerry, how often can you achieve refraining from backbiting and blaming in your university environment?" Tipene asked. It was important to be honest in my response to this question. I shared my own experiences of the need to belong and how I also need to have a secure sense of place. I can often be motivated by the need to fit in even more so than by my aspirations to become a grateful person. If I was feeling pain from how I believed that someone had treated me, or if I was stressed or tired or overworked, I found it very difficult to not engage in negative complaint.

However, I also shared that when I was in perfectionist mode, I did not forgive myself easily when I engaged in negative complaint, and this could prevent me from doing anything proactive. If, on the other hand, I could abandon self-judgement, I could come to see my negative complaint as a sign that I had gone off-track. I believe the moment we become conscious of complaining about another and resolve not to do it again we regain our integrity. I would make efforts to get back on track by trying not to complain about this person again. I was on a series of corrections – going off track and then adjusting back again. By regularly reflecting on how I could respond in a more proactive or grateful way, I was able to step into more conscious behaviour. When I was about to have a conversation with someone with whom I might be tempted to air a grievance, I would often try to picture myself refraining from complaining and rehearse a conversation in which I could show how I appreciated the person with whom I was in conflict.

This eventually led to a discussion about how much the virtues of magnanimity and altruistic love needed to be at play if we were to truly practise gratitude. Margaret Visser reminds us that gratitude requires "all that is highest in human beings". She says that,

> …From the receiver, it calls for recognition, memory, intelligence, consideration, and justice. From the giver, when generosity is met with ingratitude, it requires forbearance, acceptance, and refusal to turn sour, no matter how hurt we might feel. If memory, justice, forgiveness, and the rest are expressive of human nature at its best, then so is gratitude.[186]

It is important to remember that the person who has inflicted pain or wronged us in some way usually has a story behind their behaviour. As Rachel Carsen, the author of *Silent Springs* says: "Underneath the most annoying behaviour is a frustrated person who is crying out for compassion."[187] If we try to put ourselves in the shoes of another, and understand the situation from their perspective, we can gain insights that can help us dissipate our pain. If we put ourselves above the person and criticise them, we neglect to see that we too have faults. If we look deeply inside, our own faults may be the same kinds of faults that we are criticising in the other person!

Being an active agent of change

My few hours with the gratitude group had given me clarity about some of the underlying issues of the gratitude-resentment spectrum in their relationship with Claire and how they were seeing the conflict about the music program. I hoped to find a way to share some of this with Claire as we resumed our earlier discussion.

"Surely it's they who need to express more gratitude, not me," Claire pleaded with me, as if wanting me to side with her, or rescue her from the situation in some way. We only had another twenty minutes together before Claire had to address the school assembly. Although the situation appeared impossible to Claire, her hardships seemed to make her open to my suggestions about how to express gratitude to her 'enemy'. As I shared some of the awakenings we had just reached in the teachers' group about the impact of resentment and mistrust on student learning, Claire was eager to know what Megan Tschannen-Moran suggested to restore trust. As I named some of these elements – admitting our mistakes, apologising, asking for forgiveness, amending our ways – Claire looked away as she told me her underlying fear: "I feel there is no way back now. I've lost the respect and trust of so many of my staff, I feel that my integrity is in tatters." We discussed how building trust takes time, and often involves work behind the scenes, away from public view, and most importantly, working on change within ourselves.

I suggested to Claire that our greatest measure of change should be our view of ourselves, not how others see us. We can reflect on this in the choices we make on a day-to-day basis at the level of our inner attitude. All change has to be step-by-step, one gratitude practice at a time. Claire asked me to suggest a practice that she could take up that would make a difference. Many things ran through my mind. The image that resounded most strongly was her beautiful, broad smile.

I briefly explained the power of a practice and tried to boost Claire by reminding her that as she had such a role of influence, any gratitude practice she took up would make a big difference to the whole school. I suggested that a powerful way to positively influence the school culture would be for Claire to welcome any complaint – whether it be negative or proactive – and consciously greet it with a smile. I also put to Claire that it would be wise not to interpret others' complaint as acts of ingratitude. Claire's brow unknotted slightly and a hint of optimism appeared on her face.

"You mean that could be my gratitude practice?" she asked.

I took Claire back to the scenario of the angry parent who had stormed out of her office earlier. She admitted that she had spoken unkindly about the music teacher's actions, and was worried they would divide the school. She had asked this parent to try to see her side. I explained that if this parent was not encouraged to be proactive by coming to see her and if he did not feel listened to, there was an increased chance that he might engage in negative complaint by talking about Claire behind her back and finding fault with her leadership.

"But what do I do when I feel so personally attacked?" Claire asked. I explained the power of a smile with the words, "thank you for coming and expressing your concerns," or "I really appreciate you taking the time to come and see me".

Such words of gratitude can diminish negativity and even turn it around. This is a truly great way to begin our navigation out of the toxic waters of negative complaint.

CHAPTER 8

THROUGH THE DOORS OF ADVERSITY

March on
Do not tarry.
To go forward
is to move toward perfection.
March on, and fear not the thorns
or sharp stones on life's path.[188]

– Kahlil Gibran

This chapter describes an event in a high school where expressing gratitude in the midst of adversity seems to be an absurd notion. It clarifies that a recommendation for gratitude in difficult situations does not advocate a passive response, or an acceptance of the status quo. I am not suggesting that gratitude should be used to fix a difficult situation, but rather provide a means by which we can grow through reflection. An approach is suggested where gratitude can assist as one enters, goes through, and comes out the other side of difficult times. By using some of the challenges facing the high school teachers as the backdrop – such as violent students and low morale – the chapter explores the appropriacy, relevance, and deeper meaning of gratitude in times of adversity. I postulate the relevance of gratitude in building teacher resilience, and draw on the wisdom of writers who invite us to consider how adversity can develop our strength of character.

When gratitude seems absurd

I was shocked and perplexed at the cold response I received from a group of seventeen staff as soon as I walked into a meeting held after school on a Monday. We were to discuss the next steps for gratitude work at their school. Heads of department of each curriculum area, administration staff, and both principal and assistant principal were present. Several hundred students attended Palmwood College, a regional state school with a wide demographic. This was our third meeting. On my first visit five months earlier, all of the fifty Palmwood teachers had spent two days exploring the relevance of the practice of gratitude at their school. After this they were invited to participate in an action research project where they nominated one or two gratitude practices to students, and then took note of the effects.

When I had first introduced the pedagogy of gratitude to the principal and assistant principal, they had thought that this was a perfect time to focus on connecting with students through acts of gratitude. They could see direct links with other initiatives they had recently embarked upon – most notably, School-wide Positive Behaviour Support. They were also keen to invite teachers to reflect on the power of their inner attitude and State of Preparedness at the beginning of the day. During this visit I had conducted focus groups to explore the effects of their gratitude practices. Now I was to meet with the executive staff on the following Monday afternoon to report on the results of a previous questionnaire, as well as some initial findings from the focus groups.

On my way to the meeting I was accompanied by the principal, Steve. As we walked along the corridor we were greeted by the assistant principal, who said to Steve, "You're so lucky that you were away all day today. I just wouldn't want to wish this day on anyone!" Steve had been at a full day workshop with me and twelve other principals from the district, where we had been exploring the possibility of setting up gratitude initiatives in other schools. Steve had taken a call at morning tea about a fight that had been brewing in the school grounds, but he had not taken it too seriously, as this was a regular occurrence at Palmwood. For decades there had been families at war with each other over property, drugs, previous acts of violence and other crimes. This would often manifest in fights in the school grounds, not just between two students, but whole gangs who represented different families. The violence that ensued had sometimes led to police intervention.

As we sat down, I looked around and sensed pain and exhaustion in most of the teachers at the meeting. I wondered if we should proceed with the set agenda. I took my cue from Steve, who acknowledged that it had been a hard day, but perhaps we could learn something about how gratitude might help us deal with it. He wanted me to first outline some of the findings from the questionnaires and focus groups. Thirty teachers had put their hand up to report on the outcomes of their gratitude practice in form class during the previous term and to take up the next stage of the action research. Many of these same teachers were present amongst this group.

The atmosphere seemed to become colder as I handed out documents with graphs that represented data analysed from the questionnaires, showing significant increases in satisfactory relationships and student engagement throughout the school. Teachers described gratitude practices of meeting and welcoming students at the door, offering bright and positive greetings, and giving priority to their relationships with the students by looking out for things they could thank them for. These had led to outcomes such as students responding with more gratitude; improved relationships; calmer presence; and a friendlier atmosphere. They also talked of more relaxed, positive and respectful relationships with their colleagues. Many said that they found their job more satisfying and felt more buoyant as a result of an increased focus on expressions of gratitude.

I was hoping that seeing these findings in print might encourage greater engagement with how we could move into the next cycle of action research. However, some slumped over, some just pushed the papers aside, and others started working on their iPads. When I asked if they wanted to make any comments on what was in front of them, a long awkward silence was finally broken by Alice: "We just can't see how gratitude has anything to do with the kind of day we've just experienced. How can you possibly expect us to be positive when there's so much violence and suffering in our school? How can you think that just one practice of gratitude is going to make the slightest bit of difference in this horrible situation?" Alice's use of the word "we" and the nods of agreement around the room indicated that this group of teachers had obviously talked before the meeting about the absurdity of practising gratitude in this situation.

I wondered what had happened to their belief in the power of gratitude? It had only been on the Friday before that most had talked about being inspired by how much gratitude had turned things around for them and had created better relationships between themselves and their students. How could something that had given so much solace and encouragement to so many teachers in the past months, now seem not only irrelevant but also absurd?

As Alice was talking, some shot angry looks at the principal. I wondered if they were angry that he seemed to be trying to normalise this situation, or because he was absent when they most needed him?

I jumped in too quickly, to defend the principal and the power of gratitude, by saying that gratitude is not the same as being positive. Frowns and heads rolling indicated that this was not the time to enter into an intellectual discussion about the meaning of gratitude. My next move was, upon reflection, even more preposterous. I hoped to empower these teachers by talking about the butterfly effect and the influence that one teacher's gratitude could have on the school, hoping this would remind them of what they had said on the Friday. One teacher, Damien, got up and stormed out at this point, throwing the papers I had given him on the floor. I finally recognised the pain of that day for these teachers. I had not even heard the details of the situation – a situation I was fooling myself that I could 'fix'!

I realised that it was not gratitude I was trying to defend. It was my own ego. The best way to bring about a *reconnaissance*, to recognise these teachers, was to listen to them, to acknowledge the weightiness of their day. Perhaps this is what they wanted from their principal – they needed him to not overlook their pain as if it was part of the fabric of the school, and what they had signed up for in teaching at Palmwood. I was relieved when Steve apologised and, with head down, quietly asked them to tell him what had happened.

Steve's apology brought the circle into a less fragmented and defiant tone. They spoke of the sense of danger and conflict that had been brewing at the beginning of the day. On the weekend there had been a huge drink- and drug-driven fight between two of the families over money that was owed, and that fight was about to play itself out amongst the children of the families on the school grounds. Two girls started tearing each others' hair out, swearing, threatening to kill each other, and scratching and hitting each other. Many others joined in on each side. Other students ran for cover. It did not take long for blood to spill and then there were police vans. When they left, another student chained herself to a pole outside the canteen, threatening to commit suicide if any of her family members were put in gaol.

The fight should have been talked about at the start of the afternoon. I could have looked with them at the possibility of using gratitude as a way of exploring adversity, but the teachers had thought that I was simply trying to 'fix' the situation. The atmosphere in the room changed a bit as they opened up more fully to talk about what had happened during the day. I was grateful that these teachers were able to move a little closer to contemplating the relevance of gratitude in the midst of this situation, despite my insensitivity.

Before we can invite a discussion about gratitude in the midst of adversity, we need to speak about and name our pain, to have it heard and recognised and acknowledged. I wondered if this was the kind of recognition the feuding families and their children were seeking. Was anyone listening to their pain?

Can we welcome adversity?

I returned to the caveat that I had mentioned in my first workshop with the whole staff, the one I had initially forgotten to mention in my workshop at Eastgates Primary School: *Although gratitude for small things may help in times of great adversity, there are some situations where it may be impossible, or even perhaps inappropriate, to expect ourselves to initially respond with gratitude.* While we are in the middle of adversity, caught in the eye of the storm, it may be almost impossible to practise gratitude.

Some teachers looked relieved that I was not suggesting a formula where they would switch on gratitude when facing a very traumatic situation. It is the time *after* the event when we can contemplate areas where we might be able to respond with gratitude, to reflect on what the situation can teach us. During the trauma, it may only be possible to behave and act as calmly and rationally as we can.

I then invited the teachers to consider a parallel incident that had happened in the more distant past. As one teacher said "Albert", all seemed to agree and knew the situation this referred to. It did not take much to remember the violence and consequences of that day – a situation one of the teachers described as "warfare". They could all recall the pain and devastation that stayed with many students and teachers for weeks after that event.

I received looks of surprise when I arose from my seat and went to the whiteboard to draw a picture of some waves. I announced that this diagram represents life – the ups and downs, the peaks and troughs. We have sunshine and rain, happiness and sadness, good times and bad times. We are accustomed to judging our success in life by whether or not we are at the top of the wave. In many ways our modern culture has led us to believe that we are doing well when we are at this spot, content and happy, and with little suffering. We think we need to avoid the bottom of the wave at all costs.

This expectation to feel happy all the time is evident from the huge industry that has been built around it. We may use its strategies and devices to assist us to avoid going to the bottom of the wave. The teachers were quick to nominate some of these: go shopping, drink alcohol, play computer games, gamble, mindlessly watch hours of television, spend too long on Facebook etc, etc. Of course, there is nothing wrong with these pastimes in themselves. We often need the comfort such activities can give, especially in the midst of adversity. Where they can be problematic is when they become our only means of escape and we do not take time out to look at what is going on within the adversity, and what we need to learn from it.

I put to them that many of us do not like to face our adversity, our bottom of the wave, eye to eye. We may not have sufficient resilience to do so or we may be afraid to face it because it shows us something that needs to change in ourselves, or our situation, that we may not be willing or able to accept. It could be that it is the underlying fear of change that we are not able to face, rather than the adversity itself. We may even be afraid that we will fail the challenge that the adversity is throwing at us.

We do not need to look far to see that in the teaching profession there are many challenges at the bottom of the wave, and signs that teachers are not coping. For more than a few, teaching is no longer the joyous and fulfilling profession they signed up for when they first embarked on their career. They enter the profession eagerly, with great hope and a sense of purpose, and leave within five years because they feel undervalued, burnt out or overly stressed. They become troubled and defeated by what seems to them irresolvable and perplexing patterns in students' attitudes, in conflicts amongst colleagues, in the authority of school leadership and in relationships with students' parents. They experience the irreversible consequences of political decisions and economic expediency, forces outside the school, reverberations of constant restructuring of educational systems of governance, or micromanagement by those who know little of their reality. Work overload, lack of job security, and demand for excessive degrees of accountability, litigation and reporting – the list could go on – manifest in the everyday lives of teachers and deplete their faith in their profession. It is little wonder that teacher resilience is looming as a major issue for education today.[189]

I asked the Palmwood teachers if they were open to exploring with me a radical view of how we might address our adversity differently. At the same time,

I wanted to stress that I was not asking them to contemplate situations that were so extreme that they were impossible to bear. It was also important to acknowledge that in some situations, such as those of abuse or possible harm, it is necessary for us to exit or act straight away.

If we allow ourselves to be conscious of not totally removing ourselves from the situation when we are at the bottom of the wave, we may find that going through adversity shapes our character, gives us the greatest wisdom, and in the long term leads us to a deeper sense of happiness – one that is quite distinct from the superficial happiness we gain from things we temporarily escape from.

I asked the group about what we can do differently when we are at the bottom of the wave? Could we reflect, learn the lessons, not try to escape, look for the meaning? We might first ask: What is going on here? As we just witnessed from the teachers voicing their pain about the violence, they were able to articulate it more clearly, and understand it more deeply than if they had not taken the time out to reflect. Often, the longer we have after a traumatic event, the more we can gain clarity and understanding. Other questions we might ask are: Have we been in a similar situation before? If so, how did we escape from it or deal with it in the past? What were the consequences of our actions?

Next we might ask: What is this teaching me about something that I need to change? Instead of blaming others for what I am going through, is it time to reflect on what my part may be in it? Using the familiar adage of self-efficacy – *for things to change, first I must change* – if I could see this situation in a mirror, what would it be reflecting back to me about myself?

Finally, we might then express gratitude for the lessons learned, and for the parts of our character or life that we can try to change as a result of this adversity. Our greatest way to express gratitude is to change in the way the adversity is showing us we need to change. In this way we engage in a more deliberate and conscious relationship with the adversity, to embrace its gifts, and to acknowledge that there is a purpose in it, rather than feel that we are victims of circumstances beyond our control.

At the risk of sounding clichéd or underplaying the adversity they were experiencing, I asked if they could recall any messages that portray the perennial wisdom of adversity as our greatest teacher, our greatest friend, as they are woven through literature, art, drama and philosophy from ancient to contemporary times. All knew of examples. Some were even set for the curricula for some of their subjects. I recalled Joseph Campbell's[190] philosophy, which brings Eastern mysticism and Western science together in an intense, provocative and promising exploration of the mythological dimension of the art of living gracefully through adversity, the hero's journey. He opens us to the possibilities of finding our deepest strengths. He says: "The black moment is the moment when the real message of transformation is going to come. At the darkest moment comes the light."[191]

Then Marina spoke of the qualities Steve portrays in times of adversity, and many agreed with her. "I admire how you seem to go through strife with a quiet acceptance, an inner strength. I guess that's why we were a bit angry with you today when you weren't here." Marina identified a crucial element to being able to learn and grow as a result of difficult times. The quality of being accepting of adversity is like water that flows smoothly over rocks and around obstacles, and is crucial if we are to take on the hero's journey when we confront difficulties.

In the thirteenth century, the great Persian poet, Rumi, urged us to approach unavoidable suffering consciously, by welcoming it into the guesthouse of our being. I opened my laptop and asked if I could put up on the projector one of Rumi's poems.

> *This human being is a guest house.*
> *Every morning a new arrival.*
>
> *A joy, a depression, a meanness,*
> *some momentary awareness comes*
> *as an unexpected visitor.*
>
> *Welcome and entertain them all!*
> *Even if they're a crowd of sorrows,*
> *who violently sweep your house*
> *empty of its furniture,*
> *still, treat each guest honourably.*
> *He may be clearing you out*
> *for some new delight.*
> *The dark thought, the shame, the malice,*
> *meet them at the door laughing*
> *and invite them in.*
>
> *Be grateful for whoever comes,*
> *because each has been sent*
> *as a guide from beyond.* [192]

Jalalu'l Rumi

Rumi not only wants us to be accepting, but also grateful for whoever or whatever comes to us, because each is a guide to our living. By moving from acceptance to gratitude, we can take a different path in life's journey, one perhaps strewn with the gifts of the adversity, along which grow the seeds of willingness to receive all that may come our way. On this new path we can learn to affirm the lessons of adversity as gifts, and walk where the course of such gifts leads us. Gratitude helps us move out of a situation of blame by thanking another, even our enemy, for the gift of the lesson.

I then went back to the wave diagram and asked them what happens if we do not take the steps we had just explored. Using the metaphor given to us by Rumi, what if depression and meanness come knocking at our door and we pretend that we are not home? Do we stand the risk of succumbing to victim mentality? Without reflection on the lessons behind the adversity we may risk staying stuck in a situation we do not like, or dying inside because we are waiting for something external to do the changing for us. To try to be grateful for adversity is a powerful step toward taking responsibility for growth and change. It is a vital part of building our resilience.

If we avoid the lessons to be learned, more often than not we will find that we will meet the same adversity again, dressed in different clothes. For example, we might move schools because of difficulties or conflict and feel greatly relieved for a while, but then the same issues we thought we had escaped from arise again.

A radical act

One of the teachers then asked how they could express gratitude to the brawling students: "We might be able to offer gratitude to others in our personal life, but by offering these students gratitude we would just be saying, 'everything's alright, you can keep on doing what you're doing'."

I asked what kind of response they usually give to such students when they return to school the next day, or later, in the case of suspension.

"We usually can't look at each other in the face for a few days," one teacher replied. "I tell them how disappointed I am, or how hurt I am by their behaviour." "I warn them of what will happen if they do it again," said another. "In that last incident I was responsible for a roster where we kept the students who were involved in at lunch times for two weeks. They also had to pick up rubbish after school." Then Steve listed the repercussions that the school had in its procedures – some of which had to be created and passed through the school board, just to deal with the gravity of this kind of violence. "I just carry on as normal after that as I don't think it's my job to punish them. That's up to the police, but our relationship is never the same."

"So what were the inner attitudes behind some of these ways of dealing with the adversity?" I asked. The answers from the group revealed to them that instead of expressing gratitude they were doing the opposite – holding resentment towards the students and their parents, criticising them, blaming and shaming them, and making them feel guilt and remorse.

Most agreed that their approach so far had not been working. The violence and problems in the school were not getting any better, no matter what they did as staff to create punitive measures to stop them. In the course of our discussion, it slowly dawned on us that the claims made earlier about gratitude not working with these violent students may have been misplaced. Since they started to more consciously practise gratitude as a school, they had only practised gratitude towards students who were disengaged, but never to those whom they thought could, at any moment, "turn from innocent looking teenagers into monsters". The general consensus of opinion amongst the group seemed to be that to express gratitude to such students would mean that they were condoning their behaviour, letting them feel that they had won, that they had the upper hand, even inviting further violence and rebellion. They also did not want to leave themselves vulnerable to trusting these students only to have that trust betrayed in the future. In effect, they built a wall of protection around themselves.

"What have been the costs to you in dealing with the adversity in the ways you have been in the past?" I asked. Words came easily to describe their tiredness, stress, anxious nights, poor teaching, despondency, cynicism, strained relationships at home, loss of faith in the system, and for some, in humanity itself. They also judged themselves for not being able to cope. Their recent discovery, or indeed reminder, of the power of gratitude when they expressed it in less challenging circumstances, had made them feel that they had the answer to all their difficulties – only to feel bitterly disappointed when all they could summon in these instances was in fact the opposite of gratitude. Hearing the pain in their voices I wondered if it was their strong collegiality, the bonds connecting them to each other, that was what kept them going.

Then Steve talked about the costs to the school. "Even though we have a strong group of great teachers who really support each other here at Palmwood, we have also lost some great teachers. They gave up hoping that things would ever get better and left." Steve continued: "We also need to think of the costs to the other students who just want to focus on their learning, but then take days to recover and refocus after such events."

I suggested that when things are not working, perhaps it is better to try something completely the opposite, something that may seem illogical or even counter-intuitive. I took a deep breath before asking the group to consider something for which they could express gratitude to these students. I could see from the looks on their faces that I was inviting them into an area that was unfamiliar to most. As they suggested such things as gratitude for not going to jail, or for surviving the night, they admitted they were not being sincere and they were really struggling to move past their pain to find anything to be grateful for.

I remembered my discussion with the pre-service teachers about an ethic of gratitude that had been inspired by Noddings' ethic of care, as outlined in Chapter 6. Could we draw on the feelings of what it was like when someone expressed gratitude to us when we were going through a difficult time, to extrapolate to this next scenario? Going back to that exploration, how could we recognise the human essence inside these troublesome students? Their violent and aggressive behaviour had stopped most from seeing it.

I was sure that acts of violence and aggression from students could only be turned around with something radically different – with love, respect, listening and gratitude. Nothing else would work. I hoped to inspire them, prompt their memory, with another teacher's story, from a school where I had held a series of gratitude workshops. Christine was teaching at a high school that had a reputation for drug dealing and violence. She realised that to survive in the school she needed to move past her fears and approach her job and the students with gratitude. One day she was handing out practice exam papers to Year 9 students, and a boy pulled out a flick knife as she passed him, threatening to hurt her if she did not pass him in this exam. Everyone in the school was afraid of this student and could not find any way to control him.

When she saw the knife, instead of screaming something like, "get out and never come back to this class again", Christine responded by sitting down and asking the boy what he was angry about. As she listened to his fears and then told him what his good qualities were and how grateful she was to be teaching him, the boy was shocked, and then started to pour out more about what was happening for him and the difficulties he was experiencing at school. He completely calmed down and did not cause any trouble in that class from that point onwards. All the other students noticed this and the aggressive behaviour amongst many of them also diminished.

If we are to take gratitude as our teacher ethic that guides our relationships with all our students, how do reach into the essence, the human worthiness, of these violent students? "Perhaps we could search for what it is these students most need?" Alice asked. To this I added, "If we think about gratitude as gift-giving, what gift is it that these students are most in need of at present?" Now the atmosphere in the room changed. The radical suggestion I made before seemed less radical. Teachers want to see each of their students doing well. This is why they embarked on teaching in the first place. It was easy for these teachers to pour out suggestions of praise, encouragement, acknowledgement of their efforts, forgiveness, empathy, listening to their pain and really hearing it, not blaming them for it. "We could also be grateful to them for showing us where we have gone wrong in society, and how much further we have to go," Steve said.

"But we're not here to be counsellors or social workers!" Jeremy protested. "I just want to teach!"

I acknowledged that this was how many teachers feel – their role has been stretched way beyond just teaching. This is one of their major sources of resentment, particularly in situations where the level of problems makes it difficult to teach as much of the content as they would like, and to get through it in the orderly fashion they would hope to. One of the lines in a beautiful poem by Michael Leunig[193] is: "Give us a stray dog when we expect congratulations," where he is asking us to approach life with few expectations. The more we cling to a fixed identity of what it is to teach and a fixed agenda of getting through a certain amount of content or activities in a certain period of time, the more we inhibit that important quality of acceptance that our previous discussion highlighted as crucial to resilience in the midst of adversity.

We hear much these days of teaching to the whole student, of student-centred learning. But if we are to really achieve this in any authentic and real way, we would be teaching to the student in all their pain, in all their out-of-control behaviour. This is the student we have before us – although we try, we cannot be selective in the parts we address and those we do not. What I am suggesting here is a phenomenological view of student experience, which would, according to Troutner, include "...all kinds of experience, the aesthetic, the emotional, the noetic, the spiritual, dreams, feelings, moods..."[194] Husserl called such phenomena "essential phenomena of the human world" and, moreover, they are essential for the "meaning-making capacity" of human consciousness.[195] Given the complexity of the student cohorts in most of our schools, perhaps we need to accept that teaching is not just about the teaching of content. Teaching is also primarily about how we can change ourselves to become better people, and to model this to our students. Teaching is about *both* the character development of the teacher and the teaching of the curriculum.

Maybe we can view the challenges presented by the difficult students as opportunities to practise gratitude so that we cannot only become better teachers but better people. What would our day look like if we approached it with this view? Would we be building a trusting and safe environment, so that students feel settled enough to be able to learn?

"But just when I am getting over one incident, and getting back to my equilibrium, let alone my gratitude, another pops up and then another!" Jeremy remonstrated. I suggested that we might imagine a gratitude practice at this time, something achievable, to be a small light that grows bigger and bigger as we consciously respond with gratitude after each event. As we do so, the light gets bigger, and so does our capacity.

Anxious nights

"I think the teaching profession expects far too much of us these days," Jeremy continued, "we push ourselves too hard and then don't know when to stop. What's the role of gratitude in dealing with our personal anxiety? When we get too stressed to be able to think of anything except how to get through each day, isn't that a sign that we need to get out?"

Jeremy was right to question how gratitude could assist us in times like these, and if there is a danger that embracing it will cloud our judgement about whether it is time to leave the situation and move on. I postulated with them that perhaps if we engage in the steps of reflective practice discussed earlier, we may be able to build more personal resilience from which to make this decision.

Michelle then spoke about how gratitude had helped her become more resilient. "I was waking in the middle of the night, flooded with fears about my job, my health, and worried about some of my students. Since the first workshop, at night I now only focus on what I have to be thankful for and I've noticed my 'night terrors' lessening. I am not waking up as stressed out." She said that instead of worrying about what might happen in the future, she would think about what she was receiving from her students, the joy and sense of purpose they brought to her life, and the efforts they made. "I've been able to teach better than ever in the past few months; I've felt more alive and connected to my students and colleagues and people around me are telling me how much better I look."

In some fields of social and positive psychology, recent investigation into the effects of gratitude could inspire discussion of the relevance of gratitude to teacher resilience. Researchers have noted the potential of gratitude to dissolve regret; increase optimism; enable one to be less susceptible to emotions like disappointment, regret, and frustration; increase health and general wellbeing; improve moods; provide a source of human strength in dealing with adversity; and have a positive impact in the treatment of depression.[196]

Much of this research is based around gratitude as an emotion and is conducted under clinical conditions. Teachers who *practise* gratitude in their *everyday* working lives during my action research projects report similar outcomes to these empirical findings. Teachers at all levels of education consistently state that they feel calmer, less stressed, more positive, have a greater sense of life and work satisfaction, and are more able to connect with those around them, as they more consciously practise gratitude. As one of these teachers said, "Gratitude can, even from the inconsistent effort made to date, calm, restore and revive."

Michelle was highlighting an important aspect of gratitude in times of adversity. When we think of what we are grateful for, we take a step back from the situation and are more able to choose our response. Instead of being consumed by our anxiety, we are able to see that there is an alternative perspective. Focusing on what we can be grateful for can empower us to make different choices, choices more likely to bring about positive outcomes. Again, our gratitude can be a point on the compass by which to navigate. When we move another step, to contemplate how we might express this gratitude, we are able to distance ourselves from the pain in the situation even further. We are perhaps able to gain more objectivity and not drown in feelings of fear. In this more detached state, we may be in a better position to do something about the situation, or if needed, be able to make a clear decision about whether or not it is time to move away. It is important that we make decisions that are not controlled by anxious nights.

Into greatness

There is no surer way into greatness than through the doors of adversity. Of course we can find meaning and happiness in other ways, but greatness of character and capacity to do great things in the world requires adversity, like an oyster needs grit to create a pearl. Schools like Palmwood and Millbrook have become great because of their great difficulties. However, it is not just adversity itself that leads to greatness. For some people, their difficulties can embitter or defeat them. It is our capacity to engage in a conscious relationship with adversity that makes or breaks its potential to lead to greatness.

There is much in the way that education is currently constructed that diminishes our capacity to engage in this conscious relationship, and to reach into the wisdom and strength that gratitude can offer in times of adversity. Again, conceptions of what it is to be a teacher or to teach focus almost entirely on the delivery of content rather than the character of the person who is delivering this content. For some, teaching is merely a job for which one receives payment and accrued holidays, rather than a profession that asks for a commitment to try to become the best kind of person we can be. Taking this view, teachers can often feel that their role is interrupted, undermined, and dismantled by the rising amount of difficulties they are 'forced' to face in their classroom. Problems are often identified as something wrong with the system, or society, or the curriculum. There may not be any desire to look to aspects of our inner attitude that may need to grow and change.

If we read autobiographies of great people, a common thread is the great adversity they have endured. They contain similar messages that are in the perennial wisdom of the ages, juxtaposing opposite conditions: "no pain, no gain"; "a bitter winter brings a sweet summer"; "in every discomfort there is the seed of comfort". For many great people, their path to greatness has been a long painful process that has required enormous strength. One famous example is Nelson Mandella. He was able to withstand his twenty-eight years in jail because he had a big intention: to free his people. Importantly, he had built his capacity to endure jail by the adversity he had gone through in his younger years.

We can also learn much about the role of adversity through our observation of nature. Bamboo can only become strong by stopping its growth in height to develop strong nodes before starting to grow upwards again. Butterflies can only come out in their beauty by going through the process of pushing through their cocoon. Cherry blossoms only bloom once they have born the harsh winter. Just like building our muscles, we need to build our capacity to be grateful during adversity, and to know that each time we are grateful for what adversity teaches us, we move towards greatness.

Sometimes schools take decades to step into their greatness. We should not expect too much of ourselves, or our schools too soon. In the midst of our 'quick-fix' culture, too often, when adversity comes along we try to fix the problem, rather than reflecting on what it is trying to teach us. We may be inadvertently stopping the painful process a school may need to go through in order to become great.

Indeed, adversity is often the measure by which we judge schools as being incompetent and in need of reform – quickly and urgently. If literacy and numeracy does not improve within one or two years, the school is ordered to try new techniques, or train their teachers differently so that they can make 'the adversity' go away. Rather than develop the current program and learn from areas where it needs to improve, it gets thrown out and replaced by something bigger, better, different. We are constantly bombarded by new ideas, and teachers report a weariness to try out more new techniques.

In annual school reports we are encouraged to present glowing results and positive outcomes. Rarely would we report on, let alone celebrate, things that are not going well. In the 'publish or perish' culture that dominates most universities, we are under pressure to embark on initiatives in schools that are going to generate quick and measurable results. Some government policy has moved to measuring the success of whole countries using happiness indices, none of which refers to an individual's capacity to ride the waves of adversity. All of this encourages an approach where we look for what is going well – often based on standards that are set by others who are outside of our context – and ignore where the real gold is, in what is not going well.

Emmons and Shelton state that a "grateful person" can be characterised by how they deal with adversity.

> ...grateful individuals are not naively optimistic, nor are they under some illusion that suffering and pain are non-existent. Rather, these persons have consciously taken control by choosing to extract benefits from adversity, with one of the major benefits being the perception of life as a gift.[197]

Although an extreme example of this, we may be able to take inspiration from Victor Frankl[198], Austrian psychiatrist and survivor of atrocities committed in a World War II concentration camp. In the first half of his book, *Man's Search for Meaning,* Frankl describes the horrific experience of the camp in narrative detail. In the latter half he explores the difference between those whose spirit was destroyed by their suffering and those who took "the last of the human freedoms – to choose one's attitude in any given set of circumstances, to choose one's own way."[199]

Frankl invites us into the dimension of transcendence that seeks meaning in adversity. There are three ways to discover meaning and purpose in life: by creating a work or doing a deed; by experiencing something such as goodness, truth and beauty or by loving someone; or by the attitude we take towards unavoidable suffering.[200] Frankl's philosophy challenges those who are confronted with seemingly immovable suffering, to accept the challenge of making the effort to rise above this and become great in spite of and because of it. He invites us to connect to the suffering of others around us.

> When a man finds that it is his destiny to suffer, he will have to accept his suffering as his task; his single and unique task. He will have to acknowledge the fact that even in suffering he is unique and alone in the universe. No one can relieve him of his suffering or suffer in his place. His unique opportunity lies in the way he bears his burden.[201]

This is not an unsympathetic or masochistic type of invitation as some might think. It is not calling us to lie down, accept our suffering and do nothing about it. If the suffering is avoidable, then, as Frankl recommends, "the meaningful thing to do would be to remove its cause, be it psychological, biological or political."[202] If the suffering is unavoidable, Frankl offers us great wisdom. If we have a life of suffering, the most powerful way forward is to embrace it and allow it to teach us, and strengthen us. It is this sense of mission, or, in Frankl's terms, it is this sense of purpose in adversity, that gives people the ability to respond with gratitude, to withstand the greatest of trials and taste freedom.

With the adversities we face as nations and societies seeming to be on an exponential rise, our teachers and students may need to be great people, not just happy or well-adjusted people. Rather than trying to protect ourselves from pain, or make things easier for ourselves by trying to escape our difficulties, we need to build our capacity to go through adversity with great wisdom. If the students in our classes have already been through much adversity, we can congratulate them and admire the capacity this has already built, rather than judge them as being "off to a bad start". Through our own example, we can teach our students how to walk through the doors of adversity, gracefully learning to become great people.

TEACHING GRATITUDE

...I was now into week eight of my classes...By this stage in the past semesters I had almost burnt out by now but I felt that going to class was more entertaining and interesting than times before. One aspect that has enabled me to act like this is through the daily practice of showing 'gratitude'. In doing this I have become a lot more aware of the things around me. Instead of looking at lecturers and thinking that they were people who are just teaching me the information so I could pass my exams, I looked at them in a totally different light. I have formed relationships with all my teachers and begun to realise that they all have admirable qualities. One in particular is the teacher I have for Advertising Principles and Practice. I had this lecturer for a subject last semester and didn't give him the respect he deserved. This semester I have listened to his stories and taken note of what he has said. I have learned to be grateful for having such a knowledgeable teacher in the area I am interested in....
– Tom, Individual Project

Taking teachers' own pedagogy and their understanding of the complexity of gratitude – especially in times of adversity – as the foundation, this chapter provides a framework for introducing gratitude to students. First it explores some dimensions of student disengagement and how these impact on the learning process. I revisit the concept of 'A State of Preparedness' to show gratitude in perhaps its most powerful role: assisting students to take responsibility for the way of being they bring to their class or study situation. I argue that before we consider how we are going to introduce gratitude to our students, it is important to take account of both the developmental age of the student and the institutional readiness to incorporate pedagogy around gratitude. I establish a rationale for conceptualising gratitude as a learning strategy that can facilitate greater engagement. The chapter shows how gratitude activates a true dynamic in education where students acknowledge what they have been given, and are creative in finding ways of giving back.

Are your students awake?

"Well, are you awake?" I said, after I had greeted the twenty-four students in the Education 101, Integrated Learning class – a university elective offered to students from all faculties. "Besides having your eyes open, how would I know if you are awake?" I asked, acknowledging the humour of the metaphor – one that inspired me from Maxine Greene's[203] notion of 'wide-awakeness', and Martin Heidegger's[204] notion that in order for us to be able to think in a true and deep way, we need to be *present* enough in the thinking process. In my very first class with students – no matter what the context – I ask the question *Are you awake?* to set a standard of presence that I want from them. I invite them to contemplate a different level of presence to the mediocre one that many may have settled for in their learning. My underlying hypothesis – which I often share with them – is that most students sincerely wish to be more engaged, more present in their learning, but do not know how to be, nor how to engage in discourse around what this means.[205]

Often students – particularly in the earlier years of high school – are not interested in becoming an engaged learner. We may need to pose the question of *Are you awake?* in the context of something that is nearer and dearer to their individual interests, and then perhaps to work from there towards how they might apply this quality to their learning. They may first need to recognise that this quality is essential if they want to be a good employee, dancer, singer, soccer player, parent or partner. Once students develop a thirst for the kind of presence made famous by Mihalyi Csikszentmihalyi's[206] concept of "flow" – single-minded, joyful immersion, complete absorption in the task at hand – we can invite them to practise this in their learning so that they can then become better at it in the things they love to do, or at least would prefer to do.

"How many of you find it difficult to be awake in your studies?" A few hands rose immediately; followed soon by more.

"Let me pose this in a slightly different way," I continued, and I asked for an honest answer, *How many of you remember everything that you learned last semester?* This question came only one month after they had finished their final exam for the previous semester. One hand was raised but was quickly withdrawn. I gave the class members a few moments to consider my question. "How about 80%?" I suggested. The same hand was raised and this time joined by another. As I proceeded downwards in 10% increments, more hands were raised. It was only when I reached 20% that the majority of students raised their hands. This was my main reason for offering the Education 101 unit.

The quality of learning many of our students are reporting in their studies is very far away from that hoped for by Heidegger:

> To learn means to become knowing...one who has seen, has caught sight of something, and never again loses sight of what he has caught sight of. To learn means to attain such seeing.[207]

We are spending millions of dollars on trying to make the educational experience more technologically connected, and on improving our teaching methodologies so that students are more able to access the content in an interesting way. Yet how can students access our state-of-the-art learning and teaching methodologies, if we have not deeply considered the quality of attention that our students are bringing to them? Similarly, I cannot introduce the notion of gratitude, nor indeed any other aspect of curriculum or learning strategies, before students are able to meet the precondition of awakeness, and embrace this as their responsibility to enact.

Next I asked my quintessential question, one of the most potent I have found in my past two decades of teaching: *What stops you from being awake in your learning?* This question generates completely different answers to others we tend to ask when conducting research into student learning – questions such as "How do you learn?" or "What makes you a successful learner?"[208] In the same way as we discovered from the teachers' reactions on that fateful day at Palmwood, before we can discuss the role of gratitude for our students, we need to first hear and understand the context in which we are speculating about its relevance.

If we want our listening to be an act of gratitude, of recognition of the other, we may need to ask the right question – one that opens up the whole self, not just the parts we want to hear or that are easiest to measure.[209] When I ask this question of my students it opens up the floodgates and lets loose the awareness of the adversity they are experiencing in their learning. It also calls into question the boundaries of my role as an academic. Some of the issues that students' answers reveal are often excluded from the notions of 'student' that are at the centre of curricula and teaching methodologies. My concept of student relates to that which assists them to make meaning of their world and of the content we teach them. If I am to respectfully listen to my students' answers to the question: *What stops you from being awake in your learning?* I may need to step out of the confines of traditional concepts of teacher and learner. I agree with Parker J. Palmer's point that we need new insights if we are to truly teach our students well:

> ...We need a new diagnosis of our student's inward condition, one that is more perceptive about their needs, less defensive about our role in their plight, and more likely to lead to creative modes of teaching...[210]

I asked the students to sit with people they did not know very well, so in this case there could be a mixture of journalism, law, languages, philosophy, business studies, and psychology students at each table. I invited them to introduce themselves and then to discuss my question. As I wandered from group to group I could see that each one was relieved that he or she was not alone in their procrastination, perfectionism, poor time management, stress, exam anxiety, laziness, boredom, or lack of motivation. Some admitted it was difficult to stay awake in the literal sense as they tried to balance university with their part-time jobs. Others talked about their young children. From the edges of the circles, I heard complaints about particular lecturers and courses.

"How could anyone could stay 'awake' in lectures," they asked "where there's the constant drone of a monotonous voice reading from notes? They don't care about making it interesting for us."

Whose responsibility is it to assist you to be awake in your learning? was my next question. Answers were divided and provoked discussion about problems with the 'system'. They were part of a factory, going in one end and coming out the other with a university degree, but with little enjoyment of the process. Some of the students seemed ready to accept responsibility for their awakeness, though most felt that there should be a shared responsibility between themselves and their teachers.

Later on, when I could read their weekly journal entries, I found similar themes to those of our class discussions. These same themes had emerged in each of the seven semesters of Integrated Learning, with first year university students at other institutions, and amongst Year 11 and 12 students with whom I had worked. Their initial complaints were about the system that had failed them and the goalposts that had kept shifting. They did not know what was expected of them. They needed to move forward, but did not know how. Some were lost. They wondered if university was the place for them, did not know what to do if they dropped out, or how to manage others' expectations.

Each week we built a stronger image of a truly awake student. Perhaps these weekly class discussions where I was inviting them to take more responsibility for their awakeness grew their trust in me as their journal reader, helping many students delve more deeply into a more honest recollection of what learning was for them. Many journals described circumstances in which the narrator was distracted in some way or other. Minds were "a thousand miles away", pretending to be present and engaged, playing a game they thought was one of fooling the lecturer into thinking that they were attentive. Their words intoned being "taken over" by feelings of frustration, boredom, resentment, perfectionism, inertia, indecision, anxiety, worry, aimlessness, hopelessness, fear, stress, depression, regret, anger, sadness, guilt or shame. Metaphors such as their "cloudiness" or "fog" illustrated their condition of these feelings overcoming them whenever they went to class or sat down to study, no matter how hard they tried to be awake.

In hearing these answers I needed to be clear in my own mind, and give such assurance to my students, that my role was to be an educator, not a therapist or a counsellor. It was from their answers that I started to investigate whether or not gratitude – theirs and mine – could assist in achieving the precondition of awakeness in their studies.

Preparing students for deeper learning

Who likes to garden? I asked them as they entered their fourth week of Integrated Learning. My opening questions were phrased to deepen the discussion for fifteen minutes or so about dimensions of awakeness, before the formalities of dealing with other Integrated Learning strategies. Within the past three weeks we had considered how our 'inner condition' affected our ability to be truly present in our learning. My students' journaling had made many of them more conscious of being full of complaint about the system and processes that we believed were failing us. Their words were often about being a victim, being entitled to much more than they were receiving or paying for, being disillusioned because they had higher expectations of what their university education would be like. They volunteered that this inner condition had become a large part of their culture, entrenched in their language and ways of communicating to their peers about their learning. It was their default state from the moment they started to think about their studies at the beginning of the day.

I wanted to invite my students to be conscious of the choices they were making about the state of being they bring to their learning. Such choices would be crucial for the kind of wide-awakeness that I wished to advocate in following Maxine Greene. Greene requires that learning provokes an awareness of choice for personal freedom, "living deliberately" rather than passively and in acquiescence; with "moral agency" and "conscious engagement with the world"; with "full attention to life" in order to discover what we are living for and what gives us meaning. Such consciousness does not "come automatically; it comes through being alive, awake, curious..."[211]

In order to take the next step toward awakeness, I asked the students to consider what conditions would be necessary for seeds to grow and thrive. "Compost", "rain", "sunshine", "right soil and weather", they answered. The metaphor behind my question suggested that we need to prepare ourselves quite deliberately. If we 'prepare our being' *before* coming to class or *before* sitting down to study, we might be able to adopt our best inner attitude, and our learning would have a greater chance of taking hold. Although we might have mastered other state-of-the-art Integrated Learning strategies such as memory or reading skills, if we do not attend to the kind of inner attitude or outlook we bring to our learning, 'seeds of knowledge' might not grow, as we are sprinkling them on unfertile ground. If our inner attitude is one of complaint, we poison the soil, and deplete it of nourishment.

In the previous chapters we have explored how teachers can gain greater connectedness with their students and achieve greater presence through attending to their State of Preparedness. This opens up the importance of the realm of reflection before teaching. Similarly, we can invite our students to attend to their inner attitudes before their learning, and to investigate the impact on their level of awakeness and their learning.

I was inviting the students *to choose* their state of being, to enter through their personal choice into a place that is not determined by external events or circumstances or by forces that may well be outside their control. I was inviting them to live consciously and deliberately as a student by reflecting on how their inner condition is influenced by the choices they make in every moment of the day – not just when they come to a learning situation. They could extend this consciousness to the State of Preparedness they bring to their other roles and circumstances – at work, as a parent, as a friend. I hoped to inspire them by showing how Kwan, a student from a class I had recently worked with at another university, exercised this choice:

> *This class gave me perspective on life, something which I needed so to not become completely overwhelmed with life...I came out of that class feeling deeply reflective. In the last few months, I have been dealing with personal issues all to do with self-confidence and homesickness. I have been letting a negative attitude completely consume my life, and if I didn't do anything to change this, I would make myself sick, both emotionally and physically. While I am not saying that this class completely turned my life around, it was another perspective on what I am going through and another set of solutions in order to help myself.*

The focus for my students this week had been to reflect on the choices they had in their state of being, their State of Preparedness, as they thought about and approached their other courses. This gave the students time and incentive, before we met for our next class, to reflect on the current conditions of their soil, the reasons for not being able to be fully engaged in their studies. In this way we had 'prepared the ground' for exploring the place of gratitude in their learning.

Our 'reflection on being' was to set the stages of reflection that Froh and his colleagues advocate for gratitude to occur. We read from Froh that gratitude

> ...begins with the awareness that individuals have a choice of taking whatever attitude they prefer in a given situation. The second step requires that the individual attain a certain level of self-reflection so the necessary internal work of being grateful can occur. Following this stage, gratitude often becomes a felt experience as a result of a conscious attitude and intention to be grateful, which then, it is hoped, results in its expression through action (e.g. thanking others for their generosity).[212]

In the following class I asked my students the question: *If complaint poisons the soil, what might be an inner attitude that nourishes it?* Sometimes students came to the notion of gratitude as the antithesis of complaint. When they arrived at the word "gratitude" I just let the word lie still for a few moments, despite what for some might have been an awkward silence. From feedback in previous semesters,

I had learned not to rush to explain, narrating experiences, advancing definitions or distributing worksheets. Although I had been inspired by stories of success of previous students' applications of gratitude, I had received feedback that my initial introductions of gratitude were over-zealous and had turned some students away. I had forgotten my commitment to encourage students to use their own critical evaluation skills to assess the value of gratitude for themselves. I did not want to do this again.

I invited the students to form small groups to discuss the possible relevance of gratitude in their approach to their studies and to consider what the word means for them. The value of gratitude inherent for most was in helping them move from the habit of focusing on what they do not have, to a new habit of focusing on what they do have. It could assist them to remember to give back rather than just be in receiving mode. Some would recognise the quality of gratitude that shone through in their fellow classmates. These same students would often have stories of great adversity – some shared and some that arose from the narrative of their life thus far – refugees from war-torn countries, mature-aged students who had wanted to get back to university for many years beforehand, those who had been close to death or had endured serious illness. The high level of awakeness these students brought to their studies arose naturally from their attitude of not taking anything for granted; of treating each moment, and their education, as a gift; of wanting to give back for the gift of their life or health or loved ones that they may have been close to losing. Their whole being and their approach to their studies spoke loudly of the relationship between gratitude and learning.

It was possible to go from here into imagining what it would be like if we did not have all of the 'gifts' that make up the current learning situation. I asked my students to contemplate the billions of students around the world who would like to be in their position but who are not able to be. I invited them to watch SBS news that evening if they needed a more vivid image. This immediately made some sit up in their chair and take notice. Maybe it shook them out of a sense of complacency or a condition that is close to what Maxine Green labels as "taken-for-grantedness" – and which we could call a sense of entitlement – a condition that precludes the flourishing of gratitude.

I invited my students into a discovery of the meaning of gratitude for themselves before I introduced them to my distinctions and emphasis on gratitude as a practice of giving back for what we have received.

I also encouraged them to consider the choices they could make in different dimensions – thoughts, self-talk, words, emotions, and behaviour – in order to explore the impact these could be having on their learning outcomes. I used the following diagram to invite discussion about the impact of an inner attitude of complaint and dissatisfaction on these. So as not to present this as a formula to suppress negativity or to insist on a happy disposition, we also discussed some of the complexities of complaint explored in Chapter 7.

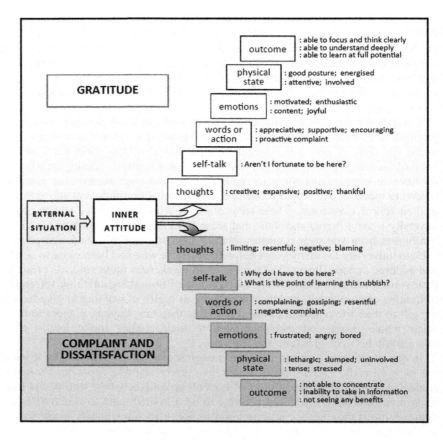

Figure 4. Dimensions of the impact of one's inner attitude.

This figure can help us examine whether our attitudes are reflected in our actions.

It is natural for our students to want us to be further ahead in our gratitude than they are themselves, so that they can learn from us and look up to us when they are struggling to practise. Where we need to model gratitude for our students, we also need to be wary of setting ourselves up to fail in our students' eyes. The moment we complain or fail to express gratitude when something goes wrong, we are open to criticism and may also cause some students to lose hope. It is therefore important from the start that we do not set ourselves up as perfect practitioners, but humbly acknowledge our own difficulties to them, as well as our successes. This will enable our students to let themselves off the hook when they find it difficult to practise gratitude, or when they try to be perfect in their own attempts.

When are they ready?

When we teach gratitude it feels best to do so in a humble, subtle, gentle, graceful way that emulates the characteristics of gratitude. This means being sensitive to our students' readiness to embrace gratitude as a way of being in their learning, and also the readiness of our institution to consider its relevance to educational goals and processes. To gain awareness of students' readiness requires a well-considered understanding of their developmental stage and the suitability of suggesting gratitude in their present situation.

In our class discussions, some students welcomed the possibility of gratitude as a learning strategy. Others were clearly suspicious and spoke of the negative connotations surrounding the word 'gratitude'. From the negative reactions the word conjures, I have come to see that too many adults have lost touch with the magnificent power of gratitude because of the way that it was 'taught' to them when they were young – particularly when they were facing adversity. They find it difficult to embrace the possible place of gratitude in their learning because, as children, they may have been forced to believe in something that they did not yet understand and to behave in a certain way that was beyond their developmental capacity. At an age when they could not compare themselves with others, they may have been expected to feel gratitude for what they had by making light of their suffering, because others were less fortunate. In the midst of their pain, they may have been 'taught' that they *should* feel grateful because of the efforts of the very same person who was unwittingly inflicting that pain. At an age when they had not yet developed the "moral memory" of what others had done for them, their 'ingratitude' may have been met with disappointment and even punishment.

It is also important to investigate whether or not gratitude is something that develops with age as a natural part of our human disposition, or whether it needs to be consciously and deliberately nurtured. Indeed our own difficulty to maintain a state of gratefulness, or to remember to express gratitude, shows us time and again that our gratitude is something that may not be innate, but rather needs regular attention and vigilance. Drawing on the work of Miller (2006), Froh and his colleagues (2007) argue:

> Experiencing gratitude does not come naturally; it is a learned process and sometimes an effortful one, and it requires a certain level of inner reflection and introspection. Gratitude must be practised and cultivated...[213]

How can we teach gratitude in ways that are suitable for the developmental age of our students and that honour the complexity and different interpretations of gratitude? Perhaps during their younger years, we can inspire children with positive associations with gratitude. We can encourage children to come to gratitude with their hearts. We can create educational experiences that call forth joy, delight, surprise, awe, curiosity and wonder. At the core of children's sense of 'giftedness', of feeling 'blessed', we can find ways to make it easier for each and every child to feel appreciated and to appreciate others. If we wish for our high school and university students to express gratitude in their learning, education itself needs to be something that incites an appreciative response.

As teachers who know our students level of maturity, we are best placed to determine when they have the cognitive, emotional, moral and social development to be able and ready to engage willingly and wholeheartedly with gratitude, in its more complete meaning. We can observe their ability to empathise, to engage in conscious and authentic acts of reciprocity, to act with clear intention. As we open up to understanding our students' capacity for gratitude, we can gain insights into the kinds of skills we might help them develop so they can move towards gratitude in its fullest expression. As Visser reminds us, "Being grateful is impossible without mindfulness, recollection and recognition."[214] I believe that many teachers would be confident about teaching these skills as precursors to teaching about gratitude.

Nowhere is there a more pronounced need for heightening our consciousness of the student's age and maturity for introducing a more complete sense of gratitude than when we teach the relevance of gratitude during and after adversity. Consider for a moment the complexity of asking all students in a Year 9 class to write letters of gratitude to their parents – parents who may have treated them badly or to whom they feel resentful. Or, in the case of some of my classes, where there are students who are refugees from war-torn countries, for whom the bag of trauma they have brought with them should only be opened at their choice.

How, when and if we introduce our students to some of the principles and possibilities we explored in the previous chapter on adversity, very much depends on our capacity and skill to listen to their adversity, and the level of choices we establish when we introduce gratitude. It would not work for instance, if we do not allow gratitude to be a voluntary exercise that students are invited to explore amongst other alternatives. I invited my students to exercise this choice in the context of Integrated Learning by providing the alternative of focusing instead on other strategies, such as working with their particular learning style.

One of the questions I am asked most frequently by teachers and other academics is whether or not students take a cynical approach to the suggestion of gratitude as a learning strategy. I believe our answer to this question depends very much on our own experience of how gratitude has assisted us in our life, and our conviction that it may have a place in our students' learning. It also depends on the readiness of our institution to embrace the possibility of gratitude. Although teachers of young students warn that they are on the lookout for anything that preaches about how to be "a better person" or to be "more positive", my experience has taught me that university-age students are more open to the relevance of gratitude than many in my teacher workshops.

In my students' answers to the question of "What stops you from being awake in your learning?" I hear the echo of a phenomenon that is commonly ignored by many educators: questions of *how to be* are *more important* for students than questions of *how to think* critically or analytically, or *how to perform well* on assessment tasks. We can see this quest for answers to *how to be* in the songs our students listen to, the books they read, the websites they populate, and the identities they struggle to find in virtual and 'off-line' communities. Directions taken to accommodate both the demands of content-heavy curricula and the seemingly strategic learner, have meant that active learning is usually constructed in terms of task-orientation. The consequence has been the silencing of the question of "how to be?" by often giving almost complete priority to the questions of "how to do?" or "how to think?". Such a stance is strongly echoed in one of the most commonplace axioms about learning 'I do and I understand'.[215] It translates in the academic context as "I critically think and I understand"; or "I analyse the information in a logical fashion and I understand". Such a focus is also characteristic of notions of "deeper approaches to learning" that have been idealised in many higher education contexts.[216] I believe the main problem with a task-oriented or 'doing-oriented' curriculum is that little attention is given to the students themselves, in all their various dimensions, in their being, and how this relates to their learning.

However, if we are to investigate the role of gratitude in addressing the ontological and existential quest of our students, it is important to reconsider the discussion provoked by Ecclestone and Hayes and many others who are against recent moves towards what they call "the happiness agenda." This discussion is echoed in many a conversation or debate I have had with university colleagues and teachers. The important question that arises is whether or not we should be teaching gratitude in our educational institutions to *all* of our students in ways that prescribe and homogenise a certain way of being. Moreover, how can we justify the introduction of gratitude in the context of the academic emphasis on critical thinking and the mastery of content? In answering these questions, it is important that our goals are clearly educational rather than therapeutic.

As Integrated Learning seemed to pave the way for important questions and answers of an existential nature, my students were challenged by the fact that this dimension was not given importance or even a mention in their other academic subjects. In most of their other units they were abiding by different rules, with clear boundaries around the kind and amount of self-exploration that was appropriate within a university setting. In some instances this did not even extend to sharing their name. In order for them to feel comfortable within my unit and for them to fulfil a key objective – to apply the underlying principles to their other units – I became aware that I needed to consider their context more fully. I needed to remember the important principle I was reminded of by the teachers at Millbrook, as we saw in Chapter 5, *gratitude lives and breathes in a context*. If we want to teach gratitude we need to be able to take the students' perspective of how it lives and breathes in their context.

Before I could show the relevance of gratitude to the academic learning context, I needed to demonstrate how the traditional thinking skills and the objectivist stance could be *enhanced* by assisting students to find answers to *how to be?* We need to teach and encourage students to attend to both their being *and* their higher order thinking skills. I therefore needed to engage my students in a dialectic, to explore a relationship between thinking and being, rather than making a radical departure from the traditional focus on the cognitive.

In order to achieve this, I embedded my pedagogy strongly in ensuring the nature of the assessment tasks required them to think critically. While the first of my tasks explored the question of *What stops you from being awake in your learning?*, the second task was to choose another unit they were studying concurrently which they found the most challenging. They were asked to embark upon an 'Individual Project' where they would apply the Integrated Learning strategies to their learning of this other unit and write a critical evaluation of how effective they found the strategies. Their third task was to write an academic essay, which would investigate some theoretical justifications for the strategies they were learning in my unit.

In the spirit of the warnings issued by Stephen Law in his text *War for Children's Minds,* where there is a healthy and respectful balance of liberal and authoritative approaches to education, we need "periods in which open, philosophical discussion of important moral, cultural, political and religious questions takes place."[217] If we are to engage students in a discussion of the relevance of gratitude, so that it is not one that Law might call, "psychological manipulation", we also need to teach and encourage the skills of critical inquiry, so that they can decide on its meaning and significance for themselves.

To this end I not only required my students to demonstrate critical thinking about the relevance of gratitude in their discussions and assessment tasks, I also introduced gratitude as one of many learning strategies and how it sits amongst these, rather than revolving the unit around gratitude alone. As well as the theory and practice of A State of Preparedness and gratitude, these strategies included exam skills, long-term memory skills, learning styles, critical thinking, overcoming procrastination, deep and surface approaches to learning, and reading strategies. I made a deliberate choice in naming this unit, *Integrated* Learning. I wanted my students to connect each of the topics to each other, to their other courses, and to their lives in general. I emphasised that I was expecting them to become true researchers and learn to critically evaluate the effectiveness of the Integrated Learning strategies – not to write about them or believe in them just because *I* wanted them to.

Gratitude as a learning strategy

Many students reported that they could not remember a time when they truly enjoyed or valued their learning. My invitation to be in A State of Preparedness by choosing to practise gratitude meant that it would be their own responsibility to change the situation, and not wait around for the system or teachers to create this change for them. Their enhanced awareness of the crippling power of complaint and the underlying victim mentality that they came to discover and articulate in their journals and class discussions, assisted these students to move past the previously negative connotations they attributed to gratitude. Most agreed to experiment with gratitude as they were coming to understand it, and to investigate whether or not it worked in their other subjects. But some were sceptical of its power. A small number chose not to apply gratitude and opted to concentrate their assignment entirely on the value of the 'more conventional' Integrated Learning strategies.

For the first fifteen minutes of every class in the following weeks, I led the students into different dimensions of fuller expressions of gratitude – humility, giving, interconnectedness, and awe, mystery and wonder. Each dimension built on the others as the weeks progressed. We explored the relevance of each dimension to other Integrated Learning strategies, which were the focus of the remainder of every class. They told me they learned the most about gratitude through how other students applied it to their studies and the struggles they had along the way. Some also said that they wanted me to share more of my own journey with gratitude and how I apply it in my teaching and own learning. I posed dilemmas, encouraged critical discussion, and invited objections about the place of gratitude in education.

I asked the students to contemplate how gratitude could assist them to move into an active engagement with their studies, and to explore ways in which they could see learning as giving, as well as receiving. In his exploration of "a curriculum of giving", Thomas Nielsen (2011) describes four kinds of giving – to self, to relationships, to community and to life. For Nielsen, gratitude falls into the final category. Importantly, research in the areas of 'service learning' shows that a focus on giving is linked to academic success as well as enhanced wellbeing[218]. Service is also at the heart of Tobin Hart's transformational notion of "understanding", which for him means, "to stand amongst". To truly understand the knowledge we have gained, we need to see how it applies in relationship to the people and things around us. For Hart, understanding "…begins to take us beyond self-interest and self-separation", and "…One of the most direct ways to experiment with understanding and empathy is through service…service also extends beyond people to include serving the task at hand."[219] Further, service "opens our consciousness, our ways of knowing. Service is a way of knowing our connection with a reality much larger than ourselves."[220]

We extended the notion of 'learning as giving' into the next week's discussion of the place of awe, mystery and wonder in our inner attitude to learning, inciting a sense of giftedness for things at the heart of their learning. For example, optometry students reflected on gratitude for their eyes, law students on gratitude for the legal system, and accounting students on gratitude for numbers. In her Individual

Project, Verona wrote about how her change in attitude and expressing gratitude for her textbook motivated her:

> *I have learned to find the best in each subject and to be grateful for all that I am able to learn and everything else around me. Because I am more grateful with what I have, I treat materials more preciously and now I am trying to read all the textbooks that I have bought since my first semester in university, which still look brand new. So far, I have read the whole textbook for my New Venture Planning subject and I am very proud of myself. I have never completed one whole textbook before.*

It seemed easy for most students to acknowledge all the material things that enabled them to be able to learn – the buildings, grounds, resources, textbooks and other materials, could be considered as gifts that they could "give back" by treating these more preciously, by valuing them in ways they had not thought of in the past. They thought of turning off the lights when they walked out; straightening the desks; picking up rubbish; and valuing their textbooks more fully by reading them. I suggested that they convert this into a 'gratitude practice', choosing just one thing and then doing it consistently over a period of time.

My students also acknowledged the many people who contributed to their ability to learn and be in the position of going to university, which they now started to describe as "a privilege". They found it easy to think of tangible ways of "giving back" to their parents, grandparents, teachers (past and present), the cleaners, and administrators. Their lists included: writing letters of thanks to their past teachers; coming to class more prepared; smiling at and greeting their tutors and others in their classes; connecting with others; helping their peers; staying back and genuinely thanking their lecturers after class; looking for good points they see in others; and treating each moment preciously by being more attentive.

As we have discussed in other chapters, it is important that students understand gratitude as a practice and that they do not fall into the trap of needing to feel grateful all the time in order for gratitude to be more fully embraced in their lives. One of the most effective ways of doing this is to embark on a practice together with our students as a class. As gratitude itself has the power to bond others together, a class practice of gratitude has a strong uniting power. It not only strengthens collaboration, but also increases the likeliness of positive outcomes, because the inner attitude of a group of people together is a powerful and transformative force. If everyone has a common goal, they can support each other, and discuss difficulties and successes. Understanding of the meaning and importance of gratitude can be clarified through the input of others.

Such a discussion would be a good opportunity to introduce our students to the difference between helping and giving. If, for example, they chose to give back by assisting second-language learners to take more comprehensive notes during the lectures, they would need to be aware that they are entering a giving and receiving dynamic, where both parties are on an equal footing. Helping would take the form of the student perceiving a lack in the other that they could fulfil, and would diminish the mutuality of relationship that is essential to gratitude. They would need to open up to how much they receive from this giving opportunity. We are not expressing gratitude because of a perceived need in the other person, but because we recognise something we have received from them. We are not trying to rescue or save another with our gratitude because we feel we have something that they do not have. Our gratitude should be expressed from a position of awe, not pity. In this example, the giver could see the second-language learner as already having at least two languages. Their courage to take up university study in a different language could also be inspirational.

Thinking and Thanking

Before gratitude could take hold in my own pedagogy, I needed to show its relevance in the university context – a secular education system that calls itself 'higher' education because it emphasises higher order thinking skills – logical, analytical and critical thinking. At the heart of this *logos* is the objective, detached learner. I gained a clearer and surer footing of the place of gratitude in this context from my students' honest and reflective responses as they applied gratitude to the other subjects they were studying concurrently with Integrated Learning. Many of these were deeply entrenched in the traditional focus on the higher order thinking skills – subjects such as accounting, tax law, philosophy, and psychology.

Their Individual Projects had spoken of the power of gratitude to 'lift the fog' of their boredom, procrastination, perfectionism, resentment and lack of motivation, so they could more fully engage with their studies. Many appreciated the power of gratitude as the antithesis of resentment, or the challenge it posed to their inner attitudes of entitlement or victim mentality. An awareness of gratitude invited some of my students to value their time at university more preciously and not squander it. It called upon others to step out of being a passive recipient by taking a perspective of actively giving back. Gratitude also assisted them to feel more connected to others and to the essence of their subjects, so that the learning moment was richer, more memorable.

It seemed that for many students their increased consciousness of gratitude may have activated their memory by reminding them of what others had given in the past, expanding their sense of connectedness and sense of involvement with others, enriching their sense of self. Many reported their enjoyment in being 'co-researchers' in the role of gratitude in their more traditional 'thinking' subjects.

My students' reports of gratitude have similar qualities to those that Tobin Hart holds to be at the core of transformational learning: a change of consciousness, and an emphasis on self-actualising, self-transcendence. In the work of André Compte-Sponville in *A Small Treatise on Great Virtues*, it is virtues such as gratitude that affirm our excellence, our humanity, "...our way of being and acting humanly...our power to act well."[221] In *Ethical Imagining*, Margaret Sommerville talks about transcendence as being essential for transformation, for "becoming our authentic selves". Christopher Peterson and Martin Seligman in their book *Character Strengths*, treat gratitude as a character strength they describe as "transcendent" in quality, and go so far as to define gratitude as that which "allows individuals to forge connections to the larger universe and thereby provide meaning to their lives" because gratitude "connects someone directly to goodness" and "the transcendent emotion of grace – the sense that we have benefited from the actions of another."[222]

I believe my students were able to embrace gratitude as a way of being because they were able to see its relevance to *their* context and an answer to *their* quest to become a better learner. They were encouraged to risk including more of their being in their thinking because of the stories of past students who had applied gratitude to their mainstream subjects and the testimonials of other lecturers who were seeing positive changes in their students. Most importantly, they were inspired by their own successes of practising gratitude in their other subjects.

However, I wonder if gratitude would have taken hold if we had not prepared the ground first by exploring its relevance to the student who is or who becomes awake? I wonder if gratitude could generate greater awakeness if students did not attend to it at their level of being, as required in A State of Preparedness?

Rather than prescribe a way of being, or a certain way of thinking, I invite my students to be 'underway' in their thinking process: to become more aware and then prepare to be able to think in a more total way. It is a process that is continually under review, an ideal to be conscious of, every time one is engaged in the academic learning process. In this way the student is joining in an education process which not only requires thinking with the higher order thinking skills, but also helps them to become better prepared to think more consciously about the impact of their state of being. That is, to think in the way recommended in A State of Preparedness is not an act of will but an act of allowing, of preparing, of being open.

Thus the approach of A State of Preparedness is not a prescription of how to be, but how to be prepared, in one's 'beingness', to hear the call to really think. University and high school education can *invite* the student to 'gather' and 'focus' their whole self on the subject matter in order that they understand, at the level of heart and mind, its essential nature and truth. As my research has shown, students accustomed to a logo-centric framework often do not know how to come to the text with this dimension of beingness. In other words, the current higher order thinking skills such as analysis, logic and critical thinking, do not, in any significant sense, prepare their being.

From their stories of becoming more present in their thinking process, we might constitute a modern-day interpretation of the etymological link between the words 'thinking' and 'thanking'.[223] Heidegger pointed out: "...The old English noun for thought is *thanc* or *thonc* – a thought, a grateful thought."[224] Indeed we see this relationship in other modern languages. For example, in Danish the word 'takke', to thank, is very similar to 'taenke', to think. In German, 'danken', is to thank and 'denken', to think.

Heidegger postulates the question "Is thinking a giving of thanks?" The more we are able to bring our whole self to the thinking process, the more we are expressing gratitude for the ability to think. Although it is not clear which comes first – thinking or thanking – Heidegger is perhaps pointing to the circular relationship between the two. Not only does gratitude promote thinking, but it is crucial to the thinking process itself. As my students showed, the more they thought with gratitude, the more they were truly thinking, because gratitude enabled them to be more present, more awake in their thinking process. In other words, when we think with thanks, we think better.

Cassie wrote to me a week after she began to bring gratitude more consciously and practically into her Masters of Music Education studies, and consequently, her teaching. Her letter speaks of a strong relationship between thinking and thanking.

The past week has been simply so exhilarating. I am astounded at the level of concentration that I am able to sustain as I am reading. I have been trying for months now to get into the routine of study and making myself sit and read for a block of time. My rationale has been one of discipline, but little did I know that what I was missing was essentially to be present and be grateful...I cannot help leaping out of bed in the mornings, anticipating with great excitement the possibility of discovering more about music. This is such an amazingly alive and fresh feeling. My thinking has been so different. The questions that I am generating seem to propel me into discovery mode all the time. And I think I am starting to grasp how to 'thanc'...Lapping up learning as I have never done before, I hope that my students can learn to live this type of learning. Thank you from the bottom of my heart – Thank you for developing "thancs" in my thinking.

CHAPTER 10

TOWARDS COMMUNITIES OF GRATITUDE

A hundred times every day I remind myself that my inner and outer life depend on the labours of other men, living and dead, and that I must exert myself in order to give in the same measure as I have received and am still receiving.[225]
– Albert Einstein

In this chapter we return to Eastgates Primary School to meet with the teachers' gratitude group for the final time that year. We explore how practising gratitude as a group had expanded their notion of gratitude and their sense of community. Our discussion leads on to how this might result in reciprocity from the community and wider society. I bring the themes of the book together as we postulate a way forward where acts of gratitude can move us to actively consider education as a 'gift'. I extend the discussion to wider areas of concern, highlighting, for example, the potential of this approach to foster a greater awareness of the need to give back to the environment, one of the directions where I strongly feel education needs to take us in the future. I conclude the chapter by summarising the educational goals of gratitude that have been demonstrated in each of the themes of this book.

Being real

As I flew into the city for my final meeting for the year with the teachers' gratitude group at Eastgates Primary School, I reflected on the profound impact our time together had had on my own gratitude. Their struggles, dilemmas, and successes helped me engage more honestly with my own understanding and practice. I was inspired to deepen my thinking as I witnessed the graciousness that gratitude gave these teachers when they practised it in times of conflict and adversity. From emails some had sent me since we last met, I sensed that although the conflict regarding the music teacher had not been any less divisive, the group was able to more consciously choose how it was going to respond.

The assistant principal, Julie's, hope at the beginning of the year, as represented by the gratitude posters on her walls and the many messages and sayings she sent out regularly in the weekly newsletters, was that the whole school would be transformed. She had remained being that candle of hope throughout the gratitude work, and the teachers thanked her often for her shining example and strong leadership.

Julie started our meeting by asking us to reflect on the important lessons we had learned in this past year of more consciously practising gratitude, and where the group would like to go from here. As I sat amongst the group I gladly felt that I was no longer leading or facilitating them. They looked to each other for wisdom that came from both a respectful knowledge that they were all facing similar difficulties and that they could draw on an understanding of gratitude from practising it within their lived experience – a life-world that I only had glimpses of in my interactions with them.

Bill was the first to respond, "Well I'm still here," he proudly proclaimed, "and I think I need another year of just focusing on what I receive instead of what I give. It's really helped me survive this year." Stacey told the group that she looked forward to the times when they met, as their meetings were "like doing yoga". Others agreed with Stacey, saying that even though they would often have to fight with the competing demands of other activities to get to their gratitude meetings, and they might feel tired or stressed, most of the time they left feeling more renewed and invigorated. They also felt 'calmer' – a word that came up often in this and other discussions about the benefits of practising gratitude – calmer classrooms, calmer students, calmer within themselves. Kathryn said that if she could not make it to their meetings, she felt that she was missing something very important. The group talked of being inspired by hearing stories of personal transformation and deepening relationships with students or colleagues.

I asked them what had made this group stay together and enabled them to sustain their practice the whole year. They talked of the agreements they had set up at the beginning and how Julie brought them back to these often. Julie pulled out the familiar card where she was collecting a list that their discussion added to as they went along: not to make anyone wrong, not to compare ourselves with others, listen well, maintain confidentiality, no put-downs, try not to judge each other or ourselves, no pulling rank, and that it is okay to speak from the heart and about life outside of school. The reverence and kindness expressed as each person spoke – or didn't speak – revealed a trusting space that had grown stronger over the year. They also shared how being part of the group kept them on their toes, and gave them the structure to keep going with their gratitude practice when there was so much that would distract them otherwise. Whenever they saw each other in the school grounds or in the corridor or staffroom, they would remember their commitment to practise gratitude.

"I've loved how we can be real with each other," Stacey continued the discussion, "how we could talk about areas where it was difficult to practise gratitude and support each other rather than receive judgement or even judge ourselves. Sometimes it was easier for us to practise gratitude at school rather than at home with our kids or partners, or our parents." Then Julie said, "I agree. Discussing gratitude as a group allows us to talk about ourselves as real people, our failings and difficulties and vulnerabilities. We've talked about how guilty some felt about leaving their young children in childcare every morning as they rushed to school, or problems they are having with their teenage children. It's not like getting together as a group to discuss an area of the curriculum or a new resource, where we don't get anywhere near any of the things that are really going on for us as people, or get to know the others in the group so intimately. This has felt like a true community, united in sharing real problems, about us as people."

I could hear in their comments that their gratitude was helping them reach into the undivided self, that Parker J. Palmer argues is at the heart of teaching with integrity, where "every major thread of one's life experience is honoured".[226] They had created a space of sharing and inhabiting lives behind their teacher role, using their discussion of gratitude to explore their authenticity and their integrity.

Then Stacey shared, "We're all busy people, but if others know that you're thankful for their presence, their words, their advice, they'll reveal a bit more of themselves to you and sometimes that's very important. I think you need to get to know the whole person rather than a little snippet of 'did you get that timetable finished?' or whatever. And I think that by having that depth, you have a much better working environment, you gel more, you appreciate one another more, and it has to have great outcomes for your own work environment and certainly for the students too. I think that's because people feel that they're able to be more vulnerable with you, because they trust you because they know that you value them." They were unanimous in their belief that their increased gratitude had helped them be less utilitarian in their relationship with their colleagues and others in the school community.

Dianne spoke next, "I've realised recently that I was receiving more favours than someone who was doing even more work and who was more diligent than I was. My gratitude to this person motivated me to bring this to the attention of the supervisor and make the situation more equitable." The group then spoke of how their increased attention to gratitude helped them become less self-interested and their consciousness of 'the other' extended and expanded. They shared that their discussion of where they were as a school on the gratitude-ingratitude continuum shone an important light on the realisation that there were those in their community who were valued more than others. Groups of parents who came to school association meetings were more valued than those who never came to the school. Parents were more valued than grandparents. Children who came from more functional families were valued more than those who did not. Teachers who were permanent and who had been in the school the longest were more valued than others – especially those who came in on relief teaching or casual contracts. Alternatively, those who were younger teachers with the more recent pedagogy and fresher approaches were more valued than the older teachers. People whom they got along with were more valued than those with whom they didn't. Those who worked in their area and shared common curricula were more valued than those who did not. The group realised that gratitude should be expressed to all, irrespective.

They spoke of how their gratitude to their support staff had become more prominent. Sam told us how he had had numerous problems with the heating system in his room and needed to continually ask the maintenance person for assistance. He decided to make it his gratitude practice to thank him when his heater was working well, not just to contact him when it was not working. Dianne spoke of how much she valued the library support person and recognised her for her love of books and her generous help when Dianne's rowdy students blasted in. Both spoke of the effects of their gratitude on building the 'social capital' in the school. Now they felt they could ask for help anytime and know that others would feel okay about asking them for help. The beneficent cycle of gratitude was spreading far and wide in this school community.

Their community of gratitude practice had led to a different kind of reflection, a deeper understanding of each other's situation, and much closer relationships with each other. In a sense, this community had its own charisma. Gratitude was not just an individual practice. Through their dialogue, it assumed a different form. The meaning of gratitude expanded, deepened and was enlivened as it travelled in different and unexpected directions that it would never have gone to if they were just practising gratitude alone. Their stories of support for each other truly showed how the sum could be greater than its parts. The more people practise gratitude together, the greater the impact.

They also talked of how their notion of 'community' had changed. A focus on gratitude had become a great leveller, a great way to reach a common core that did not rely on status or qualifications or position. Their community of gratitude practice was not a group of like-minded people who had clearly defined goals in mind. In fact they agreed that normally they would not have joined with some of the individuals in the group as they did not have much in common professionally, or in the way they approached their work. They recognised the value their differences had given them – the more diverse angles they discussed, the richer their understanding of the diversity of gratitude. The nature of gratitude itself helped them celebrate their diversity of ideas. A community of gratitude practice can actually unite those who may have difficulty getting along and bring people together in unexpected ways.

Then Katie spoke of one of her biggest difficulties: "I find that the more I consciously practise gratitude, the more some others shun me or want to put me down. Some call me a 'do-gooder' or accuse me of being too idealistic or not being real."

"It hasn't always been easy being part of 'the gratitude group' ", Stella agreed. "Some people label us and then expect far too much of us. They criticise us when they notice that we're not being grateful." They then discussed that at the beginning the gratitude group felt false and a bit forced. Trust did not always come easily, and most admitted that it had taken a year to build. But now they had opened up to a new way of being together, and they could not go back to the old way. The strengths of being together far outweighed the negatives.

"But I'm afraid about what I'm going to do next year," Kathryn said to the group. They all nodded as she told me that she was to be moved to another school where she could not imagine starting a gratitude group. "I won't have the wonderful support that we've found here." I responded to Kathryn by reiterating that we do not need a 'group' to start practising gratitude. I reminded them all that we are always part of a community, and we need to start where we are. From the moment we express gratitude to another, we open ourselves to interconnectedness, and community starts from there.

Although they could see great strength in belonging to a gratitude group, they also discussed how sometimes it was easier to work behind the scenes, to not make any proclamations about gratitude publicly. Gratitude works best, is most gracious, when it is expressed behind the scenes, when it fits into the context and does not stick out as something new or something that others do not have. They saw the wisdom in the decision they had made earlier in the year to have this group as one that supported each other in their own individual gratitude practices, not one where they would practise as a group. But they also spoke of the need to remind themselves that they were not special or necessarily doing anything better than or different to others who were choosing not to belong to their group – they needed to help each other to be vigilant about this.

I asked them to share how they would like to structure the group from here on and what kind of involvement they wanted from me. They said they were ready to take up leadership and responsibility for growing other gratitude groups in the school. They wanted to inspire people with their own example, and each bring someone else to the group next year. I acknowledged to them that communities of practice are best gathered and supported by people within the school rather than an external 'expert'. An outside facilitator might be a resource or a springboard for ideas or ways of addressing challenges, but it is wise to hand it over to those at the coal face as soon as possible. In fact, experts are not needed. A commitment to the potential of gratitude in education and an understanding of the landscape of gratitude in the school is a wonderful starting point.

Gratitude to the 'system': an ongoing practice

"I've actually started to be grateful for the education system itself since joining this gratitude group. Have you noticed that I've stopped complaining about the minister for education lately?" Stacey asked the group. "I value institutions a lot more than I used to in the past because I can see that they at least give you a framework to work in. A lot of everyday things are looked after by the system, so I don't need to worry about anything." The group agreed that complaint about the system took up much discussion time within the school. Sam continued in agreement with Stacey,

"Before, I used to think that I could only change once the system changes. But now I realise that the system has not been set up to care for people. It can't care for people. We need to care for each other. I never thought I would see the day when I would admit this, but this is what gratitude has opened me up to!"

"But the system can't work without the humanised teacher," Katie jumped in, "As teachers go on with their practice of gratitude and become brighter, maybe the system will honour ways of valuing the characteristics of the heart part of teaching, not just the delivery of the curriculum, but qualities like 'good at caring for others', or 'kindness', or 'generosity'."

"Sorry, but I just don't share your same views about the system" Bill said. "I believe it's doing an awful job of looking after us, even on a systems level. I think it's becoming more and more neglectful and punitive. I just can't find much gratitude for a system that doesn't express any gratitude for the people within it, but in fact seems to go out of its way to express ingratitude! Look at what they are trying to do now", he contested, "with all this testing of students. This data is going to determine our ranking and pay scale. What kind of message of gratitude to teachers is that?"

Tipene added, "and then the media gets hold of the so-called bad test results and publishes them! Rarely do we hear what teachers are doing right." Stacey proposed, "so society needs to learn more about what teachers do and who teachers are, and they need to learn how to critique what the media is feeding them. But I don't think our gratitude practice should have these aims, because that makes our gratitude conditional. Maybe we should focus on what teaching gives us?"

Kathryn answered this by saying, "It's the relationships that keep most of us in the profession – our relationships between our colleagues and our students and our community. That's why our gratitude is so important, as it keeps these relationships healthy". Then Dianne spoke of why she was delighted with the gratitude work as it was opening up the same kind of ethos that permeated her previous school, which, to her was "the best school in the world", even though it was by far the toughest. "I knew that my colleagues valued what I did because they would tell me, and tell me often. For example one said, 'I really need to congratulate you on how far you have brought your kids this year. Just the way they carry themselves and the way they speak and the way they are focused on their work and work really hard and the way they treat each other. And that's because of you.' It was a small school, and we were all quite good with that at our school, at just saying what we valued in each other. It came naturally. It can't be arbitrary, it has to be deliberate and worked on." Dianne's description opened the discussion to how much relationships are really important and need to be worked on and not taken for granted, meaning that gratitude needs to be more than ritualistic.

Julie suggested another point, "As we start valuing our role as teachers more, I can imagine that society will start to do so as well." They went on to discuss how much teaching as a profession was undervalued, to the point where sometimes they were reluctant to admit they were a teacher. Kathryn then shared, "When I was starting to think about going back to do teaching as my second degree – it took me a while because my kids needed to be a bit older – many people I told warned me that this choice would be a waste of my talent and my mind. Even my own mother told me that, and she's a teacher! That gave me a really good idea of how teaching is undervalued in society. Most people recognise that you get lost in the system."

"How can the system manage change better than it does now?" Bill asked the group. His question started a strong discussion where the teachers talked about feeling that new ideas and curricula were "inflicted upon them", without being asked if they wanted or needed the change. They highlighted the fact that there is much cynicism out in the teaching world because change has been managed in a disrespectful way. Teachers feel the lack of consultation as a sign of ingratitude. Even if they are good teachers, those who have been involved in many cycles of change tend to retreat to their individual corner to protect themselves, to preserve their energy and their self-esteem. They have given all their enthusiasm and energy to one change, one new curriculum, and before they have recovered, another one comes along to replace it. Julie summarised the feeling, "so what we are saying underneath all this, is that the way change has been introduced actually works against a sense of community."

What about parents?

"What about our role as it's seen by parents?" Dianne asked. "Gratitude from parents goes such a long way, just a few words of thanks, noticing that their child is learning better, or that they're happier, or that they have friends." The group discussed how they felt that gratitude from parents had declined dramatically over the past decade. They felt that they were seen as someone who was employed by the parents, rather than someone who was giving something precious to their child – further evidence of being caught in the grip of the exchange paradigm. Stacey invited us to consider this in a different way, "I think we need to be more compassionate about why some parents don't express gratitude to us. I don't think they feel they can come and talk to us on an equal footing. I find that when I open up to them about my own failings as a parent, all the barriers come down. They see you as a teacher straight away, but they don't see you as a person until you see them and show yourself as a person. If you have a difficult child in your class, that parent has a difficult child too, so for me in talking to the parent you are always allies. You unite in how you feel you can move forward. To have that relationship, there needs to be a sense of win-win, so there's no power games going on or blame being thrown around."

Then Julie said, "And haven't we noticed a dramatic effect from the parents' gratitude group?" She recalled some of the experiences of the twelve parents who had regularly met over the past year to share their practices and challenges. Many mirrored the teachers' experiences, and they too became a close-knit group who supported each other. All of the parents valued the opportunity to gather together and share their limitations as parents and took comfort in not feeling alone in their struggles.

One of these parents took leadership in organising a cross-cultural food event as a mark of gratitude to her child's school. Teachers were invited to come along for a delicious banquet, provided with gratitude and at no cost. That parent reported that her gratitude practice increased her confidence and gave her a greater sense of connectedness with the school community. Another parent had been too shy to nominate herself to be part of the school association committee, but decided to make that her gratitude practice. Being able to take such action as part of a gratitude group gave them the opportunity and pretext to take the initiative in areas that they had wanted to for some time, but felt too embarrassed.

Some parents reported turning their relationships with their children around by focusing on their good points, and not being disappointed in what they felt they were not doing. Others worked alongside the teacher of their child, where they united in a gratitude practice, and noticed marked improvements in their child's learning and behaviour. One parent took the initiative of thanking the teacher in front of their child, modelling behaviour that was eventually picked up by the child.

"It's such a privilege to have parents who have come on board so actively with the gratitude project from the start," I acknowledged to the Eastgates teachers, "and one that is perhaps quite rare." I took this opportunity to share with them the differences I had experienced with the parent communities at other schools.

Millbrook teachers recognised that they first needed to express gratitude to parents, making a bridge towards better relationships. They were seeing that small practices went a long way to improving parents' and teachers' attitudes. The principal at Palmwood College had organised a gratitude workshop for parents, and everyone was very excited about the possibilities of this being an important first step in increasing gratitude in this school community. A big pot of hot chicken soup was brewed in the hope of a big turnout, but only two parents turned up. The principal kept apologising for the small attendance, but I saw it as a statement of enormous potential for where the gratitude work needed to be directed in the future.

"Yes, we are incredibly lucky with our parent community," Julie said, "and maybe if we looked more consciously for what we receive from the parents, our music program troubles would have been put in a better perspective." The group spoke of the power of the unity between teacher, parent and child, and how deeply they valued gratitude from parents. As Dianne said, "when a parent actually comes and talks to you or when they let you into their lives, that's when it all happens. It's not about an exchange. It's just seeing it as the community it can be, and valuing it. But for this to happen we need to move past the professional distance we tend to make between ourselves as teachers, and them as parents. We are, first of all, people." Our discussion helped us recognise that we needed to extend our community of gratitude practice to parents, not just teachers.

Envisaging and remembering gratitude

I asked the group to share their vision of an education system that had active and conscious gratitude more fully at its core. They talked of a more dynamic relationship where there was a constant flow of giving and receiving from all involved; a school where staff, students and parents feel equally and genuinely valued by each other[227] – increasing self-esteem, improving health, growing resilience and reducing bullying. They imagined the words they used and the tone of their communication would reflect truth, goodness and beauty. Staff and students would be more confident and skilled in expressing their complaint in proactive ways. As they progressed through high school and beyond, students would be engaged in their learning, taking responsibility for their State of Preparedness and what they can give to their learning situation. Everything would matter, time would not be wasted, and there would be nothing that was taken for granted. All the materials would be treated more preciously. Education would be treasured. Communities would feel more cohesive and supportive. We knew that this was reaching toward an ideal, but we also knew that it was a wonderful goal to strive for.

Our discussion highlighted how strong the metaphor of education as "the gift" is in the giving and receiving dynamic of teaching and learning. I asked how we could express more gratitude for education so that it was treasured as a gift. If we do not proactively celebrate education as a gift, we stand to lose what we value most about it. So many great aspects of education seem to disappear because the gift was valued only by the people involved, who did not take the extra step to publicly celebrate and value what they treasured. We cannot wait until governments announce that they are going to shut schools before we publicly acclaim what we are grateful for in them. The best way to express gratitude to our schools and our teachers is to publicly celebrate them often and in as many forums as possible – to continually remember to express our gratitude.

Most teachers feel that education is not only a right, it is also a privilege. But if education were to be packaged as a gift, rather than a commodity, would people be more willing to open it up and look inside with wonder and awe? If we were to celebrate the gift of education within our communities, would more people be willing to protect what we value in education when it is threatened with removal? For example, if we did so, next time there is a new program that is going to be introduced that does not represent what we hold as valuable for our students' learning, we may be in a stronger position to voice our concerns because of the informed understanding of the community about what is going to be replaced. Or, when a casual teacher is valued and the community is publicly alerted to the gifts they bring, there would be a ground force of support for retaining that teacher if his or her job was going to be taken away.

The group then spoke of ways in which they could celebrate education more fully than they do at present, by exuding more joy and passion for their curriculum area and the art of teaching, informing parents at parent-teacher nights what they are grateful for in their role, or celebrating the less obvious and tangible successes in the staff room or in newsletters. They also talked of teachers and school leaders who were shining examples of doing this well.

"Although there are some good examples of people at Eastgates who celebrate the gift of education, on the whole we've lost the art of celebrating what we have," Tipene spoke. She went on to relay something that was also discussed by Afke Komter.[228] In the Maori culture a fundamental rule of gift giving is that the thing that is given and received is active, it has a life. Whenever one is given something, they must find a way to continue the chain of giving by giving back in some way, but it must be of greater value than the gift they were given, and one must give of themselves, not just an inanimate object. "So we need to revive the power of the gift as something very vibrant and alive, not something dead and packaged in documents and procedures," Tipene said.

She then went on "but now we're so busy and so performance driven we've forgotten to do this when we have truly great learning happening in our school." And then Katie added, "Yes, but when we do celebrate our successes or what we value in our teaching, people sometimes think that we're boasting. Our ego and the resultant vulnerability stop us from celebrating what we value in education."

"But we are vulnerable to losing too much if we're not courageous enough to move past what people think of us, and to stand up humbly and honestly for what we value the most in education and what we do! The gift of education needs our custodianship," I spoke to them passionately. Our lack of public expression of gratitude for the gift of education is making it so silent and invisible that its very essence seems too easily replaceable. I shared with them that in my context the rapid introduction of on-line teaching was a classic example of this for me. I admitted that the world of on-line learning and associated technologies has brought great advantages and created educational opportunities for many who would not have otherwise been in a position to engage in these. However, this does not take away from the fact that because we did not publicly value the gift of the embodied dynamic of the teacher-student relationship[229], we did not value the teaching moment where we could powerfully recognise our students, it became easy for our teacher presence, in its fullest and most educationally potent form, to be replaced by a machine.

Gratitude to the environment

How we could express gratitude to the environment was a topic that arose nearly every time we met as a group. Because we did not express enough gratitude for, and publicly value, our ecosystem and the many wonderful species of plants and animals, many have now been lost, some never to return. The increased consciousness of gratitude amongst this group of teachers made them more aware of how much materials were being wasted, lights being left on unnecessarily, paper being thrown out without being recycled, food in the canteen being discarded. Some had embraced the notion that gratitude for materials meant acting on what we valued, so they would make it their gratitude practice to treat materials preciously. They felt even more passionate about modelling this to their students.

"Do you know that at the high school where my wife teaches," Sam continued the discussion, "they now need to get a special cleaner in on the weekends to pick up all the rubbish, as the maintenance people that are employed by the school just can't deal with it anymore. Apparently the students see it beneath them to pick up rubbish or to dispose of it in a civil way. If the teachers get the students to pick up rubbish, they have parents phoning up to complain, saying, 'I'm not sending my kid to school to pick up rubbish!' Yet those same students are doing big projects on saving the planet, or stopping deforestation!"

"But we need to help our students to see that what they're doing makes a difference, and that we are part of a much bigger picture. Most of the time they can't see past their self-interests," Dianne suggested. "But we adults can't get past our self-interests either, so how can we expect our youth to be able to?" Katie replied. "It's really interesting looking at the carbon tax thing at the moment. It amazes me the way people complain about it, and see it all in economic terms. Even for so many wealthy people, it all comes down to how much it's going to cost them, rather than it being seen as an opportunity to repay the environment, to treat it as a gift."

"It would require us to hold a vision where we are happy to make self-sacrifices," Julie continued. "One of the important things I've learned by being involved in the gratitude work this year, has been how satisfying and rewarding it is to go beyond our selves. The old way of thinking is that if we go out of our way to connect with someone else, to value them, then we would lose out, because it may inconvenience us. But I've found giving more consciously to others to be so much more rewarding and satisfying."

Then Katie asked the group: "How do we teach gratitude for the environment? Now that is the trillion dollar question that we must all find creative ways to answer!"

"I think it starts with our empathy with the students," Sam suggested. "You have to care about people properly before you can care about the environment properly.

People think they can go and save the planet by going to social action meetings but then come back and scream at their partner or fight with their colleagues. Perhaps more gratitude between teachers will model that caring empathy, so that students can exude this more fully themselves." Then Katie continued along the same lines, "Perhaps there's even an earlier step than this. First we need to value ourselves, and then we will know how to value others. Then you can empathise with other people better, and see the impact you have on other people, and this would just naturally extend to having empathy for the environment."

I suggested that we need to be able to see the beauty and value in nature in order to be motivated to protect it. Our gratitude helps us to see and feel its sacredness. As Marion Schiltz and her colleagues write, "when we see the sacredness of all life, we naturally want to care for it..."[230] It is from appreciating nature that we can inspire more gratitude in our students – gratitude for their senses, for their bodies, for the beauty around them. Nature can teach us so much of what we need to learn about humility, acceptance, resilience, beauty, and connectedness. Nature is calling us all the time to take note of its beauty, but our distraction stops us from hearing that call.[231] Gratitude can also play a vital role in removing the clouds of resentment and worry so that we can be more present to being connected to nature. We need to invite our students into A State of Preparedness, where they are more able to be moved by the magnificence of nature and more humble in recognition of their reliance on its offerings. Again, an inner attitude of gratitude is a precursor to taking action and seeing the big picture.

As the time to finish was drawing near, we agreed that this was a very fitting point to reach. "This is such a big topic, and so important, why don't we make it our goal for the gratitude group next year?" Julie suggested to the teachers, and they agreed.

I thanked them all for what they had given me, and what they had taught me about gratitude in education, and their inspiration of how a gratitude community could set the tone of a whole school. In my parting words to them, I recalled the "ethical imagining" that Margaret Somerville invites us into, where we shift our culture from that of entitlement to one of responsibility. She says, "making that shift is crucial to our own protection, and to the protection of nature, far into the future".[232] Such responsibility can only come from a sense of connectedness to what we owe others rather than what we are owed, vitalised by approaching our lives as a quest for what we can give back. Taking this responsibility calls for our vigilant celebration as a community of the gifts we have received from each other and nature...with gratitude.

Gratitude and its educational imperative

As I was nearing the end of writing this book, many asked me why it took nearly a decade to develop. I feel that to deepen my understanding of gratitude in the context of education, I have needed every moment of contemplation, every incident of personal adversity, every critique from my protagonists, and every interaction with the hundreds of people I have had the privilege of working with. I am also asked what has kept up my interest. I reply by saying that this topic will continue to be my life's work, but it feels like I am only just starting. It is a jewel as a practitioner and researcher in the field of education to find a topic that I believe offers so much to such a wide cross-section of people in the educational community – students, parents, teachers at all levels of education, counsellors, leaders and administrators. Each time they discuss gratitude it comes alive in a different form, as more questions are asked that delve more deeply into its meaning.

How gratifying it is to be working in an area that goes beyond the traditional divide between private and public worlds, and that allows me to bring every major thread of my life experience to it. How liberating it is to be working within a field that goes beyond the traditional focus on narrow conceptions of content and curriculum. How fortuitous to be researching in an area, which only a decade ago was dismissed by so many academics whom I met, but is now overlapping topics that are gaining key prominence in the renewed focus on character, citizenship, and values education.

Some teachers wonder why we need a whole book on the importance of gratitude in education. For them, gratitude comes so easily and naturally that it is already part of their teacher ethic. They do not see the need to emphasise it, or discuss it in such depth. However, when I invite them to move beyond a focus on their own individual practice, and to consider the place of gratitude in educational communities, many are quick to identify what I have discussed in this book as a "malaise". My work on gratitude has shone a torch on a discourse that is a common theme throughout every community that I have worked in: the malaise of toxic complaint and the largely unrecognised impact of this on the learning and teaching moment. As I have said in various chapters in this book, when teachers are full of negative complaint, their inner attitude flows to their students. When students have an inner attitude of complaint, they cannot be present enough to learn.

For those who consider the primary purpose of education to be the delivery of content or information, my position on the importance of gratitude may be too radical a view. But if we look for a moment at the possibility of how much that information can come alive, can be more deeply felt and understood, if students were invited into a deeper and more embodied appreciation of its very essence, it may not be as big a jump as it first appears. For example, how can an optometry student be awake in their study of the science of the eye and how to care for other people's eyes, if they have not first gained a deep appreciation for the gift of sight and the eye itself?

Of course, gratitude may seem more relevant for those who aspire towards transformational goals such as personal re-formation or self-actualisation.

The dimensions of my work that further these goals are the importance of A State of Preparedness, the pre-condition of awakeness, the invitation to step into a giving paradigm, to unashamedly step into our sense of indebtedness, and in fact to celebrate it.

It is important to stress that I am not saying that gratitude is the only transformative force for healthy educational communities or enacting powerful pedagogy. Nor does it stand in its own right, separate from the many other qualities of a good teacher or student or community.

Tobin Hart says that in the process of transformation, something is lost and something is gained. If we ask what is lost if we practise more gratitude in education, we may see that we lose an all-consuming focus on the content and task, and a performance-driven view of the student and teacher. If we ask what is gained, we may see that we gain a focus on the interrelationship between thinking and being, the integrity of an undivided self, and a heightened recognition of our interconnectedness. We move away from an exchange paradigm that sees education as a 'bargain across the counter', one of receiving that generates a sense of entitlement, and we move towards a gift paradigm that sees education as a dynamic interplay of giver, receiver and gift, that creates a flourishing community.

For gratitude to have a role in education's move into the gift paradigm may require us to take a radical view. This is one where gratitude is not easy to define or contain or measure by empirical means, and certainly one that looks different for each individual and context. We need to understand gratitude through our hearts and through our practice to fully realise its potential in our lives. To access it only as a theory may not allow it to play its transformative part in our teaching and learning. Expressing gratitude to people and in situations that we do not like is often the most radical and counterintuitive option, but it is one that gives moral cohesion to our communities and creates environments of trust, so that our students can be present enough to learn.

The notion of 'student-centredness' has gained popularity in current discourse, and this is certainly a healthier perspective than the teacher-centred models of the past. However, I believe this image has done us a disservice in some ways. If we think of the community as a circle, a hoop, with the students at the centre receiving from those around them, we may be robbing our students of the opportunity to take responsibility for what they can give to their learning community. Perhaps a healthier perspective is one where we require them to be able to take different positions within the hoop at different times, and to connect more fully with those outside their own selves, allowing them the opportunity to move from receiving to giving mode?

Our starting point is not trying to fix students or "coach them in emotions" of happiness. Our imperative is educational not therapeutic. Ecclestone and Hayes argue that:

Calling education 'transformative' is shorthand for the transformative power of human beings to try to change the world, and, in doing so, to change themselves. In the present climate, the focus has shifted completely away from changing the world towards changing yourself in order to accept your vulnerability and human frailty and then to be coached to have 'appropriate' emotions associated with wellbeing.[233]

When we ask students to consider practising gratitude, our starting point is not one of "vulnerability" or "human frailty". Rather it is one that invites our students to seek out a higher level of presence in their learning and to explore the role of gratitude in achieving this.

With our own gratitude practice at the heart of our pedagogy, we are not so much masters of theory or philosophy about gratitude, but simply practitioners who realise that it takes a lifetime to grow. Our initial focus would not be on embedding gratitude in the content of a curriculum. First, we need to establish the conditions within ourselves and within our classrooms, to create the right environment for gratitude to flourish in its own time, at its own pace. The conditions for teaching gratitude arise from our own commitment and lived experience of its true educational value, our State of Preparedness, and our recognition of our connectedness to the human essence of the other.

The educational imperative relates to us encouraging our students to be awake in their learning and to bring this quality of awakeness to other areas of their lives. Our goal becomes one of inviting our students to contemplate the role gratitude may play in this process and to engage in critical thinking about its value for them as the author of their own life. As Li, one of my students who was studying optometry, recognised:

I think that showing gratitude for the simple things in life is important in the optometric profession. Although most people do not give much thought to their eyes, optometrists have been trained to care for the health of the communities' eyes. The skills I learnt in this tutorial have not only helped me to become a better university student, but will eventually help me to become a better optometrist. Despite being a mere first-year, I have learnt that sight is a blessing – taking into account all the beautiful things we see. I hope that the patients I will see as an optometrist feel the positive attitude I attain from showing gratitude toward life....

NOTES

Chapter 1

[1] Visser (2009, p. 327).
[2] See Lovat, Toomey, Clement, Crotty, & Nielson (2009).
[3] See Gibbs (2006).
[4] For examples of applications of positive psychology to education, see: Chan (2010); Froh, Miller, & Snyder (2007); Froh,, Kashdan, Ozimkowski, K., & Miller, N. (2009); Froh, J., Yurkewicz, C., & Kashdan, T. (2009); Froh, Bono, & Emmons (2010); McCraty & Childre (2004); Seligman (2009); Seligman 2011; Seligman, Ernst, Gillham, Reivich, & Linkins (2009); Unsworth, Turner, Williams, & Houle (2010).
[5] Taylor (1989).
[6] Giddens (1990, 1991).
[7] Tarnas (1991).
[8] Barnett (2004).
[9] For good overview of the influences of some of these thinkers see Harpham (2004, p. 19-36).
[10] Bono, Emmons, & McCullough (2004, p. 473) discuss these states at greater length.
[11] This was cited in Dale, M. (2004, p.66).
[12] Dale (2004, p. 67).
[13] Vaughan & Estola (2008, p.24).
[14] Taylor (1989).
[15] As the sociologist Anthony Giddens (1991) remarks, we live in a time where many are left with "a feeling that life has nothing worthwhile to offer".
[16] Dale (2004, p. 67).
[17] Williams (2011).
[18] Anne Game and Andrew Metcalfe also discuss the notion of the gift as it relates to education. For example see Game & Metcalfe (2010).
[19] Vaughan & Estola (2008, p. 24).
[20] Roberts (2004, p. 65).
[21] Ecclestone & Hayes (2009a, 2009b).
[22] Ecclestone & Hayes (2009b, p. x).
[23] Ecclestone & Hayes (2009b, p. xii).
[24] John Van Maanen (1988) describes this as 'impressionist tales', where "...Reflective, meditative themes may develop from the story and spin off in a number of fieldworker-determined directions. The story itself, the impressionist tale, is a representational means of cracking open the culture and the fieldworker's way of knowing so that both can be jointly examined...The epistemological aim is then to braid the knower with the known..." p. 102.
[25] Where appropriate and necessary, I have always sought permission and ethics approval for these to be recorded.

Chapter 2

[26] This is a pseudonym as are the names of other schools in the book.
[27] For a more detailed account of the impact of gratitude for school leaders see Howells (2009).
[28] Palmer (2007).
[29] Palmer (1998, p. 10).
[30] Emmons & Hill (2001, p. 88).
[31] Emmons & McCullough (2004).
[32] This is a summary of findings from researchers as documented in Emmons & McCullough (2004).

NOTES

33 McCraty & Childre (2004, p. 248).
34 Emmons & Crumpler (2000, p. 59).
35 Emmons & Hill (2001, p. 20).
36 Fiumara (1990).
37 Fiumara's work on a "philosophy of listening" suggests a way of being with the thinking process which she calls "dwelling", which requires an "orientation towards openness", which the logo-centric tradition, in its search for certainty, destroys. This demands a relationship with thinking which does not revolve around grasping, mastering and using, but rather one which is "anchored to humility and faithfulness". It requires that "we dwell with, abide by, whatever we try to know; that we aim at coexistence-with rather than knowledge-of" (1991, p. 15).
38 Quoted in Emmons (2004, p. 12).

Chapter 3

39 As discussed by McCullough, Kirkpatrick, Emmons, & Tsang (2001).
40 O'Sullivan (2001).
41 Hart (2001).
42 Palmer (2007).
43 Ferrer & Tarnas (2001).
44 Solomon (2004, p. 282).
45 Atwood (2008, p. 1).
46 Cousens (2010).
47 McCullough, Emmons, & Tsang (2002, p. 115).
48 Erenreich (2009).
49 Emmons (2004, p. 5).
50 Seligman, Ernst, Gillham, Reivich, & Linkins (2009, p. 304-305).
51 See McCullough, Kirkpatrick, Emmons, & Tsang (2001).
52 Emmons & Crumpler (2000).
53 Harpham (2004, p. 21).
54 Emmons (2004, p. 4).
55 ibid. (p. 4). Here he is citing Pruyser.
56 Komter (2004, p. 201).
57 This is discussed extensively in the literature on gratitude and ethics. See for example Berger, 1975; Camenish, 1981; Fitzgerald, 1998; Knowles, 2002; Lyons, 1969; McConnell, 1993; and White (1999).
58 I have recently explored the notion of gratitude in the context of pre-service teaching, see Howells & Cumming (2012).
59 Emmons & Crumpler, (2000).
60 This definition was first published in Howells (2007).
61 Buck (2004, p. 11).
62 Visser (2009).
63 Compte-Sponville (1996).
64 Taylor (1989).
65 Greene (1988).
66 Greene (1988, p. 22).
67 Sommerville (2006, p. 14).
68 MacKinnon (2011) taken from extract published in Sunday Times, Perth, July 24, 2011, p. 95.
69 For a full exploration of different cultural interpretations and nuances, please see Visser (2009).
70 Hart (2001, p. 86).
71 ibid. (p. 10).
72 Singer (2007, p. 28).
73 Mugerauer (1998, p. 13).

Chapter 4

[74] Suzuki (1995, p. 141).
[75] Shelton, C. (2004, p. 273).
[76] Suzuki, S. (1983, p. 18).
[77] Dewey (1933, 1938).
[78] Fitzgerald (1998, p 120).
[79] Steindl-Rast (1984, p. 27).
[80] ibid. (p. 22).
[81] Jones & O'Neil (2003, p. 5).
[82] Steindl-Rast (1984, p. 27).
[83] Fredrickson (2004, p. 151).
[84] ibid. (p. 65).
[85] Peterson & Seligman (2004, p. 526).
[86] Schlitz, Veitan, & Amorok (2007, p. 93).
[87] ibid. (p. 93).
[88] ibid. (p. 92).
[89] McCullough, Kirkpatrick, Emmons & Tsang (2001); McCullough, Emmons & Tsang (2002).
[90] Stewart-Robertson (1990).
[91] Komter (2004, p. 195).
[92] Friere (1993).
[93] Harpham, E. (2004, p.21).
[94] Buck (2004, p. 110).
[95] Steindl-Rast, D. (1984, p.19).
[96] White, P. (1999, p. 48).
[97] Harpham (2004, p. 19).
[98] Quoted in Schlitz, Veitan & Amorok (2007, p. 110).

Chapter 5

[99] In Knowles (2004, p. 845).
[100] Maslow held that gratitude is one of the characteristics of self-actualisation where those who reach this level have the ability to " 'appreciate again and again, freshly and naively, the basic goods of life with awe, pleasure, wonder, and even ecstasy, however stale these experiences have become' " (cited in Emmons & Shelton, 2002, p. 460).
[101] Williamson (1992, p. 190).
[102] Johnson (2005).
[103] For an example of a critique see Miller (2009).
[104] Fredrickson (2004, 2009).
[105] Fredrickson (2004, p. 147).
[106] ibid. (p. 149).
[107] ibid. (p. 149).
[108] ibid. (p. 149).
[109] ibid. (p. 149).
[110] ibid. (p. 150).
[111] ibid. (p. 150).
[112] ibid. (p. 153).
[113] ibid. (p. 153).
[114] ibid. (p. 151).
[115] ibid. (p. 151).

NOTES

Chapter 6

[116] Palmer (2007, p. 16).
[117] Visser (2009, p. 389).
[118] ibid. (p. 389).
[119] ibid. (p. 389).
[120] ibid. (p. 390).
[121] ibid. (p. 391).
[122] Noddings (1999, p. 192).
[123] This is also called a "flow-on effect" and is consistent with other literature on gratitude. For example, see Fredrickson 2004; McAdams & Bauer, 2004; Toledo-Pereyra, 2006; and Wood, Froh, & Geraghty, 2010.
[124] White (1999, p. 47).
[125] Buber (1947, 1958).
[126] Jung (1983).
[127] Taylor (1989, 1995a, 1995b).
[128] Sommerville (2006).
[129] Kiekegaard (1962).
[130] See, for example, Fox (1979); Heubner (1985); Miller (1993, 2000); Palmer (1993).
[131] Visser (2009, p. 374).
[132] Taylor (1989, p. 27).
[133] Sommerville (2006, p. 2).
[134] Taylor (1989, p. 59).
[135] See Taylor (1995b).
[136] Taylor (1995a, p. 63).
[137] Simmel (1996, p. 45).
[138] Many researchers in the field of positive psychology report on the pro-social effects of gratitude, where it can contribute to building healthier relationships and enhance social behaviour. For example, empirical studies have confirmed that there is a correlation between a grateful disposition and "prosocial" states such as empathy, forgiveness, emotional support, and willingness to help others (McCullough, Emmons & Tsang (2002); Tsang (2006)). Also see Bartlett & DeStono (2006).
[139] ibid. (p. 45).
[140] ibid. (p. 46).
[141] Saul (2001, p. 127).
[142] Noddings (1992).
[143] Noddings (2002, p. 2).
[144] Noddings,.(1998, p. 187) cited in Smith (2004).
[145] Rodgers & Raider-Roth (2006, p. 265).
[146] ibid. (p. 274).
[147] ibid. (p. 270).
[148] Palmer (1998, p. 10).
[149] Palmer (2007, p. 16).
[150] ibid. (p. 16).
[151] Holmes (1991, p. 11)
[152] Midgley (1991, p. 44).
[153] Visser (2009, p. 374).
[154] Emmons & Shelton (2002, p. 446).
[155] Emmons & Hill (2001, p. 5).
[156] Bono & McCullogh (2006).
[157] Other examples of how this is discussed is as the opposite of resentment (Roberts, 2004; Fitzgerald, 1998); vengeance (Solomon, 2004), and complaint (Bowen, 2007; Stein, 1989). Emmons (2003) also discusses the impact of some of these states in the workplace.
[158] Schon (1984).

[159] Burch (1990).
[160] Greene (1988, 1995).
[161] Greene (1988, p. 9).
[162] Ibid. (p. 9).
[163] Visser (2009, p. 390).
[164] Some also like to write in the mornings to engage their State of Preparedness. As Max Van Manen (1990) notes, "To write is to exercise self-consciousness". For him, writing is a way of revealing to the writer a reality that cannot be seen until it is written. Letting words flow freely on the page, free of an inner critical voice, can help us celebrate the joys that an increased gratitude is generating in our lives, and capture events that would otherwise be lost in the busyness of competing demands. In writing we take notice, and celebrate what we see, in a more embedded form.

Chapter 7

[165] Roberts (2004, p. 68).
[166] Komter (2004, p. 196).
[167] Visser (2009, p. 321-2).
[168] Buck (2004, p. 110).
[169] Fitzgerald (1998, p.127).
[170] Ibid. (p. 120).
[171] As described in Baron (1995).
[172] Covey (2006).
[173] ibid. (p. 4).
[174] Tschannen-Moran (2004).
[175] ibid. (p. 15).
[176] ibid. (p. 19-20).
[177] ibid. (p. 135).
[178] Visser (2009, p. 374).
[179] Rodgers & Raider-Roth (2006, p. 277).
[180] Roberts (2004, p. 66).
[181] ibid. (p. 68).
[182] ibid. (p. 67).
[183] Einstein (1956).
[184] Jung (1983).
[185] Capra (2010, p. 31).
[186] Visser (2009, p. 312).
[187] Cited in Covey (2006, p. 12).

Chapter 8

[188] Kahlil Gibran.
[189] Unsatisfactory relationships with colleagues and school leaders are cited as even more significant causes of stress and burnout than teacher-student relations (Nias, 1996; Tronman, 2000). A focus on teacher emotion should not only consider social relationships but also how emotion is "embedded in school culture, ideology, and power relations" (Zembylas, 2003, p. 113). Many reasons have been proposed in the literature for why collegiality is declining in schools. Declining autonomy; loss of control and self-efficacy with increased managerialism and constant restructuring (Dearlove, 1997); work overload and diversification, and lack of job security with increased casualisation of the workforce (Tronman, 2000) are just a few. For recent exploration of teacher causes of teacher stress, also see Guglielmi & Tatrow (1998); Hargreaves (1998); Howard & Johnson (2004); Kyriacou, (2001).
[190] Campbell (1945, 1988, 2004).
[191] Campbell (1988, p. 46).

NOTES

[192] In Barks (2004, p. 109).
[193] Leunig (1990).
[194] Troutner (1974, p. 152).
[195] McPhail, (1995).
[196] For reference to some of these findings, empirical research on the effects of gratitude suggests that it can create peace of mind and have a positive effect on stress levels (Emmons & McCullough, 2003; Roberts, 2004). In addition, stress levels may also be reduced by the practice of gratitude due to its ability to enhance feelings of wellbeing (Emmons & McCullough, 2003; McAdams & Bauer, 2004; Watkins, 2004); improve moods (Watkins, Woodward, Stone, & Kolts, 2003); dissolve regret (Roberts, 2004); enable one to be less susceptible to "such emotions as disappointment, regret, and frustration" (Roberts, 2004)); have a positive impact on depression; and increase optimism (Emmons & Shelton, 2002).
[197] Emmons & Shelton (2002, p. 468).
[198] Frankl (1985).
[199] ibid. (p.131).
[200] ibid. (p. 133).
[201] ibid. (p. 99).
[202] ibid. (p. 136).

Chapter 9

[203] Greene (1997).
[204] Heidegger (1968).
[205] The kind of awakeness and the ways in which one can assist students to attain this are many and varied. Here I am discussing what has been effective for university and Year 11 and 12 students. For those students in the younger years, it may be as basic as caring for their nutritional needs before they are able to concentrate enough to learn. The main point here is to ensure that we have attended to this first, before starting to teach content.
[206] Csikszentmihalyi (2000); Csikszentmihalyi & Csikszentmihalyi (1992).
[207] Heidegger (1971, p. 143).
[208] These were the questions that dominated research into the deep/ surface distinctions in approaches to learning, e.g. Marton, Dall-Alba & Beatty (1993).
[209] As was illustrated in the quote from Troutner in the previous chapter.
[210] Palmer (1998, p. 42).
[211] Greene (1988, p. 9).
[212] Froh, Miller & Snyder (2007, p. 7).
[213] ibid (p. 9).
[214] Visser (2009 p. 312).
[215] As identified by Laurillad (1993).
[216] See Marton, Dall-Alba & Beatty (1993).
[217] Law (2007, p. 166).
[218] Nielsen (2011).
[219] Hart (2001, p. 10).
[220] ibid. (p. 107).
[221] Comte-Sponville (1996, p. 3).
[222] Peterson & Seligman (2004, p. 524).
[223] Visser (2009) and Steindl Rast (2004) also discuss the relationship between thanking and enhanced thinking processes.
[224] Heidegger (1968, p. 139).

Chapter 10

[225] Einstein (1956, p. 1)

[226] Palmer (1998, p. 16).

[227] At tertiary level the triad is management, teachers and students.

[228] Komter (2004).

[229] There were so few articles or pedagogy around the ontological dimension of the teacher, about the significance of their embodied presence in the classroom, perhaps because this could not be measured, that we lost a sense of its importance. In her book, Digital Hemlock, Tara Brabazon (2002) astutely captures many dimensions of what we have lost, and says so much in her one statement: "It is a tough era for a teacher with a body." p. 103. And that, "…one of the reasons it has been so easy to celebrate online education is because we have neither theorised nor admitted how flesh, blood and bone function in our classrooms…"p. 104.

[230] Schiltz, Veitan & Amorok (2007, p. 187).

[231] Red Indians, Aborigines and other indigenous people have always had that connection with nature perhaps because they do show gratitude to the earth.

[232] Sommerville (2006, p. 66).

[233] Ecclestone and Hayes (2009, p. 161).

REFERENCES

Atwood, M. (2008). *Payback: Debt and the Shadow Side of Wealth*. London: Bloomsbury.

Barks, C. (2004). *The Essential Rumi: New Expanded Edition*. CA: HarperOne.

Barnett, R. (2004). Learning for an unknown future. *Higher Education Research and Development*, *23*(3), 247–260.

Baron, M. (1995). *Kantian Ethics almost Without an Apology*. Cornell: Cornell U.P.

Bartlett, M., & DeStono, D. (2006). Gratitude and prosocial behaviour: Helping when it costs you. *Psychological Science*, *17*(4), 319–325.

Bartlett, R. (2003). Souls without longing. *Public Interest*, *150*, 101–115.

Becker, L. (1986). *Reciprocity*. London: Routledge.

Berger, F. R. (1975). Gratitude. *Ethics*, 85, 298–309.

Blackburn, S. (2001). *Being Good: A Short Introduction to Ethics*. Oxford: Oxford University Press.

Bono, G., Emmons, R., & McCullough, M. (2004). Gratitude in practice and the practice of gratitude. In A. Linley & S. Joseph (Eds.), *Positive Psychology in Practice* (pp. 464–481). New Jersey: John Wiley & Sons.

Bono, G., & McCullough, M. (2006). Positive response to benefit and harm: Bringing forgiveness and gratitude into cognitive therapy. *Journal of Cognitive Psychotherapy*, *26*(20), 147–159.

Bowen, W. (2007). *A Complaint Free World: Take the 21-day Challenge*. New York: Doubleday.

Brabazon, T. (2002). *Digital Hemlock*. Sydney: UNSW Press.

Buber, M. (1947). *Between Man and Man* (R. G. Smith, Trans.). London: Kegan Paul.

Buber, M. (1958). *I and Thou* (R. G. Smith, Trans.). Edinburgh: T. & T. Clark.

Buck, R. (2004). The gratitude of exchange and the gratitude of caring: A developmental-interactionist perspective of moral emotion. In R. Emmons & M. McCullough (Eds.), *The Psychology of Gratitude* (pp. 100–122). Oxford: Oxford University Press.

Burch, R. (1990). 'Phenomenology and lived experience: Taking a measure of the topic'. *Phenomenology and Pedagogy*, *8*, 130–160.

Camenish, P. (1981). Gift and Gratitude in Ethics. *Journal of Religious Ethics*, *9*, 1–34.

Campbell, J. (1945). *The Hero with a Thousand Faces*. New York: Pantheon Books.

Campbell, J. (1988). *The Power of Myth*. New York: Doubleday.

Campbell, J. (2004*). Pathways to Bliss: Mythology and Personal Transformation*. CA: Novato.

Capra, F. (2010). *The Tao of Physics: An Exploration of the Parallels Between Modern Physics and Eastern Mysticism* (updated edition). CA: Shamballa.

Chan, D. (2010). Gratitude, gratitude intervention and subjective wellbeing among Chinese school leaders in Hong Kong. *Educational Psychology*, *30*(2), 139–153.

Cohen, A. (2006). On gratitude. *Social Justice Research*, *19*(2), 254–276.

Coleman, J. (2009). Well-being in schools: Empirical measure, or politician's dream? *Oxford Review of Education*, *35*(3), 281–292.

Comte-Sponville, A. (1996). *A Small Treatise on the Great Virtues: The Uses of Philosophy in Everyday Life*. New York: Holt.

Cousens, A. (2010). Positivity. Song from the CD *free flowin' footsteps*.

Covey, S. M. R. (2006). *The Speed of Trust: The One Thing That Changes Everything*. New York: Simon & Schuster.

Csikszentmihalyi, M. (2000). *Beyond Boredom and Anxiety*. San Francisco: Jossey Bass.

Csikszentmihalyi, M. & Csikszentmihalyi, I. (Eds.). (1992). *Optimal Experience: Psychological Studies of Flow in Consciousness*. Cambridge: Cambridge University Press.

Dale, M. (2004). *Tales In and Out of School.* In D. Liston & J. Garrison (Eds.), *Teaching, Learning and Loving* (pp. 65–79). New York: RoutledgeFalmer.

Dearlove, J. (1997). The academic labour process: From collegiality and professionalism to managerialism and proletarianisation? *Higher Education Review, 30*(1), 56–75.

Dewey, J. (1933). *How We Think.* USA: D.C. Heath & Co.

Dewey, J. (1938). *Experience and Education.* New York: Collier Books.

Ecclestone, K., & Hayes, D. (2009a). Changing the subject: The educational implications of developing emotional well-being. *Oxford Review of Education, 35*(3), 371–389.

Ecclestone, K., & Hayes, D. (2009b). *The Dangerous Rise of Therapeutic Education.* New York: Routledge.

Einstein, A. (1956). *The World as I See* It. NY: Citadel Press.

Emmons, R. (2003). Acts of gratitude in organizations. In K. S. Cameron, J. E. Dutton, & R. E. Quinn (Eds.), *Positive Organisational Scholarship* (pp. 81–93). San Francisco: Berrett-Koehler.

Emmons, R. (2004). Introduction. In R. Emmons & M. McCullough (Eds.), *The Psychology of Gratitude* (pp. 3–15). Oxford: Oxford University Press.

Emmons, R., & Crumpler, C. (2000). Gratitude as a human strength: Appraising the evidence. *Journal of Social and Clinical Psychology, 19*(1), 56–70.

Emmons, R., & Hill, J. (2001). *Words of Gratitude: For Mind, Body and Soul.* Pennsylvania: Templeton Foundation Press.

Emmons, R., & McCullough, M. (2003). Counting blessings versus burdens: An experimental investigation of gratitude and subjective well-being in daily life. *Journal of Personality and Social Psychology, 84*(2), 377–389.

Emmons, R., & McCullough, M. (2004). *The Psychology of Gratitude.* Oxford: Oxford University Press.

Emmons, R., & Paloutzian, R. (2003). The psychology of religion. *Annual Review of Psychology, 54,* 377–402.

Emmons, R., & Shelton, C. (2002). Gratitude and the science of positive psychology. In C. R. Snyder & S. Lopez (Eds.), *Handbook of Positive Psychology* (pp. 459–471). Oxford: Oxford University Press.

Erenreich, B. (2009). *Bright-sided: How the Relentless Promotion of Positive Thinking is Undermining America.* New York: Metropolitan Books.

Ferrer, J., & Tarnas, R. (2001). *Revisioning Transpersonal Theory: A Participatory Vision of Human Spirituality.* NY: SUNY.

Fitzgerald, P. (1998). Gratitude and justice. *Ethics, 109*(1), 119–153.

Fiumara, G. (1990). *The Other Side of Language: A Philosophy of Listening* (C. Lambert, Trans.). London and New York: Routledge.

Fox, M. (1979). *A Spirituality Named Compassion: And the Healing of the Global Village, Humpty Dumpty and Us.* Minnesota: Winston Press, Inc.

Frankl, V. (1985). *Man's Search for Meaning.* New York: Simon & Schuster.

Fredrickson, B. (2004). Gratitude, like other positive emotions, broadens and builds. In R. Emmons & M. McCullough (Eds.), *The Psychology of Gratitude* (pp. 145–166). Oxford: Oxford University Press.

Fredrickson, B. (2009). *Positivity: Groundbreaking Research Reveals How to Embrace the Hidden Strength of Positivity, and Thrive.* New York: Random House.

Fredrickson, B., & Joiner, T. (2002). Positive emotions trigger upward spirals toward emotional well-being. *Psychological Science, 13*(2), 172–175.

Friere, P. (1993). *Pedagogy of the Oppressed.* New York: Continuum Books.

Froh, J., Bono, G., & Emmons, R. (2010). Beyond grateful is beyond good manners: Gratitude and motivation to contribute to society among early adolescents. *Motiv Emot, 34,* 144–157.

Froh, J., Kashdan, T., Ozimkowski, K., & Miller, N. (2009). Who benefits the most from a gratitude intervention in children and adolescents? Examining positive affect as a moderator. *The Journal of Positive Psychology, 4*(5), 408–422.

Froh, J., Miller, D., & Snyder, S. (2007). Gratitude in children and adolescents: Development, assessment, and school-based intervention. *School Psychology Forum: Research in Practice, 2*(1), 1–13.

Froh, J., Yurkewicz, C., & Kashdan, T. (2009). Gratitude and subjective wellbeing in early adolescence: Examining gender differences. *Journal of Adolescence, 32*, 633–650.

Game, A., & Metcalfe, A. (2010). Presence of the gift. *Cultural Studies Review, 16*(1). http://epress.lib.uts.edu.au/journals/index.php/csrj/index.

Gibbs, J. (2006). *Reaching All by Creating Tribes Learning Communities.* California: Centre Source Systems.

Giddens, A. (1990). *The Consequences of Modernity.* Cambridge: Polity.

Giddens, A. (1991). *Modernity and Self-Identity.* Cambridge: Polity.

Gray, J. (1968). Introduction. In M. Heidegger (Ed.), *What Is Called Thinking?* New York: Harper & Row. First published in 1954.

Greene, M. (1988). *The Dialectic of Freedom.* New York and London: Teachers College Press.

Greene, M. (1995). *Releasing the Imagination: Essays on Education, the Arts, and Social Change.* San Francisco: Jossey-Bass.

Greene, M. (1996). A rereading of Dewey's art as experience: Pointers toward a new theory of learning. In D. Olson & N. Torrence (Eds.), *The Handbook of Education and Human Development: New Models for Learning, Teaching and Schooling* (pp. 56–74). Oxford: Blackwell.

Greene, M. (1997). 'The lived world, literature and education'. In D. Vandenberg (Ed.), *Phenomenology and Educational Discourse* (pp. 169–190). Johannesburg: Heinemann.

Griffith, J., Steptoe, A., & Cropley, M. (1999). An investigation of coping strategies associated with job stress in teachers. *British Journal of Educational Psychology, 69*, 517–531.

Guglielmi, R. S., & Tatrow, K. (1998). Occupational stress, burnout and health in teachers: A methodological and theoretical analysis. *Review of Educational Research, 68*(1), 61–99.

Hargreaves, A. (1998). The emotional politics of teaching and teacher development with implications for leadership. *International Journal of Leadership in Education, 1*, 315–336.

Harpham, E. (2004). Gratitude in the history of ideas. In R. Emmons & M. McCullough (Eds.), *The Psychology of Gratitude* (pp. 19–36). Oxford: Oxford University Press.

Hart, T. (2001). *From Information to Transformation: Education for the Evolution of Consciousness.* New York: Peter Lang Publishing.

Heidegger, M. (1968). *What Is Called Thinking?* (F. Wick & J. Gray, Trans.). New York: Harper & Row.

Heidegger, M. (1971). *On the Way to Language.* New York: Harper and Row.

Heubner, D. (1985). 'Spirituality and knowing'. In E. Eisner (Ed.), *Learning and Teaching the Ways of Knowing* (pp. 159–173). Chicago: The National Society for the Study of Education.

Holmes, E. (1991). *A Dictionary of New Thought Terms.* CA: Devorss Publications.

Howard, S., & Johnson, B. (2004). Resilient teachers: Resisting stress and burnout. *Social Psychology of Education, 7*, 399–420.

Howells, K. (2004). The role of gratitude in higher education. *Research and Development in Higher Education, 27*, 164–173.

Howells, K. (2007). Practising gratitude to enhance teaching and learning. *Education Connect, (8),* 12–15.

Howells, K. (2009). Strengthening relationships and resilience through practices of gratitude. *Principal Matters, 80*(Spring), 2–6.

REFERENCES

Howells, K., & Cumming, J. (2012). Exploring the role of gratitude in the professional experience of pre-service teachers. *Teaching Education, 23*(1), 71–88.

Hughes, R. (1994). *Culture of Complaint: The Fraying of America*. London: HarperCollins.

Johnson, L. (2005). *Teaching Outside the Box: How to Grab Your Students by their Brains?* San Francisco: Jossey-Bass.

Jones, A., & O'Neil, J. (2003). *Seasons of Grace: The Life-Giving Practice of Gratitude*. New Jersey: John Wiley & Sons.

Jung, C. (1983). *Memories, Dreams, Reflections*. London: HarperCollins.

Kiekegaard, S. (1962). *Works of Love*. NY: Harper Torchbooks.

Knowles, D. (2002). Gratitude and good government. *Res Publica*, 8, 1–20.

Knowles, E. (2004). *The Oxford Dictionary of Quotations*. Oxford: Oxford University Press.

Komter, A. (2004). Gratitude and gift exchange. In R. Emmons & M. McCullough (Eds.), *The Psychology of Gratitude* (pp. 195–212). Oxford: Oxford University Press.

Komter, A. (Ed.). (1996). *The Gift: An Interdisciplinary Perspective*. Amsterdam: Amsterdam University Press.

Kyriacou, C. (2001). Teacher stress: Directions for future research. *Educational Review, 53*(1), 27–35.

Laurillard, D. (1993). *Rethinking University Teaching: A Framework for the Effective Use of Educational Technology*. London and New York: Routledge.

Law, S. (2007). *The War for Children's Minds*. New York: Routledge.

Leggo, C. (1999). Research as poetic rumination: Twenty six ways of listening to light. *Journal of Educational Thought, 33*(2) (August 1999), 113–133.

Leonard, T. (1997). *Working Wisdom*. Austin: Bard Press.

Leunig, M. (1990). *A Common Prayer*. Victoria: HarperCollins.

Lovat, T., Toomey, R., Clement, N., Crotty, R., & Nielsen, T. (2009). *Values Education, Quality Teaching and Service Learning*. NSW: David Barlow.

Lyons, D. (1969). The odd debt of gratitude. *Analysis, 29*, 92–97.

McAdams, D., & Bauer, J. (2004). Gratitude in modern life: Its manifestations and development. In R. Emmons & M. McCullough (Eds.), *The Psychology of Gratitude* (pp. 81–99). Oxford: Oxford University Press.

McConnell, T. (1993). *Gratitude*. Philadelphia: Temple University Press.

McCraty, R., & Childre, D. (2004). The grateful heart: The psychophysiology of appreciation. In R. Emmons & M. McCullough (Eds.), *The Psychology of Gratitude* (pp. 230–256). Oxford: Oxford University Press.

McCullough, M., Emmons, R., & Tsang, J. (2002). The grateful disposition: A conceptual and empirical topography. *Journal of Personality and Social Psychology, 82*(1), 112–127.

McCullough, M., Kirkpatrick, S., Emmons, R., & Tsang, J. (2001). Is gratitude a moral affect? *Psychological Bulletin, 127*, 249–266.

McCullough, M., Tsang, J., & Emmons, R. (2004). Gratitude in intermediate affective terrain: Links of grateful moods to individual differences and daily emotional experience. *Journal of Personality and Social Psychology, 86*(2), 295–309.

Mackinnon, B. (2011). *The Liam Jurrah Story: From Yuendumu to the MCG* (pp. 94–95). Melbourne, Victory Books. (extract published in Sunday Times), Perth, July 24, 2011.

McPhail, J. (1995). Phenomenology as philosophy and method: Applications to ways of doing special education. *Remedial and Special Education, 16*, 159–165.

Marton, F., Dall-Alba, G., & Beatty, E. (1993). Conceptions of learning. *International Journal of Educational Research, 19*, 271–300.

Midgley, M. (1991). *Wisdom, Information and Wonder - What is Knowledge for?* London and New York: Routledge.

Miller, A. (2009). A critique of positive psychology – or 'The new science of happiness'. In R. Cigman & A. Davis (Eds.), *New Philosophies of Learning* (pp. 221–238). Oxford: Wiley-Blackwell.

Miller, J. (1993). *The Holistic Curriculum*. Toronto, Ontario: OISE Press.

Miller, J. (2000). *Education and the Soul: Toward a Spiritual Curriculum*. Albany: State University of New York Press.

Mugerauer, R. (1988). *Heidegger's Language and Thinking*. Atlantic Highlands, NJ: Humanities Press International.

Nias, J. (1996). Thinking about feeling: The emotions in teaching. *Cambridge Journal of Education, 26,* 293–323.

Nielsen, T. (2011). A curriculum of giving for student wellbeing and achievement – 'How to wear leather sandals on a rough surface'. In D. Wright, C. Camden-Pratt, & S. Hill (Eds.), *Social Ecology: Applying Ecological Understanding to Our Lives and Our Planet* (pp. 151–164). UK: Hawthorn Press.

Noddings, N. (1984). *Caring, a Feminine Approach to Ethics & Moral Education*. Berkeley: University of California Press.

Noddings, N. (1992). *The Challenge to Care in Schools: An Alternative Approach to Education*. New York: Teachers College Press.

Noddings, N. (1999). Two concepts of caring. *Philosophy of Education*. Retrieved August 27, 2011, http://www.ed.uiuc.edu/EPS/PES-yearbook/1999/noddings.asp.

Noddings, N. (2002). *Starting at Home. Caring and Social Policy*. Berkeley: University of California Press.

O'Sullivan, E. (2001). *Transformative Learning: Educational Vision for the 21st Century*. London: Zed Books.

Palmer, P. J. (1993). *To Know as We are Known: Education as a Spiritual Journey* (2nd ed.). New York: HarperOne.

Palmer, P. J. (1998). *The Courage to Teach: Exploring the Inner Landscape of the Teachers' Life*. San Francisco: Jossey Bass.

Palmer, P. J. (2007). *The Courage to Teach: Exploring the Inner Landscape of the Teachers' Life* (2nd ed.). San Francisco: Jossey Bass.

Peterson, C., & Park, N. (2004). Classification and measurement of character strengths: Implications for Practice. In A. Linley & S. Joseph (Eds.), *Positive Psychology in Practice* (pp. 433–446). New Jersey: John Wiley & Sons.

Peterson, C., & Seligman, M. (2004). *Character Strengths and Virtues: A Handbook and Classification*. New York: Oxford University Press.

Quick, S., & Lesueur, A. (2004). "Gifts of gratitude and blessings" universe of possibilities. *University of Kentucky Cooperative Extension Service, 10,* 1–10.

Roberts, R. (2004). The blessings of gratitude: A conceptual analysis. In R. Emmons & M. McCullough (Eds.), *The Psychology of Gratitude* (pp. 58–79). Oxford: Oxford University Press.

Rodgers, C., & Raider-Roth, M. (2006). Presence in teaching. *Teachers and Teaching: Theory and Practice, 12*(3), 265–287.

Saul, J. R. (2001). *On Equilibrium*. London: Penguin Books.

Schimmel, S. (2004). Gratitude in Judaism. In R. Emmons & M. McCullough (Eds.), *The Psychology of Gratitude* (pp. 37–57). Oxford: Oxford University Press.

Schlitz, M., Veitan, C., & Amorok, T. (2007). *Living Deeply, The Art and Science of Transformation in Everyday Life*. CA: New Harbinger Publications.

Schon, D. (1984). *The Reflective Practitioner: How Professionals Think in Action*. CA: Basic Books.

Seligman, M. (1992*). Learned Optimism*. Sydney: Random House.

Seligman, M. (2011). *Flourish*. North Sydney: William Heinemann.

REFERENCES

Seligman, M., Ernst, R., Gillham, J., Reivich, K., & Linkins, M. (2009). Positive education: Positive psychology and classroom interventions. *Oxford Review of Education, 35*(3), 293–331.
Shelton, C. (2000). *Achieving Moral Health.* New York: Crossroad.
Shelton, C. (2004). Gratitude: Considerations from a moral perspective. In R. Emmons & M. McCullough (Eds.), *The Psychology of Gratitude* (pp. 257–281). Oxford: Oxford University Press.
Simmel, G. (1996). Faithfulness and gratitude. In A. Komter (Ed.), *The Gift: An Interdisciplinary Perspective* (pp. 39–48). Amsterdam: Amsterdam University Press.
Singer, M. (2007). *The Untethered Soul: The Journey beyond the Self.* CA: Noetic Books.
Smith, A. (1759). *The Theory of Moral Sentiments* (D. Raphael & A. Macfie Eds.). Indianapolis: Liberty Classics.
Smith, M. K. (2004). Nel noddings, the ethics of care and education', *the encyclopaedia of informal education.* www.infed.org/thinkers/noddings.htm. Downloaded August, 25th, 2011.
Solomon, R. (2004). Foreword. In R. Emmons & M. McCullough (Eds.), *The Psychology of Gratitude* (pp. v–xi) Oxford: Oxford University Press.
Sommerville, M. (2006). *The Ethical Imagination: Journeys of the Human Spirit.* Melbourne: Melbourne University Press.
Stein, M. (1989). Gratitude and attitude: A note on emotional welfare. *Social Psychology Quarterly, 52*(3), 242–248.
Steindl-Rast, D. (1984). *Gratefulness: The Heart of Prayer.* New York: Paulist Press.
Steindl-Rast, D. (2004). Gratitude as thankfulness and gratefulness. In R. Emmons & M. McCullough (Eds.), *The Psychology of Gratitude* (pp. 257–281). Oxford: Oxford University Press.
Stewart-Robertson, C. (1990). The rhythms of gratitude: Historical developments and philosophical concerns. *Australasian Journal of Philosophy, 68*(2), 189–205.
Suzuki, S. (1983). *Nurtured by Love: The Classic Approach to Talent Education* (2nd ed.). Miami: Sumi-Birchard Inc.
Suzuki, S. (1995). *Zen Mind, Beginner's Mind.* New York: Weatherill.
Tapscott, D. (1998). *Growing Up Digital: The Rise of the Net Generation.* New York: McGraw Hill.
Tarnas, R. (1991). *The Passion of the Western Mind.* New York: Crown Publishers.
Taylor, C. (1989). *Sources of the Self: The Making of Modern Identity.* Cambridge: Harvard University Press.
Taylor, C. (1995a). The dialogical self. In R. Goodman & W. Fisher (Eds.), *Rethinking Knowledge: Reflections Across the Disciplines* (57–66). Albany: State University of New York Press.
Taylor, C. (1995b). *Philosophical Arguments.* Cambridge, Mass.: Harvard University Press.
Taylor, G. (1993). 'A theory of practice: Hermeneutical understanding', *Higher Educational Research and Development, 12*(1), 59–72.
Toledo-Pereyra, L. (2006). Gratitude. *Journal of Investigative Surgery, 19*, 137–140.
Tronman, G. (2000). Teacher stress in the low-trust society. *British Journal of Education, 21*(3), 330–353.
Troutner, L. (1974). Toward a phenomenology of education: An exercise in the foundations. *Philosophy of Education, 30*, 140–164.
Tsang, J. (2006). Gratitude and prosocial behaviour: An experimental test of gratitude. *Cognition and Emotion, 20*(1), 138–148.
Tschannen-Moran, M. (2004). *Trust Matters: Leadership for Successful Schools.* CA: Jossey-Bass.
Unsworth, K., Turner, N., Williams, H., & Houle, S. (2010). Giving thanks: The relational context of gratitude in postgraduate supervision. *Studies in Higher Education, 35*(8), 871–888.
Van Maanen, J. (1988). *Tales of the Field: On Writing Ethnography.* Chicago: University of Chicago Press.

Van Manen, M. (1990). *Researching Lived Experience: Human Science for An Action Sensitive Pedagogy*. Ontario: SUNY Press.

Vaughan, G., & Estola, E. (2008). The gift paradigm in early childhood education. In S. Farquhar & P. Fitzsimons (Eds.), *Philosophy of Early Childhood Education* (pp. 24–41). Victoria: Blackwell Publishing.

Visser, M. (2009). *The Gift of Thanks: The Roots and Rituals of Gratitude*. Boston: Houghton Mifflin Harcourt.

Watkins, P. (2004). Gratitude and subjective well-Being. In R. Emmons & M. McCullough (Eds.), *The Psychology of Gratitude* (pp. 167–194). Oxford: Oxford University Press.

Watkins, P., Scheer, J., Ovnicek, M., & Kolt, R. (2006). The debt of gratitude: Dissociating gratitude and indebtedness. *Cognition and Emotion, 20*(2), 217–241.

Watkins, P., Woodward, K., Stone, T., & Kolts, R. (2003). Gratitude and happiness: Development of a measure of gratitude and relationships with subjective well-being. *Social Behavior and Personality, 31*(5), 431–452.

White, P. (1999). Gratitude, citizenship and education. *Studies in Philosophy and Education, 18*, 43–52.

Williams, R. (2011, August 11). Speech given to the House of Lords. http://www.archbishopofcanterbury.org/articles.php/2152/archbishop-speaks-in-house-of-lords-on-unrest downloaded September 5, 2011.

Williamson, M. (1992). *A Return to Love: Reflections on the Principles of a Course in Miracles*. New York: HarperCollins.

Wood, A., Froh, J., & Geraghty, A. (2010). Gratitude and well-being: A review and theoretical integration. *Clinical Psychology Review, 30*, 890–205.

Zembylas, M. (2003). Caring for teacher emotion: Reflections on teacher self-development. *Studies in Philosophy and Education, 22*, 103–125.

Zournazi, M. (2002). *Hope: New Philosophies for Change*. Annandale: Pluto Press.

CPSIA information can be obtained
at www.ICGtesting.com
Printed in the USA
BVOW06s0630060417
480407BV00003B/33/P

9 789460 918124